Johnny Cash
and Philosophy

D0850937

Popular Culture and Philosophy®
Series Editor: George A. Reisch

Popular Culture and Philosophy®

Johnny Cash and Philosophy

The Burning Ring of Truth

Edited by

JOHN HUSS

and

DAVID WERTHER

OPEN COURT
Chicago and La Salle, Illinois

Volume 31 in the series, Popular Culture and Philosophy®, edited by George A. Reisch

To order books from Open Court, call 1-800-815-2280, or visit our website at www.opencourtbooks.com.

Open Court Publishing Company is a division of Carus Publishing Company.

Copyright © 2008 by Carus Publishing Company

First printing 2008

Johnny Cash's lyrics are quoted by permission of Bug Music.

All rights reserved. No part of this publication may be reproduced, stored in a retrieval system, or transmitted, in any form or by any means, electronic, mechanical, photocopying, recording, or otherwise, without the prior written permission of the publisher, Open Court Publishing Company, a division of Carus Publishing Company, 315 Fifth Street, P.O. Box 300, Peru, Illinois, 61354-3000.

Printed and bound in the United States of America.

Library of Congress Cataloging-in-Publication Data

Johnny Cash and philosophy : the burning ring of truth / edited by John Huss and David Werther.
    p. cm. — (Popular culture and philosophy ; v. 31)
    "Philosophers explore the meaning and continuing importance of Johnny Cash's music and legacy"—Provided by publisher.
    Includes bibliographical references and index.
    ISBN-13: 978-0-8126-9645-5 (trade pbk. : alk. paper)
    ISBN-10: 0-8126-9645-X (trade pbk. : alk. paper)
    1. 1. Cash, Johnny. 2. Country musicians—United States—
    Biography. I. Huss, John, 1963- II. Werther, David.
ML420.C265J66 2008
782.421642092—dc22
                                                            2007052449

To Bruce and Luan Werther
They introduced me to *Johnny Cash at San Quentin*

To Joanna Trzeciak
I Love You Because

Contents

Introduction

On trial for corrupting the youth of Athens, the ancient Greek philosopher Socrates famously claimed that he wasn't corrupting anybody—all he was doing was asking questions. Two thousand years later, on stage before the youth of Athens, Georgia, Johnny Cash might have claimed he wasn't corrupting anybody either—all he was doing was asking "What is Truth?"

The stage in question was actually in Nashville, Tennessee, so the previous sentence is a lie, not the truth. But before we get too philosophical, let's be honest: Johnny Cash was no philosopher. We all know what he really was, or at least we think we do. Cotton-picker. Enlisted man. Appliance salesman. Rock'n'roll pioneer. Loving husband and father. Two-timing drug addict. Patriarch. Christian and hellion. Patriot and protester. The voice of convicts, the poor, veterans, American Indians, and others whose voices too often went unheard. He was country. He was comedy—remember "Chicken in Black"? He was folk, gospel, and swing.

Johnny Cash was a paradox—a walking contradiction, Kris Kristofferson called him. And you can bet that wherever there's a paradox, there's a philosopher nearby either posing it, pointing it out, or peeking behind it: if the world was created by a benevolent God, how can it contain evil? If "I" am constantly changing (as Johnny Cash often claimed he was), where is the enduring "I" that is undergoing the transformation? If justice is defined by the rule of law, what is an unjust law? These are some of the paradoxes we explore in this book.

But as Cash himself might have said, for every philosopher paralyzed by paradox, out front there needs to be a Man in Black pointing out what's true or right or important, but easily forgotten or overlooked. There is Cash the social critic, calling out those who are so heavenly minded that they're "No Earthly Good," lobbying government officials to reform our correctional system in his concerts at San Quentin, Folsom, and other prisons, and raising money for new schools on Indian reservations. But there was also the Cash who understood the power of simplicity, embodied in the boom-chicka-boom of Luther Perkins's guitar propelling songs like "I Walk the Line," "Big River," and "So Doggone Lonesome." "Get rhythm when you get the blues," he tells us. Is this philosophy? Good question. Either way it's advice even a philosopher can use.

But the authors of the chapters in this book are not just philosophers—we are Cash fans. Cash fans are a varied lot today and always have been. Consider the scene at a crowded Cash concert in Arthur, Illinois, described in Tom Dearmore's 1969 *New York Times Magazine* cover story. It was the sweltering summer of 1969, and bearded hippies with unwashed feet were rubbing shoulders with bearded Amish in flat-brimmed hats, a starry-eyed waitress, college boys in Bermuda shorts, a deeply tanned heavy equipment operator, plaid-clad mods, American Gothics, and cab drivers down from Chicago. Over the decades punks, goths, soccer moms, alt.country types, metrosexuals, and hipsters became part of the mix. Perhaps it is because Cash himself had so many sides that people of such varied persuasions are drawn to him. And that is the case in this book too. Here you will find philosophical explorations inspired by the life and music of Johnny Cash—and even June Carter Cash—written by philosophers of many different views and voices. And just like at a Johnny Cash concert, there's a little something for everyone. We welcome you to join in and think along.

PART I

Self

1

Cash Value:
The Authenticity of
Johnny Cash

JESSE W. BUTLER

> The image is one thing, but the man is another.
> —Elvis Presley

> He's a walking contradiction, partly truth and partly fiction.
> —Kris Kristofferson

Imagine Johnny Cash as a guest on the Dr. Phil show. He walks out to greet Dr. Phil, uttering "Hello, I'm Johnny Cash" while offering a firm but warm handshake. After both men take a seat, the following dialogue ensues:

Dr. Phil: So, isn't your name really J.R., and not Johnny?

Johnny Cash: Well, that's what my mama and daddy called me, and some of my family still call me J.R. Depending on how she's feeling about me, June calls me John, Johnny or Cash, but you can just call me Johnny, like most folks do.

Dr. Phil: But why should I call you that if it is just a made-up name? You see, J.R., the point isn't really about your name. It's about your true self. Here you are living the life of a star named Johnny Cash, with people believing you are some kind of rebel that has been to prison, and you dress in black to fit the part. But isn't this all a kind of fantasy life? What I'm getting at is that we need to identify the real person that is *really* you, not this image of Johnny Cash. Don't you think that maybe some of the problems you've had in your life could be addressed if you got in touch with who you really are, J.R.?

JOHNNY CASH: Look man, I don't know who you think I am, but I *am* Johnny Cash and I wear black because I want to, for my own reasons. Some folks may think I've been to prison because of some of the songs I sing, but that's not something I deceived anybody about. Besides, those songs speak to real people and their real lives, and that's what's really important here, isn't it? Maybe people get the wrong impression sometimes, but that doesn't change the fact that I am who I've become by singing my songs and living my life as I see fit.

Of course no such dialogue really happened, but the issues it presents are real.[1] The persona, or public image, of Johnny Cash exhibits a strong impression of authenticity, appearing as a unique and real man, the "Man in Black." Yet the songs and other events and characteristics that form the persona of Johnny Cash contain prominent features that are either fictitious or were projected onto the man by the society around him. As one noteworthy example, the popular song "Folsom Prison Blues" tells the tale of a murder and imprisonment that Johnny Cash did not experience at all. However, this song, along with the content it portrays, was a key factor in Cash's career and even paved the way for him to perform the song at Folsom Prison itself. As the live recording of this performance rose up the music charts, it played a large role in the formation of Cash's now iconic persona and became a significant component of who the general public understood him to be.

What are we to make of this situation? Is the Johnny Cash that we all know from his songs and other public manifestations somehow just an inauthentic image, as the imagined Dr. Phil seemed to suggest, or can we regard the Johnny Cash persona as the authentic identity of the flesh-and-blood man that lived his life as Johnny Cash? I don't know about you, but I prefer the second option. In fact, I think the life and identity of Johnny Cash provide an excellent illustration of authenticity.

---

[1] I am not suggesting that Dr. Phil really thinks that Johnny Cash is a fake. The dialogue between Cash and Dr. Phil is purely hypothetical. However, as we will see, Dr. Phil's general view of the authentic self could lead to such an assessment.

Being an authentic person does not involve shedding an external persona as if it were a false mask, but rather involves actively vesting one's persona with value as it takes shape throughout life, much in the same way that cash money takes on value through its use. As we'll see, Johnny Cash is a remarkable example of how this can happen.

The Making of Johnny Cash

Let's look at three key events that played a crucial role in the development of Johnny Cash into a cultural icon. In all three cases, Cash takes on new characteristics through processes that are initiated and shaped by social forces external to the man himself. Through these examples, we'll see how the persona of Johnny Cash took on a life of its own, irrespective of the preceding facts and characteristics of the actual man's life.

Our first event is the creation of the secular recording artist Johnny Cash. In 1955, J.R. Cash (going by the name John at this point in his life) and two of his friends paid a visit to Sun Records, in hope of becoming gospel music performers. After hearing them perform, Sam Phillips, the head of Sun Records who was at that time paving the way for Elvis Presley's rise to stardom, told them that he could not sell gospel music but that if they came back with some original music of their own he could perhaps record them and put out a record, which of course they did. Already we see the appearance of an external social force that prominently shapes the construction of what will become the Johnny Cash persona. John Cash and his band wanted to play gospel music, but a record industry leader prompted them to go in another, more secular, direction, strongly shaping the trajectory of Cash's career from that point forward. As Cash himself later stated in a 1988 interview, "I always wanted a hit gospel song, but God gave me "A Boy Named Sue" instead, and I'm happy with it."[2]

---

[2] P. 242 in Steve Turner, *The Man Called Cash: The Life, Love, and Faith of an American Legend* (Nashville: W Publishing Group, 2004). For a detailed account of Cash's early formative history, also see Marshall Grant's book *I Was There When It Happened: My Life with Johnny Cash* (Nashville: Cumberland House, 2006).

Upon the initiation of this recording career, the issue of what to call the band inevitably arose. Cash's suggestion was simply the *Tennessee Three*, which did not single him out as the focal point of the group. However, the producer Sam Phillips proposed another name, *Johnny Cash and the Tennessee Two*. Cash had not gone by the name of Johnny before, and was reportedly reluctant to take on the name, but Phillips persuaded him to adopt it for the purpose of marketing his music. As stated in Steve Turner's authorized biography:

> Sam Phillips suggested he change his first name to Johnny because *John* sounded old and boring whereas *Johnny* sounded young and rebellious. Marlon Brando had played a character called Johnny in *The Wild Ones; Johnny Guitar* was a recent movie directed by Nick Ray; and the R&B singer Johnny Ace had killed himself on New Year's Day in a backstage game of Russian roulette. Cash thought that at twenty-three he was too old to be a Johnny, but Phillips persuaded him otherwise and the name went on the label.[3]

So, the name Johnny Cash was chosen and imposed by another person, for the purpose of presenting a particular iconic image based upon the rebellious connotations it evoked at the time. Considering this, the Johnny Cash persona can be seen as a manufactured entity from the very beginning, strongly shaped by forces external to the man himself.

Our next event in the construction of the Johnny Cash persona concerns one of Cash's earliest and most famous songs, "Folsom Prison Blues." This was the third song recorded by Johnny Cash and the Tennessee Two, and it undisputedly became an identity-defining element of Cash's career and persona. As you probably already know, this song is the first-person narration of a man imprisoned in Folsom for murder. Johnny Cash himself, however, clearly experienced no such thing. In fact, Cash was never sentenced to prison, and by all personal accounts was as clean as possibly could be at this point in his career.[4] Moreover, "Folsom Prison Blues" borrowed heavily both

---

[3] *The Man Called Cash*, p. 53. Also reported in *I Was There When It Happened*, p. 39.

[4] As all autobiographies and biographies of Cash attest, he was arrested a few times later in his career, due to his problems with amphetamines, but he was never sent to prison as a result. For more details on this aspect of Cash's life

lyrically and musically from two preceding songs, Jimmie Rodgers' "Blue Yodel No. 1 (T for Texas)" and Gordon Jenkins' "Crescent City Blues," to such an extent that a case for plagiarism can, and has, been made.[5]

Despite these factual separations between Cash and the content of his song, "Folsom Prison Blues" has come to be closely identified with Johnny Cash by the general public. If you aren't aware of this already, consider the fact that Cash himself reported that being asked about his time in prison was the number one topic among his various interview experiences.[6] This was perhaps partially due to the fact that Cash performed and recorded the song at Folsom Prison itself, creating one of the most influential live recordings of all time and paving the way for associations between himself and the social outsiders found in prison. As documented in Michael Streissguth's detailed account of the Folsom Prison album, there is some reason to believe that this associational effect was intentional, especially on the part of Cash's recording engineers and producers. As one example of evidence for this intention, there is an overdubbed yelp of excitement that appears on the recording after the unforgettable lyric "I shot a man in Reno, just to watch him die," but which did not actually occur during Cash's performance of the song.[7] Clearly, given the context of the recording, the intent is to draw attention to the dark nature of the song and its theme of criminality, which over time became projected onto the public image of Cash himself. So, again we see that a central element of the Johnny Cash persona was constructed by social forces outside the man himself and his own personal decisions, without accurate correspondence to and representation of his actual life.

Our third and final example in this brief overview of the making of the Johnny Cash persona is the fact that Johnny Cash

---

see *The Man Called Cash* and *I Was There When It Happened*. The former, in particular, provides a variety of evidence that the young John Cash, prior to his later engagement with drugs, was a very clean-cut young man that straightforwardly abided by a Christian morality and lifestyle.

[5] Michael Streissguth, *Johnny Cash at Folsom Prison: The Making of a Masterpiece* (Da Capo Press, 2004), p 21. See also *The Man Called Cash*, p. 61.

[6] Johnny Cash with Patrick Carr, *Cash: The Autobiography* (New York: Harper Paperbacks, 1997), p. 76.

[7] *Johnny Cash at Folsom Prison*, p. 89.

is often known as the "Man in Black," in reference to his dressing in black and also connoting his associations with the darker aspects of life and society, with outlaws, outsiders, and the down-trodden. This is a central aspect of the general public's image of Johnny Cash.[8] Yet again, however, we have an instance where the persona of Johnny Cash does not originate from the representation of a pre-existing facet of the man himself. As both Marshall Grant and Cash himself have stated, this association with the color black was simply the result of unplanned circumstances. Speaking about his first performance, which was for an audience of ladies at a Memphis church, Cash states that

> Unfortunately, none of us had any clothes a "real" band would wear—I didn't own a suit, or even a tie—but each of us did have a black shirt and a pair of blue jeans. So that became our band outfit, and since the folks at the church seemed to like us and musicians are deeply superstitious—if they tell you otherwise, don't believe them—I suggested we stick with the black.[9]

Cash himself gradually came to identify with and dress in the color black, and even wrote a song about his reasons for being "The Man in Black," but as we see here the origins of the image are less than monumental and do not reflect anything substantial about Cash himself. Instead it was merely an accidental event that only took on a significant meaning as it became identified with Johnny Cash over time.

Taken together, the three central facets of the Johnny Cash persona outlined above provide a strong case for regarding the Johnny Cash persona as a social construct, meaning that it is not derived from accurate representation of J.R. Cash but rather is a product of social forces and circumstances that lie outside the intrinsic personal characteristics of Cash himself, as a real

---

[8] In conducting an informal survey concerning people's conceptions of Johnny Cash, I found that 26 out of 32 people mentioned the fact that Cash wore black or the phrase "The Man in Black" itself, without any solicitation or prompting of this aspect of Cash's persona. While perhaps not the strongest evidence, this underlines the strong associations people have between Johnny Cash and the "Man in Black" moniker.

[9] *Cash: The Autobiography*, p. 86. Grant's account of the origin of the "Man in Black" image differs from Cash's, but is equally accidental in nature. See *I Was There When It Happened*, p. 100.

man.[10] Cash himself personally invested in and gave life to this persona as it developed, thereby incorporating it into his identity, but it originated from and was continually shaped by various external social factors, from the individual decisions of significant people involved in the formation of his career to the general public that got to know him as his popularity and fame grew.

Becoming the Man in Black

So what are we to make of these observations? If the Johnny Cash persona is a social construct, what does this tell us about Johnny Cash's identity as a man? There's a tendency to think of a persona as something fundamentally unreal, as a mask that covers up the reality of the person beneath, for the very reasons we have encountered: a persona does not necessarily match up to the facts of a person's life. In illustration of this perspective, the psychologist Carl Jung (1875–1961) stated that

> Fundamentally the persona is nothing real: it is a compromise between individual and society as to what a man should appear to be. He takes a name, earns a title, exercises a function. . . . In a certain sense all this is real, yet in relation to the essential individuality of the person concerned it is only a secondary reality, a compromise formation, in making which others often have a greater share than he.[11]

From this understanding of the persona, we might conclude that the Johnny Cash that we have come to know through his songs, performances, and other public characteristics is something of a fake or shadowy mirage, something other than the real man that lies hidden beneath. However, I think that this would be a mistake.

---

[10] I do not endorse strong claims of social constructionism, such as the idea that reality itself is socially constructed. The social constructionist claim I make here is limited to the domain of public personas only, in regard to the relatively uncontroversial view that they emerge from various social processes. For more on social constructionism, see Kenneth Gergen, *An Invitation to Social Construction* (Sage Publications, 1999) and Ian Hacking, *The Social Construction of What?* (Harvard University Press, 2000).

[11] Carl Jung, *The Relations between the Ego and the Unconscious* (Princeton University Press, 1935), p. 158.

Johnny Cash himself sincerely took on this persona and made it come to life. In other words, he gave it social currency. He invested it with value by becoming it, in the sense that he sincerely identified himself as Johnny Cash and actively engaged in living his life as Johnny Cash, the singer/songwriter/Country superstar. Considering this, it does not seem appropriate to understand Johnny Cash as a fake. His persona was socially constructed and engineered, but this does not necessarily entail that he was pretending to be someone or something that he was not. Irrespective of the origins of his image, he embodied it and made it a reality; he relentlessly lived the life of this Country music icon across the vast expanse of his career, singing, writing, and performing day after day and night after night with heartfelt passion for the content of his songs and the real-life issues they addressed.

In other words, the persona of Johnny Cash came to be constitutively integrated into the actions and identity of the man J.R. Cash himself, such that what was initially projected upon him from outside was gradually incorporated into himself and his real life. Consider for instance the "Man in Black" example. While this image appears to have initially emerged by accident, simply due to the social circumstances of Cash and his band, Johnny Cash took on the image and invested it with personal meaning over time. The label gradually took on real connotations that represented and exemplified what Johnny Cash stood for and really cared about, as the lyrics of the song "Man in Black" testify.[12] So, rather than simply being a social construct that was imposed from outside, this aspect of his persona is one that Johnny Cash took on in such a way that it became incorporated into his identity.

This may seem like an unusual event in the making of a unique person's identity, but actually it's quite ordinary. We all encounter social forces that strongly impact who we are and what we become, with labels, stories, personal characteristics, and so forth being projected onto us by other people and being incorporated into our actual identity over time. Consider the rel-

---

[12] "Oh, I'd love to wear a rainbow every day, And tell the world that everything's okay, But I'll try to carry off a little darkness on my back, Till things are brighter, I'm the Man in Black."

atively simple example of being given your name at birth, and how this event compares to the origins of the name Johnny Cash. When born, people are given a name by their parents, with absolutely no input on the matter. Yet in nearly all cases people quite automatically take on their given names and the various connotations they may have, gradually integrating them into their own conceptions of themselves and their identities as they persist over time. So, taking on the manufactured label of Johnny Cash cannot be taken to be an instance of fakery. Although it originated through external social forces, it is an ordinary type of event that can be accommodated into the normal formation of a person's identity.

This highlights an important facet of what it means to be a person and, simultaneously, a member of human society. People have images and conceptions projected onto them by external social processes, and sometimes there are notable differences between what society projects onto a person and the actual facts of that person's life, but over time these social projections can take on real value in people's lives and become constitutively integrated into their actual identity. In this sense, personas have a kind of "cash value" in people's lives. Just as the initially valueless (relatively speaking) paper and metal that constitute money come to take on value through the social exchanges in which they are utilized, the labels, stories, and characteristics that constitute public personas take on value through the impact they make on our lives and our social exchanges with other people. And just as Johnny Cash took on his public persona and invested it with value through the actions of his life and career, people in general also take on the various social projections and roles they encounter, making them a real, constitutive aspect of their identity.

As the American philosopher George Herbert Mead (1863–1931) put it, a person

> enters his own experience as a self or individual . . . only by taking the attitudes of other individuals toward himself within a social environment or context of experience and behavior in which both he and they are involved.[13]

---

[13] George Herbert Mead, *Mind, Self, and Society* (Chicago: University of Chicago Press, 1934), p. 138.

And, similarly, the contemporary social psychologist Kenneth Gergen states that

> . . . if the social environment continues to define a given individual in a specified manner, we may reasonably anticipate that, without countervening information, the individual will come to accept the publicly provided definition as his own.[14]

The example of Johnny Cash confirms these conceptions of what it means to be a self or person. Being a person involves being embedded within social processes that construct and shape constitutive features of that person. As I have used it, the term "persona" refers to the effects of these processes, in regard to the public image of a person that they create. Although such personas originate from social processes and external forces, they nonetheless become important aspects of who we are and who we are understood to be, both by ourselves and by others, through their gradual integration into our lives. This is exactly what we find in the above analysis of the Johnny Cash persona and its integration into the identity of the actual man himself. Although his persona originally emerged from the particular social structures surrounding his life and actions, Johnny Cash incorporated this persona into his life in such a way that it became constitutive of his actual identity and concrete existence as a human being.

Authentic Cash

We have reached a point now where something can be said about Johnny Cash's authenticity, as well as the nature of authenticity itself. Authenticity is commonly understood as being true to oneself, such that one identifies with and lives according to a "real" self that lies within. As the television personality Dr. Phil puts it,

> The authentic self is the *you* that can be found at your absolute core. It is the part of you that is not defined by your job, or your function, or your role.[15]

---

[14] Kenneth J. Gergen, "The Social Construction of Self-Knowledge," p. 375 in Daniel Kolak and Raymond Martin, eds., *Self and Identity: Contemporary Philosophical Issues* (New York: Macmillan, 1991).

[15] Phillip C. McGraw, *Self Matters: Creating Your Life from the Inside Out* (New York: Free Press, 2001), p. 30. For an interesting critical account of this

However, if we are to use this conception of authenticity to assess Johnny Cash, we will be led to deny his authenticity. As we have seen, the Johnny Cash known by the general public originated from external social processes, such as the intentional marketing strategy behind the coining of the name 'Johnny Cash' itself. However, this is precisely the part of the self that Dr. Phil would have you believe is not the true, authentic self that existed within the man himself, at his essential core. From this perspective of authenticity, the Johnny Cash that identified himself as a singer / songwriter / "Man in Black" appears to be just an inauthentic façade, defined by a public role.

Fortunately, however, we can understand authenticity in another way. Rather than being true to some internal self or essence that lies hidden beneath the various social processes that surrounds one's life, authenticity can be understood as active engagement with the social processes that impact the shape of one's life, such that the authentic person does not merely go along with these processes in a passive manner but rather takes an active and involved role in how those processes develop and manifest themselves over time.

As we have seen with Johnny Cash's life, a person's identity develops through various social processes over time, being shaped by the significant events that occur across the course of one's life. This can happen in two general ways: either the person just passively goes with the flow, accepting the processes that determine the course of his or her life, or the person actively engages with the process, becoming an efficacious agent in the construction of his or her own identity. It is in the latter case that a life can plausibly be regarded as authentic.

We're all shaped by social forces that play a role in determining who we are, but the authentic person becomes involved with how those forces impact their life and thereby embodies them in a lived, meaningful way that is lacking in people who just passively accept who society determines them to be. Considering this, the affirmation of Johnny Cash's authenticity can be found in his engagement with and participation in the social processes behind the development of the public persona

---

idea, which helped shape the content of my own view of authenticity, see Charles Guignon, *On Being Authentic* (New York: Routledge, 2004).

outlined earlier. Cash willingly, and even enthusiastically, embraced the identity that formed around him over time, thereby making Johnny Cash a lived, genuine reality rather than merely an externally imposed persona.

Consider, for instance, Cash's active engagement with the role of being a singer/songwriter. Throughout his life, Cash learned and sang the songs of others, becoming a virtual repository of American folk culture over time. He actively and passionately participated in the tradition of American folk and country music, thereby becoming an authentic member of the tradition. As many commentators on his music have stated over the years, when Cash sang the songs of others he convincingly sang them from a heartfelt position, as if they were his own. Cash wrote his own songs as well, but as we saw with "Folsom Prison Blues," even his individually-authored songs drew heavily on the traditions and musical patterns of others in such a way that his individual contributions to the world of music cannot be cleanly separated from the various social factors surrounding his life, despite the fact that he was actively involved in carving out an undeniably unique persona from within the traditions in which he participated.

In light of such observations, the misleading distinction between a true internal identity and an external persona fades away, and active reciprocal engagement between an individual and the surrounding society comes to the fore. This helps us to make sense of authenticity in a way that accommodates the impact of social forces on individual human lives. Johnny Cash was an authentic person due to his active embodiment of the public persona that formed around him, through processes that were larger than himself and his individual existence as a man. In other words, he invested the public persona of Johnny Cash with authentic value by engaging with it and living his life through it.

A dollar bill is, in itself, simply a piece of paper. But, by vesting it with a functional role for society, it becomes something more, something that takes on real "cash" value, in virtue of that social role. Similarly, J.R. Cash was just a man, a flesh and blood animal like millions of others that existed before him and after him. But, by his active embodiment of the public persona that developed through various social processes in his life, this man brought into reality something more than a flesh and blood animal. He actively participated in the making of a cultural icon that had, and continues to have, vast significance for many people across many different facets of society, thereby filling this iconic image of Johnny Cash with real, authentic value.

2

Stitches and Yarns: The Stories of Johnny Cash

CRAIG LINDAHL-URBEN and
CHARLES TALIAFERRO

> The one who likes stories is a kind of philosopher.
> —ARISTOTLE, *Metaphysics*

We sometimes think that a person's lifetime, from birth to death, is a single story and that personal development over time involves a growing awareness of that overriding narrative. Whether for good or ill, if you have a biographer, she or he will have to weave a story that includes your childhood, education, loves and hates, worth, success, perhaps even your reading this book, in which the various parts of your life are all explained by other parts and an overall structure. In the case of Johnny Cash, however, any such neat biography is jeopardized by his contradictory episodes, and Johnny's own doubts about where he stood in relationship to the many stories about him.

The life of Johnny Cash seems to be made up of many stories, and they don't seem to fit together. In *Literary Cash: Unauthorized Writings Inspired by the Legendary Johnny Cash*, Leigh H. Edwards suggests there was no single Johnny Cash:

> From rockabilly badass to country music elder statesman, Johnny Cash embodied paradoxes. No single Johnny Cash existed. Full of inconsistencies, Cash always changed, whether he played the drugged rock star trashing hotel rooms or the devout Christian touring with Billy Graham. He was the "Man in Black": a progressive voice for the disenfranchised and the Southern patriarch performing at Nixon's White House. Cash embodied the rebel outlaw

hillbilly thug and later symbolized the establishment. At the heart
of all these ambiguities lies Cash's appeal. (Benbella, 2006, p.159)

Brian Mansfield supports a similar portrait of an ever changing,
fluid life.

> Cash was seen as a poet, patriot, preacher, and protestor. He
> absorbed the images the way black absorbs light. He was all those
> things—and, by being the sum of them, he became something
> entirely different. Cash, with his overpowering presence, was large
> enough to encompass such paradoxes . . . Did he contradict
> himself? Very well then, as Walt Whitman might have said of him,
> he contradicted himself. He was large. He contained multitudes.
> He was, after all, Johnny Cash. (*Ring of Fire: A Tribute to Johnny
> Cash*, pp. 5–7)

How does the private person, whom we will refer to as J.R. Cash
or simply J.R., encompass such contrasts and still remain the
person we know—still remain whole as Johnny Cash the public
persona? How do we create a greater story, an overriding narrative like the Johnny Cash persona, that explains or describes
the single individual that we think is the center of each story?
Does he think of himself as "writing" the story of his life with
his actions past, present and future, or does he just live life now
and leave the story telling (or songs) for later?

We contend that the private person, J. R. Cash, the person
behind the performances, lived the life that later became known
in terms of the Johnny Cash story through his songs. It is
through his songs that we think his persona was most real, most
central to what he cared about in the moment. Behind the performing, public persona we can glimpse a person, J.R., who was
more than any of the stories he narrated. Our goal, then, is to
find J.R. and to locate him in relationship to the many stories of
Johnny Cash.

The Stories We Tell

When we explain things, or other people or even ourselves, we
often do so with stories that have characters (often with us as
the lead), plots, conflicts, a climax and a conclusion. We might
tell the story of the tree in our yard that was planted when our
son was born, and that story of the tree might have as much

drama as Tolstoy's *War and Peace*, and it might even be made into a poem or a song—especially if your boy was named Sue. (But not just anyone could tell that story of the man, as Johnny Cash relates in "It Takes One to Know Me.")

Philosophers recently have focused on how our thoughts of ourselves involve stories or some form of narrative. Do we see ourselves as a character in time flowing from the past into the future, always the lead in a possible story about our life? Or, are we just *here now*, aware of a past, but not feeling like we really know the person with our name that was there in the past and certainly not aware of how we might be in the future?

In the current debate, two major schools of thought have emerged. And the difference between them turns on how a person identifies his or her real self. On the one side there are philosophers who claim that we should see ourselves as entities that move through time in a unified narrative (*the diachronic theory of personal identity*) and on the other side there are philosophers who contend that people only truly know themselves as here and now, the rest is just a memory and the future doesn't exist yet (*the episodic theory*). Those who fit the diachronic model and think of themselves as moving through time find it easy to tell stories about their lives, and those who feel themselves as only *now* don't really see the purpose of *a grand narrative*—although they can certainly see that others might think there's some value in such a unified story.

Finding J.R.

All of us can tell stories, but the important thing is how we think of ourselves in relation to the stories we're telling. If we enjoy telling stories and use them as refinements to our definition of ourselves, then we are identifying with a self that passes through time—a diachronic self. The stories are just further descriptions of us. Much like saying "I am tall," the story provides for us an enlargement or a clearer view of "me." If you are a diachronic, a story about you is clearly a new contribution to be folded into your identity along with your name and height.

If, on the other hand, you tell those stories in much the same way one would tell a fairy tale, as fun, interesting perhaps, but not really an accurate description of the storyteller (at least as he or she is now), then you think of yourself existing principally in episodes and are episodic. If we are episodics, we cannot see ourselves, as we are now, in the story about the past, even if the story is about our High School Prom where we danced the night away. We're certainly telling the story at this moment, and we do know that the world sees this story as one about the storyteller, but we just don't feel like we are the person in the story. Many years separate us from that person in the story—perhaps decades—and we aren't even sure that this story represents in any way the real, in the flesh person who is telling the story—even though this real flesh and blood person has the memories that allow the telling of the story.

Those seem to be the primary ends of the spectrum in the current debate about the self. You see yourself as existing through time adding more each year to the story of your life and expanding your self, OR you see yourself in the current moment with memories that bare a strange fictional element to them—you're either diachronic or episodic. Some philosophers hold that we're all fundamentally diachronic and that being episodic is a rare, dangerous condition—an affected way to escape the responsibility of living a mature life.

The British philosopher Galen Strawson argues instead that we are fundamentally episodic and that there are dangers of pursuing a grand narrative. He might say a would-be diachronic misses out on the existential moment-by-moment nature of simply being alive. According to Strawson, diachronics are so busy composing a life story that they forget to live. In our view, the diachronic-episodic debate neglects a third option. We suggest that J.R. shows us another option that contains the other two and finds a resolution or center in art.

In his art, J.R. was somehow able to be wholly in different episodes as well as play a part in a grand narrative. The reason J.R. was able to do this was because there is a sense in which *the real J.R. was not fully temporal, or completely defined by the temporal dimension of either the grand narrative or concrete episodes.* Rather than articulate this with reference to Western and Eastern thought (in the West, Plotinus (A.D. 205–270), Bishop George Berkeley (1685–1753), Immanuel Kant (1724–1804), and, today, Howard Robinson (b. 1945), and in the East, some Hindu philosophers defend the non-temporal nature of the self), let's stick with J.R. and Johnny Cash.[1]

Out of Time Altogether

There's no doubt that J.R. does not fit easily in a grand story of his life. The view that J.R. had trouble finding himself in a story or an opinion that defined him is supported by Batchelor and Streissguth as well as by June Carter Cash. "John's not left and he's not right. He once said to me, 'Don't ask me what I think about anything unless you want to know about the next five minutes. My mind changes all the time. I believe one thing one month and the next month I believe something else. I'm changing. I'm growing. I'm becoming."[2] But there are at least two reasons to think that the private person J. R. didn't see himself as merely in the moment not associated with past moments (which would earn him the episodic label from some philosophers).

One is the Man in Black (MIB) reason: Johnny Cash was consistently drawn to an overall conception of himself as an outcast, someone who could identify with a fugitive, someone who did wrong and suffered wrong. Perhaps he did so because he was aware that we can all relate to this feeling of alienation, and he wanted to make his stage persona—Johnny Cash—easy to relate to for his audience.

So, Johnny Cash wore black, a color of mourning in the West, a color that sets you apart (if you don't happen to live in Manhattan). And when he came on stage he supported this with the defining announcement: "Hello, I'm Johnny Cash." Johnny Cash was the Man in Black. Johnny Cash was the performer and the story. The overall coherence of this artificial narrative that seems to go beyond the moment does not mean that J.R. Cash identified this as his whole self—it was his stage persona. Johnny did not appear to be wholly invested in this

---

[1] For a formal defense of the view that there is a non-temporal dimension to personal identity, see Howard Robinson's "The Self and Time" in *Persons: Human and Divine*, edited by Peter van Inwagen and D. Zimmerman (Oxford: Clarendon, 2007).

[2] Garth Campbell, *Johnny Cash: He Walked the Line, 1932–2003* (London: John Blake, 2003), p. 175.

overarching story of his identity, and there is evidence that the MIB identity was porous and fluid but nonetheless real to his audiences. This overall narrative unity known to all his audiences is displayed in the biopic *Walk the Line*, directed by James Mangold. His upbringing, the death of his brother, military service, first marriage, first hit, drug and alcohol abuse, religious faith and June, courtship and second marriage all fit into a single narrative structure—the Johnny Cash Story, or more simply Johnny Cash. Of course, this is the result of a story-teller/film maker showing us his view of what happened, a story constructed from various accounts of that period in the life of Johnny Cash, woven together to great dramatic effect. But if J.R. Cash had been unable to participate in crafting Johnny Cash, the Man in Black, or some other similar persona (that is, wholly and radically episodic), no such film could have been made. And he probably wouldn't have been the beloved performer he was.

Our second reason for resisting the claim that Cash lived only in the moment (and that he was radically episodic) is that J.R. Cash actually points to a third possibility. In his performances, the private person J.R. Cash seems to become wholly invested in the stories, as though he and we—his listeners—are actually present to the tragic or comic actors in the story. The performer Johnny Cash becomes this or that character, but without somehow losing his sense of being a self (J.R.) that underlies the performance. A Johnny Cash performance gives us a glimpse of someone who is able to move in and out of a story as though he were able to travel in time and space—a self that is not limited by time, the time of the moment or the time of the story. Batchelor's portrait of J.R. provides some evidence of this third, non-diachronic and non-episodic self or soul.

> He [J.R.] describes navigating his performance of identity:
> "I prefer to meet people before my shows, not after. When I walk off that stage I'm no longer the character I was in the songs I sang—the stories have been told, their messages imparted—but often it's a while before I'm J.R. again. When I meet people, it's important for both of us that I'm J.R.
> His comments register how authenticity is always a constructed idea that depends on the context, since he and his audience both

need to be aware of his narrative persona, "Johnny Cash," as a character he slips on and then gradually sheds. (*Literary Cash*, p. 169)

This J.R. is a self behind all the stories, able to slip in and out of the temporal context of the moment but not identified with it. J.R. was able to put on the garments of the moment not believing for a moment that the clothes make the man, and not believing the moment or story make the self. Here you have a glimpse into J.R. Cash.

Johnny Cash on the other hand—the story, that walking contradiction as Kristofferson called him—is like that old country quilt, each swatch a different moment in the time of his life. Not quite striped and not quite solid, not quite silk and not quite cotton, Johnny Cash was a beautiful quilt—an attempt to put J.R. Cash in a framework that the public would understand. Johnny Cash was, after all, a public commodity to be marketed aggressively and only he could run out of time—J.R. Cash was already identified with a self outside of time. Like the ancient Ship of Theseus, at the end of his journey Johnny Cash was no longer any of the original pieces of J.R. Cash because all of them were replaced, refitted or added, but somehow he still identified with the self behind the changes: he was still J.R (for more on personal identity in the face of wholesale replacement of one's parts, see Chapter 15 in this volume).

Being J.R.

For J.R., each swatch of a life was special. There are abundant reasons for thinking that for J.R., each person was valuable, saint and sinner alike: St. Paul and the man who shot someone just to watch him die. J.R. seemed to operate with the philosophy that some part of a person is deeper than what we know about the person, more essential even than what we see or what the person did—good or bad. J.R. knew the troubles and he knew the joys, but he also knew the deeper part that witnesses them all—what some like to call the true self. The self that stands behind, that is beneath the other "selves" with which we might identify. This self is not the same as all the ideas or conceptions we might have about the self. Those ideas and conceptions, the identities we assume, may be expressions of this real self—costumes we put on for tonight's performance—but they are not it.

Throughout his life and especially in his singing, J.R. made you feel as if he had been there, he had suffered as you had, that he knew the pain personally—as if he had been many selves. He understood the suffering of St. Paul and the man in Folsom or any other prison who hears that train rolling on by. Even though he never spent time in prison it was commonly believed that he had. But J.R. seemed to assume instinctively as only an artist does that we are all the same, deep inside, and if you let out what's in you, you will be singing in harmony with those around you, because, as he might have said, "it's all God's beautiful creation." He did not have to become a prisoner to sing like one.

J.R. didn't need to know the same pain as his audience, he only needed to know what we all must learn—what survives the pain, what is untouched by the pain. On stage J.R. became Johnny Cash and could feel the pain in the song. Only someone who has been there, who has felt the pain, can think in terms of surviving or transcending it. That's why his performance was authentic. His voice made you know that he felt it. And the rock in his voice made you certain that something survived. No matter what temptations knocked you off the path, you could pick yourself up and get back on the straight and narrow just as he had done time and again. And that's what his songs say to us and that's what his comedy and pranks reveal as a profound faith of his—no matter what, we still abide, so the wounds need to be stitched and the holes darned and we carry on. This reveals a man whose very complexity demonstrates the relationship between the true self, not fully defined by some temporal moment, and the story or narrative about the self, and leaves you wondering which character you should identify with and call your self. Even if you believe that there is no self outside of time, no self beyond the diachronic/episodic distinction, there's a sense in which Johnny Cash's voice calls us to hope there is something more than just troubles and worries—something deeper than the mere story of you.

His songs and his life constantly remind us that when we are pulled apart and come together our recovery is often due to an underlying personal identity that is unbroken no matter how shattered it seems. When our lives are shattered J.R.'s performance as Johnny Cash reminds us that each of us is a core self who can serve as a center and place for recovery. He finds us all by the railroad tracks and gives us hope because we can tell he knows how to pull it together—we've watched and heard him do it. J.R.'s Johnny Cash was there when a life was shattered, he was there in the poverty before picking time, he was there during the descent into darkness, he was there when death visited, he was there when love was lost, he was there for sinning and still is, he was definitely there when it happened, and he has passed through the little fires of life and sings to us that we are still here and that pickin' time arrives every year—the cycle is unbroken. This testament lets us see straight through to a self that is beyond these trials, untouched by them, that we need to be able to see and speak to in every person. J.R. did this intuitively, rather than through any sort of sophisticated account of time and personal identity. In a sense, J.R. was himself a natural philosopher.

We suggest J.R. believed that each of us is the bird on the wire, trying in our own way to be free despite our mistakes, crimes, losses or the pain and suffering we cause ourselves and others—the many episodes of our lives—we want to come back to the self we never left, that has always been there underneath it all—truly untouched by the suffering:

> "There's a lot of things blamed on me that never happened," says Johnny Cash. "But then there's a lot of things that I did that I never got caught at. So I guess it cancels out."[3]

And what is left when it's all cancelled out? Some would like to believe it is the true self and not just the self (important as it is) about which stories are told.

A Modest Conclusion

Although we're tempted to place our portrait of J.R. and Johnny Cash in the context of a monumental account of the self as transcending time, we close with a less ambitious suggestion. Put to one side the speculation that the "true self" is eternal or alto-

---

[3] Christopher Wren, *Winners Got Scars Too: The Life and Legend of Johnny Cash* (New York: Dial, 1971), p. 119.

gether beyond temporality. We will settle instead on the supposition that all of us (episodics and diachronics) must live our lives above the time line of instants (an "instant" is like a point, a slice of time with no duration). If "now" or "the present" had to refer to an instant, then none of us could think or act now or in the present because thinking and acting take up time. So, there's a trivial, common-sense respect in which all of us may be said to get above a rigorous time line of bare instants. There is also a fairly common-sense respect in which we may be said to transcend time when making a free choice. In choosing a future course of action, it seems we are able to imagine two different futures and to decide which future will come to pass.

Back to our hero: J.R. may occupy a place no less familiar than we ordinarily occupy or where we go when we make free choices or engage in sustained reflection. Where J.R. may differ from us is that—paradoxically—he more often located himself outside of ordinary time, enabling him to drop into the ever changing Johnny Cash from time to time, much to our delight.

3
The *Dao* and Duality of Johnny Cash

STEVEN F. GEISZ

Listen to a Johnny Cash song—it's best with the radio turned up and the windows down, and driving just a bit too fast—and you can have yourself a mystical experience. That, I assume, is uncontroversial. Figuring out just what such an experience amounts to is a bit trickier. I'm going to try to understand that mystical experience by stealing a notion from Chinese philosophy and thinking about a *dao* of Johnny Cash.

The notion of a *dao* is so thoroughly engrained in contemporary pop consciousness that it might seem to be beyond the need for explanation. That is, aside from a comment about spelling: The Chinese term '道' can be spelled either as '*dao*' or as '*tao*'. Either way, it's pronounced like 'dow'. It means, of course, a *way*. It can refer to a *literal* path or a roadway, the sort of thing on which you can walk or drive a car, or even run a train. Like a trail in the woods, perhaps, or even a road out of town, you might have a hard time finding a *dao* in the first place. Even if you find it, you've got to be careful not to lose it and then have to find your way back. Beyond just a literal roadway or path, '*dao*' can also refer to a *way of doing things*. (As in, "Buddy, that's not the way we do things around here.") And even more broadly, the term can refer to some *mystical* Way (usually spelled with a capital 'W') that people can tap into, somehow, if they get lucky.

In classical Chinese philosophy—that is, Chinese philosophy from the late 500s B.C.E. to the founding of the Qin Dyanasty in 221 B.C.E.—there was not a single, agreed upon *dao*. Rather, there were numerous conflicting schools of thought, each with its own ideas about the proper *dao* to follow. As far as we're concerned, two of those schools were most important: the Confucian school and the Daoist school. The Confucians were the followers of the influential teacher, scholar, and would-be political advisor known to Westerners as "Confucius" (551–479 B.C.E.) and to modern speakers of Mandarin Chinese as "Kongzi 孔子." The Confucians focused on how to get by in society, and their *dao* was one of the human world. In contrast to the Confucians, the Daoists sought after a *dao* of the natural world, a path unconstrained by the niceties that so occupied the Confucians.

I Walk the Line: The Social Dao of Confucius

Following the Confucian path required working hard and mastering an exquisitely subtle set of social rituals, or rites (*li* 禮). A good Confucian had to live life in accord with long-standing rituals and traditions that Confucius thought were neglected in his own day.

Confucius was big on tradition, to be sure, but that's easy to misunderstand. While later Confucians came to represent a rigid status quo in Chinese society, Confucius himself drew upon tradition in order to reform society, and many of his reforms were (at least arguably) progressive, even by today's standards. Yes, Confucius himself framed his reforms as a way to return to a better age in the distant past, so his *dao* can be said to be conservative, perhaps by definition. However, it's probably better to liken the Confucians to hipster fans of neo-traditional Honky Tonk and rockabilly. Like those *No Depression* hipsters of underground Americana, Confucius defended noble arts and aesthetic values that were neglected in his day, and he did so in the hopes of fashioning a better way of life out of such retro stylings. The Confucians advocated a kind of throw-back cool, albeit with a very uncool earnestness and sincerity.

Beyond attention to ritual and tradition, the Confucian *dao* required those on the path to develop a set of character traits that Confucians saw as essential to living well in a properly ordered society. These character traits—the Confucian virtues—included a very demanding form of *humaneness* (*ren* 仁) that was supposed to guide all of one's behavior, an intense *respect for one's parents* (*xiao* 孝—often translated as 'filial piety' by contemporary scholars), and a reverential attitude toward *learning* (*xue* 學). Also thrown into the Confucian mix were the virtues of *loyalty* (*zhong* 忠), *wisdom* (*zhi* 志), and *standing by one's word* (*xin* 信—a Chinese character that seems to show up in all kinds of tattoos these days).

To follow the *dao* of Confucius meant you had to pay close attention to your place in a properly ordered society, with all of its strict rules and regulations, and to make a strenuous effort to exhibit the difficult-to-master Confucian virtues at all times. It wasn't easy, and you had to work your butt off. The person who managed to put it all together and get it right was referred to as a *junzi* 君子 (that is, a "gentleman" or "exemplary person," depending on the translation). A *junzi* was hard to come by in real life, but he (and, yes, for the classical Confucians the *junzi* was a he) was the model of someone who had mastered the Confucian *dao*.

Following the Confucian *dao* meant seeing your life as a metaphorical journey, or at least as something that progressed in stages. Arguably, the very use of the term '*dao*' (in the sense of a roadway) in describing how to go about life requires one to think of life in terms of a journey, but the Confucians took it a step further. If you wanted to be a Confucian, you had to spend your life mastering the Confucian way, and this required finding a teacher, submitting to that teacher's instruction and discipline, studying classical literature, working to master the complex rituals that defined meaningful human interactions, and incessantly examining yourself to see whether or not you were acting at all times in a manner that was guided by the virtues of benevolence, filial piety, etc. It was a tough road. A young Confucian-in-training was not expected to master the program all at once, or even over the course of a few short years. You had to struggle to become a *junzi* by the end of your lifetime. As Confucius himself said regarding his own progress,

> From fifteen my heart-and-mind was set upon learning; from thirty I took my stance; from forty I was no longer doubtful; from fifty I realized the propensities of heaven; from sixty my ear was attuned; from seventy I could give my heart-and-mind free reign without overstepping the boundaries." (*Analects* 2.4).[1]

---

[1] See *The Analects of Confucius: A Philosophical Translation*, translated by

If we realize that the Confucian way required a whole life-time to master, we go a long way toward appreciating the famous Confucian respect for the elderly. If anyone has a shot at being a decent Confucian human being, it's going to be some-one who has some years under the belt.[2]

What Do I Care? The Easygoing *Dao* of the Daoists

In contrast to the Confucians, the rather eclectic tradition we now know as Daoism (a.k.a. Taoism) had a different idea of what *Dao* to follow. (As we will see, for the Daoists we should use 'Dao' with a big 'D.') Whereas Confucians emphasized the stuff of society, the early Daoists emphasized nature and living a life free from what they considered to be the constraining social rules of the Confucians and others. For the Daoists, the model to emulate was not that of a Confucian gentleman. Instead, the Daoist ideal was that of a reclusive sage (*sheng* 聖), rambling freely through the world, unconstrained by social con-vention and in touch with nature and natural spontaneity. The Daoist sage was part mystic hermit, part hands-off political leader, and part happy-go-lucky wanderer—a chilled out kind of proto-Grizzly Adams, living on cloud-covered Mount Tai rather than roaming the American West.

For the Daoists, the idea of the Way also was a central meta-physical notion. Ultimate reality was described as a *Dao* (here with a big 'D'), thus making the metaphor of a path or roadway central to understanding not only how to live a life, but also how everything really *is*. According to the Daoists, reality itself is a path, a road to be traveled. (Figuring out just how *every-thing* could really be a path between two or more places—each

---

Roger T. Ames and Henry Rosemont, Jr. (New York: Ballantine, 1998). I have slightly changed the Ames and Rosemont translation, using 'heaven' for '*tian*' (in spite of the fact that Ames and Rosemont would presumably dislike that move) and dropping an explanatory parenthetical inclusion of '*tianming* 天命.'
[2] While *Analects* 2.4 is a frequently quoted passage and the fact that the Confucian way of life emphasizes respect for the elderly is obvious, my appre-ciation and understanding of the issues of this paragraph owes much to Daniel A. Bell. And while we're at it, when writing this whole thing I benefited from feedback I received from Brook Sadler and from the two fine editors of this volume, John Huss and David Werther.

of which has to be a *part* of everything, as does the very path itself—appears not to have been a problem in the eyes of the Daoists. They used the path metaphor, but didn't much stress about those sorts of details.) While the Daoists *were* concerned with how to live, they weren't so much concerned to figure out how to live *in society*. Rather, they focused on getting in touch with the Great Cosmic Way that was thought to constitute the ultimate nature of everything there is.

Many non-specialists who know something of Daoism are familiar with the *Daodejing* 道德經 (a.k.a. the *Tao Te Ching*), that mystic-poetic text attributed to the sage Laozi 老子 (a.k.a. Lao Tzu or Lao Tse). The *Daodejing* opens with the famous lines '*dao* 道 *ke* 可 *dao* 道 *fei* 非 *chang* 常 *dao* 道 / *ming* 名 *ke* 可 *ming* 名 *fei* 非 *chang* 常 *ming* 名', or, in one English rendering, "A Way that can be followed is not a constant Way. / A name that can be named is not a constant name."[3] Throughout the *Daodejing*, ultimate reality is said to be beyond all words, although words are helpful in perceiving (and perhaps even in creating or constructing) the particular "ten thousand things" (*wan wu* 萬物) that make up the ordinary stuff of the world.

To follow this Daoist *Dao* and get by in the world, the poetic language of the *Daodejing* recommends adopting a broadly submissive, more-or-less easy-going attitude, and it includes many famous, contradictory-sounding claims about the weak overcoming the strong, the soft overcoming the hard, and all kinds of stuff like that. This contradictory-sounding material is sometimes talked about in terms of the "unity of opposites" or in terms of notions such as *complementarity*.[4] In the world of the *Daodejing*, there are polar oppositions embedded throughout reality—oppositions between two things or forces or concepts or whatever that at least seem to be mutually exclusive in terms of their properties or contents. At some level, however—perhaps only at the level beyond or before words and concepts—the *Daodejing* sees those opposites as really being one and the same. At the very least, the *Daodejing* sees the two poles of

[3] *The Daodejing of Laozi*, translated by Philip J. Ivanhoe (New York: Seven Bridges, 2002).
[4] For a detailed account of complementarity in the *Daodejing*, see Karyn Lai, "The *Daodejing*: Resources for Contemporary Feminist Thinking," *Journal of Chinese Philosophy* 27:2 (June 2000), pp. 131–153.

each of these pairs of opposites as being intertwined in some intimate and counterintuitive manner.

For example, with regard to pairs of opposites such as the weak and the strong, the hard and the soft, or the masculine and feminine, the *Daodejing* seems either to do one of two things. On the one hand, the *Daodejing* sometimes seems to deny that the contrast between each of the linked opposites is really as strong as it might seem, that there really is no stark contrast between the weak and the strong or between the masculine and the feminine, since anything that seems to be strong is really infused with weakness, and everything that is masculine also contains non-trivial feminine aspects. On the other hand, the *Daodejing* also seems to insist that, while there *is* a contrast between the pairs of opposites, the typically undervalued one of each contrasting pair is bound to win out in the end. Thus, the weak will overcome the strong and the soft and submissive will take down the hard and domineering. In many ways, the Daoists stuck up for the underdog.

In the cosmology of the classical Chinese tradition, there is that famous tension between the *Yin* 陰 and the *Yang* 陽, between that which is dark, submissive, passive, feminine, and quiet (the *Yin*) and that which is bright, striving, active, masculine, and speaks (the *Yang*). As anyone who has ever set foot in a head shop knows, the *Yin* and the *Yang* came to be represented in Chinese iconography with the swirly image known as the *taiji* symbol. According to the *Yin-Yang* cosmology, all phenomena are, somehow, tied to both *Yin* and *Yang*, and these two forces are in opposition and tension, with one being dominant at some times and the other at other times. How exactly this *Yin-Yang* cosmology works in the details is a big question, but even the vague, pop-cultural understanding of there being two forces in dynamic opposition in all things is good enough for us at this point. It can help us understand complementarity in the Daoist *Dao*.

The text of the *Daodejing* uses the terms '*Yin*' and '*Yang*' only once (in Chapter 42), but the complex interrelationship between opposites is a major take-home message of the entire text. Again, it is not entirely clear what the *Daodejing* thinks of the pairs of opposites: Sometimes the distinction between seeming opposites is denied, while at other times the supposedly weaker of each pair of opposites is held up as being the one that is, shall we say, truly down with the *Dao*. Whatever the exact scholarly details (they're best saved for another discussion), that great tango of *Yin* and *Yang*—the subtle complementarity of opposites—is part and parcel of the Great *Dao* of the *Daodejing*.

Oh, What a Dream: Johnny Cash and Zhuangzi

If we think only of the Confucian *dao* of traditional Chinese society or the wordless, contradiction-laden, metaphysically spooky *Dao* of the *Daodejing*, we might be hard pressed to see what the heck the notion of a *Dao* has to do with Johnny Cash. (And that's regardless of whether the word is spelled with a big 'D', a little 'd', a 'T', or whatever.) To begin to sort things out, let's look to another figure of classical Daoism, lesser known outside of China or narrow academic circles, whose version of Daoism provides an easier point of departure. This figure is Zhuangzi 莊子 (a.k.a. Chuang Tzu), the iconoclastic storyteller who emphasizes free wandering, who defends the value of being useless, and who mixes logic and absurdity to create a kind of Daoist intellectual stew. We can use similarities between Zhuangzi and the path and persona mapped out in the songs of Johnny Cash as a kind of stepping stone to understanding Cash in terms of the notion of a *Dao*. (Don't worry: We'll get back to the *Daodejing* and Confucius eventually.)

To make things easier, I'll set aside questions of authorship, both for Zhuangzi and for Cash. In spite of what scholars say about the authorship of the *Zhuangzi*, I will assume that the entire text we now have was written by a single figure named "Zhuangzi." I will also pretend that the oeuvre of Johnny Cash consists in songs that, for our purposes at least, involve his own words (regardless of who gets songwriting credits). With both Zhuangzi and Cash, we have collections of stories of ruffians and folk heroes and people who are in one way or another down on their luck and doing what they can to get by and flourish. With both Zhuangzi and Cash, we have tales of people dealing with life, death, and hardship in distinctive and often inspiring ways—ways that form a distinctive *Dao* in each case: the *Dao* of Zhuangzi and the *Dao* of Cash. Worrying about authorship or songwriting credit would only muck things up.

Let's start by looking at some striking parallels between the stories of Zhuangzi and those of Cash—parallels that can be seen if one looks with the right kind of eyes (to steal a phrase from the great Hunter S. Thompson). The opening chapter of the *Zhuangzi* is titled "Free and Easy Wandering," and in it Zhuangzi puts forward marvelous stories about characters rambling the world in complete, unrestrained freedom. There is the tall tale of a giant bird named Peng, who flies extraordinary distances at unbelievable heights—heights so high that the sky not only looks blue above, but blue down below, as well. Other creatures cannot understand Peng's grand wanderlust, and they deride it as useless or wasteful. There is a story of the mythic sage Leizi (not Laozi), who travels from place to place, unconstrained by "the trouble of walking." (Leizi, so the story goes, gets around by flying on the wind—good work if you can get it.) There's a story about the grumpy philosopher Hui Shi complaining about some giant gourds he's got that he can't figure out what to do with. In that story, Zhuangzi ribs Hui Shi for not understanding useless things, telling Hui Shi that he should have fashioned one of the apparently useless gourds into a sort of tub and used it like a boat to float aimlessly. Such stories of wanderings have analogies in many, many Johnny Cash songs, from "I've Been Everywhere" to "The Wanderer" (on U2's *Zooropa*) to just about every other song in between.

In the third chapter of the *Zhuangzi* text, there's a story about Cook Ding and his marvelous butchering skill. Ding is so masterful in his use of his carving knife that he never needs to change or sharpen his blade. He simply swings his knife, using his perception of the subtle *Dao* to find the almost non-existent spaces between the parts of the ox, cutting away in perfect harmony with the task at hand. Such a tale of astounding physical skill is echoed in John Henry's use of his hammer in Cash's version of "The Legend of John Henry's Hammer." In that song, the folk hero John Henry swings his hammer with such speed and force that observers fear the mountain he's working in (he's driving spikes into rock to bore a railroad tunnel) is going to cave in. In fact, it's just John Henry's hammer "suckin' wind."

There are other places where one can find parallels between Zhuangzi and Cash, if one is willing to find them. There are Zhuangzi's numerous accounts of physically broken and oddly shaped people, on the one hand, and Cash's description of the haphazardly produced, strange-looking car in "One Piece at a Time," on the other. There's the logic-defying narrative structure in the early *Zhuangzi* text and Cash's time-bending narrative mistake about how many minutes are left in the live rendition of "Twenty-Five Minutes to Go" on the *At Folsom Prison* album. (For those who missed it, at one point there's eight minutes to go before the hanging, then there's five, and then there's seven minutes left.) There are Zhuangzi's charismatic criminals—be they larger-than life scofflaws such as Robber Zhi or the numerous compelling individuals who have had their bodies mutilated as punishment for running afoul of the powers that be—and the Cash characters who will confront a jailer and then laugh in his face and spit in his eye.

These parallels between the *Zhuangzi* and Johnny Cash establish at least some minimal commonality between the iconoclastic Daoism of the *Zhuangzi* text and the proto-Outlaw country of Johnny Cash. Still, those familiar with the *Zhuangzi* might protest that although there are some superficial points of analogy, the *Zhuangzi* presents a very different worldview than do Cash's songs. And, of course, that's right. Zhuangzi, in spite of the cast of crazy characters in his stories and the rebelliousness found in many places throughout his tales, advocated a kind of quietude that isn't present in Cash, even if one takes into account the somber defeatism one can find in many late Cash songs. And Cash's Christian themes of sin and redemption are absent from classical Daoism.[5]

Overall, the *Zhuangzi* does present a different worldview than Cash's songs do, and I don't want to deny that. Still, there are important commonalities. In a nutshell, neither Zhuangzi nor Johnny Cash see the good life as requiring getting much in the way of a good break along the way, and they both present their ideas about the good life with humor and with a streak of rebelliousness. As I see it, the *Dao* of Cash is one of good-hearted laughter in the face of deep trouble, and the vision that is associated with this *Dao* is one that is in significant ways similar to that of Zhuangzi.

---

[5] However, Thomas Michael argues in *The Pristine Dao: Metaphysics in Early Daoist Discourse* (Albany: SUNY Press, 2005) that the notion of a soteriology— that is, the notion of an account of salvation or redemption, a notion whose application is most obvious in Christian contexts—is also appropriate for discussions of classical Daoist metaphysics.

The *Dao* of the Man in Black

So, what then *is* this *Dao* of Cash, exactly? Well, first of all, this *Dao*—this Way—is a *road*way. It involves roads and highways, and even railroads and seaways. It's about traveling and freedom, about moving from somewhere to somewhere else, and about all the potential that's involved in that. But unlike the "free and easy wandering" of Zhuangzi's sage, who roams without any kind of worry, in most of Cash's songs the ideal of the road and the movement it entails is edged with trouble. Those who do the traveling are often criminals being hounded by the law, and even if they're not, they're usually running from something. Yes, for Cash there *is* an important kind of freedom on the road—on that particular modern day paved *dao*—and there's the thrill and joy of travel, too. But it's freedom defined against a background of the chains that are being fled, whether they're the literal chains of imprisonment or the more sticky chains of a guilty conscience.

Thus, for Johnny Cash the road and the act of traveling are loaded with dual significance. And of course, given the Christian imagery and iconography that run throughout his songs, this is unsurprising. Cash's Christian imagery is an imagery of Fall and Redemption, and often of a fall again. It provides what scholars call a "soteriology"—an account of salvation and how it happens—but it's a soteriology that's especially applicable to the lives of Honky Tonk rogues.

Still, unlike many of the fire-and-brimstone ways in which the Christian imagery of Fall and Redemption gets used in other contexts, in Cash's songs there is an upbeat quality to much of it. Even in particular songs where the mood is dark and the content is bleak as it can be, even in those songs where the voice is of someone defeated by his own self, the very fact that it is *Johnny Cash's* voice that is doing the singing reminds us of the humor and the lightheartedness of his other songs. There is, even in the darkest and saddest of his songs, the presence of the easygoing side of Johnny Cash, sitting there in his voice and our memories.

There is even something of the *Dao* of the *Daodejing* in the *Dao* of Johnny Cash's songs, a country music version of the *Yin* and the *Yang*. It's something not unlike what the band the Drive-By Truckers call "the duality of the Southern thing." The lightness in the darkness and the laughter in the suffering form an Americana version of the unity of opposites. True, Cash isn't much interested in the particular polarities of the *Daodejing*, but his songs have their own mysterious, complementary pairs, and the life described in the songs is a life that constantly bumps into those pairs. There are the polarities of the criminal and the man of the law ("He said Willy Lee your name is not Jack Brown / You're the dirty hack that shot your woman down" in "Cocaine Blues"), of the son and the father (for example "Boy Named Sue"), of man and woman (think of any just about any duet he does with June Carter),[6] of sin and repentance (there're too many songs to mention on that one), and of God and humanity (everywhere). Cash has freedom of the road, on the one hand, and being chained down as your past catches up with you, on the other.

For each of these pairs of opposites (and there are other pairs, too), there cannot be one extreme without the other—if not in the literal sense that the criminal and the man of law are in fact one and the same at every moment, then at least in the sense that anyone who plays one of the roles is going to get sucked into the other, in one way or the other, eventually. When the judge in "The Long Black Veil" asks, "Son, what is your alibi?", the judge really seems to sympathize with that lonely avatar of Johnny Cash who appears as the singer of the song, sitting on the witness stand, trying to defend himself against accusations that might be wrong in the detail but are right on the mark in spirit. (The character in the song didn't commit the crime for which he is on trial, but he is guilty of something: At the time of the crime, he was, after all, with the wife of his best friend.) In so many of Cash's songs there is this central duality in things, this irresolvable tension: Freedom is there, but only against the backdrop of the possibility (or even the palpable threat) of being imprisoned, damned or simply found out. At the same time, there is—even in the darkest moments of punishment and suffering—an exuberance that's sometimes defiant, sometimes endearing, but always there, at least under the surface.

---

[6] The masculine-feminine duality is in the *Daodejing*, but it has a different flavor in Cash's music.

One Piece at a Time: And What a Hodgepodge *Dao* It Is

Let's bring this high-flying language—what Zhuangzi might call "big and useless words"—back down to earth and talk specifics. Think of the song "I've Been Everywhere," from *Unchained*. As Cash sings with abandon about all the places he's been, he sneaks in the following: "I'm a killer." It's easy to miss, but it's there: the darkness behind the supposedly free wandering.

Think of more obvious examples. Take "Folsom Prison Blues." Obviously, it's a song about imprisonment and the longing for a freedom that won't be had in this lifetime. But even there, in that song about punishment and being trapped, there's a good-natured defiance—from the claim that he killed a man "just to watch him die" to the very tone of Cash's voice throughout the entire performance. Here we have the theme of wandering-tinged-with-constraint of other songs turned on its head. It's not a song of the road, haunted by the possibility of being caught. Rather, it's a song of being locked up already, aching for the impossible chance to run once more. It's constraint aching for freedom.

That's the duality of freedom and punishment. Now consider Cash's other prominent dualities. Think again about the duality of Fall and Redemption. This is, of course, the center of what we might call the Christian *Dao*, and it might seem to have little to do with any *Dao* that's inspired by Daoism. But the fact that sinning and being redeemed form their own polarity, and that for Cash redemption is tied to the crimes that make it possible, allows for us to think of sin and redemption as part of Cash's *Dao*. Fall and Redemption are central to the *Yin* and *Yang* of Cash's world.

Beyond the Fall-Redemption pair, there's the closely related duality of love and violence. Fidelity and betrayal, too. These polarities overlap in messy ways, but if we're willing to look at Cash's songs with a keen eye to the tensions between opposing forces that somehow depend upon each other for their existence (or at least their significance), they jump out at us. Notice how seamlessly violence is linked to love—and to the rest of life, for that matter. Delia is gone, Cash sings on *American Recordings*, and she's gone, of course, because the person who is the voice of the song shot her. Otherwise, as the song says, he would have had her for his wife. And there's "Cocaine Blues" again, too: "Early one morning while making my rounds / I took a shot of cocaine and I shot my woman down." Violence and love, fidelity and betrayal: It's everywhere for Cash.

Now, if the only songs about love and transgression were songs like "Delia" and "Cocaine Blues," we might dismiss them as merely Cash's version of the dark, misogynistic self-loathing of so much twentieth-century American pop culture rather than seeing them as part of the *Yin* and *Yang* of a distinctive *Dao*, but there are other songs in which the tension between men and women and the tension between heterosexual desire and heterosexual betrayal find a different balance. Consider "Jackson." Cash threatens to head down to Jackson to "mess around," and June tells him to "go ahead and wreck your health" and "make a big fool of yourself." Cash replies with a boast: The women in Jackson are going to make him "teach 'em what they don't know how." June is not cowed, of course. They both sing about the fire in their relationship going out, but in the way they deliver the lyrics we can see that the fire is really still burning—even if it is only the threats and the sexual tension of possible betrayal that keeps it burning. Here, we've got not only the polarity of fidelity and betrayal, but all the polarities of man and woman, of husband and wife, and of desire and boredom, as well. They're all wrapped up and mixed together. There are multiple, interrelated dualities on this stretch of the *Dao* of Cash.

Consider "I Hung My Head," one of the great, bleak songs from *The Man Comes Around.* Here Cash sings about the absurdity of one awful motion—was it even an action?—that resulted in a bullet being fired across the plain and killing a lone rider on a horse. He sings, "My brother's rifle went off in my hand / A shot rang out across the land / The horse he kept running, the rider was dead / I hung my head, I hung my head." The singer gets caught (but only after running away—the polarity of the freedom of the road and imprisonment again!) and goes before the judge. The judge says, "Explain to the courtroom what went through your mind / And we'll ask the jury what verdict they find." We don't have romantic-love-and-violence or fidelity-and-betrayal here. Instead, we have the intertwining of the criminal and the man of the law. The judge, that paragon of the Law, sincerely wants to help the accused to tell his story. In this song, serious as all get-go, Johnny Cash sings of an ultimate trans-

gression—the killing of someone—and does so in a way that
brings out the apparent absurdity of so much seemingly intentional action.   Or maybe it's about the slippery boundary
between what you do and what you just let happen. In the end,
we find that it is by doing (or is it "letting happen"?) this awful
act of killing that the singer eventually manages to be saved, and
saved by the very figure he wronged. As the singer approaches
the gallows, the lyrics go, "And out in the distance a trick of the
brain / I see a lone rider crossing the plain / He's come to fetch
me to see what they done / We'll ride together 'til Kingdom
come." In the end, the opposites of sin and redemption, of
action and non-action, of death and life, of perpetrator and victim—they all come together in the most sincere of musical
moments.

I Still Miss Someone: The Self and Its Travels
Along the Way

I've been pulling lyrics from Cash, tossing in all kinds of dis-
parate themes and lumping them together under the Daoist version of the unity of opposites, and I've arguably been none too
careful in the process. But don't forget that the classical Daoist
texts weren't very systematic, either, and we're talking about
country music, anyway. In spite of the free and easy path we've
cut through Chinese thought and country music, there are
enough similarities between Cash and Zhuangzi and between
Cash and the *Daodejing* that we can at least get *something* out
of thinking of the *Dao* and the duality of Johnny Cash.

Let's think a bit about the notion of the *self* and how it plays
out in the material we've been discussing. Zhuangzi, when talking about the Daoist sage, writes, "The Perfect Man has no self;
the Holy Man has no merit; the Sage has no fame."[7] As Burton
Watson points out in his translation, all three clauses are about
the Daoist sage. Zhuangzi is saying that one who is down with
the *Dao* does not even think about his or her *self*, does not care
to receive credit for the good he or she does, and does not have
any desire for a reputation. Combined with the other stories
throughout the *Zhuangzi*, a Daoist ideal emerges according to

---

[7] Burton Watson, translator, *The Complete Works of Chuang Tzu* (New York:
Columbia, 1968), p. 32.

which following the true *Dao* requires that one lose all self-consciousness. One must, somehow, forget oneself and simply be free.

On the *Dao* of Johnny Cash, in contrast, full-blown forgetfulness of the self is not in the cards. There may be a yearning to escape from one's past, present, or future, or even a yearning to escape from one's very self. But it doesn't happen, or at least it doesn't happen for long. In Johnny Cash's world, the self is a burden that one has to carry, and the best one can do is to hope for some help from above and, in the meantime, to share one's pain by singing and telling one's story. Cash doesn't usually paint a picture of the self having all its sins and demons drop away. You're stuck with that stuff. But he does sing songs of pain and laughter and craziness and love—songs that, when you listen to them in the right way, can make you realize that you're not alone. There're others on that path, too, and if Johnny Cash is or was one of them, well, that is not bad company to keep.

Let's return to the Confucians and their social *dao*. They saw a human life as consisting in a progression, a long struggle to master all the aspects of the Confucian path. The Confucian *dao* involved traveling a temporal path through a human lifetime. It was a path that required strenuous effort from everyone who followed it, but it was a path of progress and growth, at least for those who worked hard at it.

For Cash, too, there is a common theme of an individual moving—though maybe not progressing—along a path through a lifetime. Many of the voices in his songs are those of older characters reflecting on their lives' journeys, often from the last moments of life or even from beyond the grave. There's an implicit commitment to a view of the human self as something that travels (both literally and metaphorically) and changes through time. For most of Cash's characters, the self collects sin, guilt, and regret along the way, to be sure, and it falls off the straight and narrow more often than it would like. But the self finds its way back to the Way.

But maybe that's not quite it. Perhaps it's better to say that the Way of Johnny Cash is a lot wider than the straight and narrow path of traditional morality, and that it's really pretty hard to wander off of it at all. We might even say that for Cash the *Dao* is a very wide superhighway, and that what's called the "straight and narrow" is merely a single, poorly marked lane on it. No matter how far you drift out of your proper lane, no matter how much you screw up your life, you can take comfort in knowing that you're still on that Big Highway. (Of course, it might be that you're riding on the shoulder, or perhaps you're out of gas, or maybe even you're all turned around and heading the wrong way. But don't worry: There'll be help along eventually, and in any case the Man in Black understands your troubles and has been down this road before.)

Whether or not any of these extensions of the *dao*-metaphor work (or whether the metaphor has reached its useful limit here), the point is that Cash, like the Confucians, emphasizes what we might call the temporality of the self—the idea that one's self exists on a path in time, and that the self changes as it travels along that path. But of course, the Confucians more often than not see their path as one of steady, even if slow and arduous, progress, while Cash's *Dao* involves fits and starts, to say the least.

Those fits and starts and Cash's tolerance for them can remind us of the more easygoing, flawed Daoists, with their delight in the imperfect individuals who've managed to tap into the Great Way of things. But then again, while the Daoists' *Dao* is one of softness and spontaneity and nature, Cash's is one of the indulging of desires, of periodic self-loathing, of both regret and the joy of the sin, of excitement and loss and the open road and the jailhouse all rolled up into some massive, multi-layered mess of dualities.

For those of us who have momentarily lost ourselves in a Johnny Cash song, who have found something of our own persona in one of Cash's many characters—well, thinking in terms of a distinctive Way running through it all might help us get a little further on down the line from whatever place we happen to be trying to get away from. That ain't too bad.

PART II

Life

4

Cash and Work

SAMUEL A. BUTLER

I've never picked cotton. Johnny Cash did, and my parents did, and to hear them talk about it there's something about that sort of work that stays with you, even years after the scratches on your hands have healed, years after cotton has long since been overthrown as king.

Part of it is the experience of poverty. People don't pick cotton for fun. Poverty can make work seem like a form of slavery—the difference between making furniture as a hobby and making furniture for three dollars a day when you're twelve years old. Johnny Cash grew up in Depression-era poverty somewhat alleviated by what he called New Deal "communalism," working long days in the fields as a boy trying to get some cotton out of the Mississippi Delta mud they called "gumbo."

If he sometimes worked hard, he was also often hardly working. He tells in his autobiography of listening to the radio on the sly at night, his father yelling at him to go to bed so as to be able to work in the morning. He was out fishing the afternoon his brother Jack, working to augment the family income, was killed by a table saw. When he was trying to get a foot in the door of the music industry, he half-heartedly held down a job as an appliance salesman, spending his "workday" listening to the radio in the car or some local front porch music.

If we're talking about Johnny Cash, it's not obvious that you can just assume that work and music are opposed. Sure, we say that people "play" music and "play" is the opposite of work. Sure, there are Ray Cash's admonitions to young J.R. that the music on the radio isn't "real", like the work in the fields. On the other hand, Johnny Cash wrote in *Cash* that the first time his father expressed pride in him was after he had achieved some success as a recording artist. In the same book, he begins his account of himself first with a family history, followed immediately by a work history prior to becoming a professional musician. Johnny Cash's own history is fascinating; bringing it together with what he wrote about work and workers makes the questions even more intriguing: what did work mean to Johnny Cash? How might that change the way we ourselves think of it?

Why Work Matters

Quite a lot rides on what we mean by "work." In "Workin' Man Blues," Merle Haggard sings, "a working man like me's never been on welfare, and that's one place you will not be—if you're working." Of course, nowadays we don't have anything like New Deal "communalism" in this country. Most people on welfare are required to work for the state, and they usually work at well below the minimum wage. Even those who aren't required to participate in workfare often do things like take care of children, and it makes a big difference whether taking care of children is considered "working" or not.

"Working" is often seen as an important way of participating in and contributing to society. What we call "working" and what we refuse to call "working" is, then, in some sense a way of saying who we think is contributing to society and who isn't. Calling something "work" is, to some extent, a way of honoring the activity and by extension the person who performs it.

What Is Work?

It seems to a lot of people—including Ray Cash—that something like playing music becomes "working" when you get your first royalty check. If you can get paid for it, it's work. If you can't, it isn't. Oddly enough Socrates, the first philosopher, distinguished his own activity from that of rival teachers by pointing out that he steadfastly refused payment for asking questions and engaging in arguments with his fellow citizens. For Socrates, to get paid for doing philosophy would show that it wasn't really philosophy but some sort of pyramid scheme. The people who did charge for their teachings in Classical Athens were called

"Sophists", and it's from Socrates's opinion of them that we have the derogatory word "sophistry."

There are a lot of problems with this sort of market-driven definition. Let's say I'm a baker. I worked as a baker before I went to graduate school. I made okay money, a little more than minimum wage, enough to cover my half of the rent of a small apartment and to go out with friends every once in awhile. I liked baking. So much so that I would often make bread at home. I didn't get paid for making bread at home, but the market-driven definition would call my making bread at home "non-work," while the bread I made at the bakery would be called "work." While the context in which an activity is performed probably has something to do with whether or not it's work, the market-driven definition doesn't seem to have anything at all to do with the activity itself.

This isn't to say that context isn't important. It is. When Luke has to move his dirt out of Boss Kean's ditch in *Cool Hand Luke*, it seems strange to suggest that it is "work." It's punishment. It's punishment that is harsh because the exertion is so obviously pointless. The activity itself is largely the same as when the chain gang is spreading sand over the road to be tarred, but it seems that the purpose of the activity makes a lot of difference. Purpose seems to come from both the activity itself (it does or achieves something particular) and the context in which it is performed (that something particular is useful).

Several philosophers have tried to identify work by looking at the various purposes we are trying to achieve by undertaking various activities. Aristotle includes in his *Politics* a discussion of the sorts of work that must be done in an ancient Greek city-state, and descriptions of the sorts of people who do them. The idea that work shapes us and that we are made for certain kinds of work has a long history. In the twentieth century, Hannah Arendt (1906–1975) described *The Human Condition* as being divided into three areas of activity: labor, work, and action. Labor consists of providing for sustaining life—making things like food which stay in the world only briefly before they are consumed, making it possible to start laboring again. Work is the creation of a humanized world—our cities and monuments, maybe landfills and Styrofoam as well, unfortunately.

We often think of work just as something that makes life possible. On this version of things, the point of doing work is to be able to stop, to be able to pursue leisure with which to spend time with family or friends, to play music or to read. All of these "leisure activities" invest life with meaning in some sense or another. I work around the house so that my family can live in it, but that work is only worthwhile insofar as it makes it possible for me to spend time and develop relationships with my family.

The Value of Work

This looks like a promising direction, but one shortcoming still remains—sometimes work can play a role in giving meaning to one's life, too. It would be silly to suggest that Johnny Cash's music—assuming it counts as work—didn't have anything to do with who he was; the same could presumably be said of a preacher or maybe even a philosophy professor. If meaning can come from at least some forms of work, then maybe work can be valuable in two ways: on the one hand, it might have value that comes from its being paid labor, or from its producing a useful result. Since this value comes from something outside of the work itself (namely, whomever has hired me, or the list that's lying around of "stuff that needs to be done"), this can be called "extrinsic value." On the other hand, just performing the work might seem like a worthwhile thing, regardless of what it gets done, regardless of whether I get paid for it. Since this value seems to come from within the work itself, it can be called "intrinsic value."

If work has intrinsic value, then it adds something to my life, simply by virtue of the fact that I perform it. When we make children do chores, at least part of what we want to do is to teach them responsibility. What it adds to their lives is presumably a large part of why we do it. For adults, our work might be an important part of who we are. Thinking about the intrinsic value of work in this way takes us a good bit past a conception according to which work is just "doing stuff" or "making stuff," but it seems like it's an important part of the way that we think about work.

Love's Labor

Somewhere in between the idea of work as extrinsically valuable and the idea of work as intrinsically valuable is a form of work that seems to combine the two in a very direct way. When a preacher visits a parishioner in the hospital, presumably that is work. Why is it valuable? The same question might be asked of a parent caring for a child or a teacher teaching a student. All of these are examples of what some philosophers—including Eva Kittay, in *Love's Labor*—talk about under the heading of "care work." Care work is a form of work that doesn't seem to really produce anything, and for the most part it is either badly paid or not paid at all. Preachers and teachers are paid worse than people with similar levels of education working in industry; parents aren't paid at all. All of these people, however, seem to find their work to be extremely valuable in ways that don't show up in their paychecks. What's more, the people towards whom their work is directed seem to share their appraisal: many of the most powerful experiences of childhood, experiences that shape the rest of our lives, were interactions and relationships with parents and teachers. Churchgoers are often able to make it through particularly difficult parts of their lives because of the intervening care they receive from preachers who visit them in hospitals, or who listen to their frustrations when no one else is interested. Finally, I take it that people who work in these ways would usually list these activities as of chief importance in shaping who they are. If you've been close personal friends with someone for years, know all about her hobbies and her interests, and only then find out that she has two children, you probably assume that she's not the greatest mother.

Care work is a useful concept insofar as it brings together so many of the ways in which we define work: it has some role to play in the production of valuable things like relationships and functional adults. It is a particularly good example of the way in which work can be an important element in developing who we are and extending what we can do. It is contextual in the sense that different societies care for each other in different ways, with many different structures, but it is a pervasive phenomenon in the sense that it's hard to imagine any society being able to exist without performing care in some sense or another.

Another Day Older and a-Deeper in Debt

Up to this point, I have the idea that work can play an important part in making us who we are, but it's also true—at least in our society—that work often keeps us from being who we want to be. We might not be able to move to a different place because we aren't sure if we can get a job there. Working long hours might take us away from our families, or prevent us from keeping up with our friends. Since work is connected to things like the availability of food and shelter (you have to work to pay rent and to buy groceries), work exercises a certain necessity over our lives.

Necessity in this sense is often opposed to freedom. If I didn't have to work, I might spend more time with my family. I might move back down South, or start playing guitar again. It's difficult for me to imagine doing this because the necessity of working imposes constraints on my freedom. I—and I don't think this is idiosyncratic—am often envious of people who seem to be able to make their work work for them rather than working for their work, people who decide what they want to do with their lives and then find work along the way. These are people, I take it, who have been able to exercise freedom in the context of work. I think Johnny Cash was one of these people, and I think it shows in the way that he talks about work.

Work and Identity

Cash's work, was a large part of who he was. Even when he covers songs, he covers them because they say something he wants to say. His decisions about what sort of music to perform and record, his struggles with record companies, are a testament to the pains he took to make his music an expression of himself. He struggled with Sam Phillips to record gospel music, and eventually was able to record quite a lot of it. He spent most of his career as an artist who didn't really fit on the pop charts, but didn't really seem to be part of the rhinestone jumpsuit country crowd, either. These struggles extended over a large part of Cash's career, probably best expressed in the 1984 self-parody, "Chicken in Black." Cash was able to continue the struggle, winning battles here and there (playing "The Ballad of Ira Hayes" in front of Richard Nixon, getting his several concept albums pressed). He finally won the war with the large amount of material he recorded with Rick Rubin, some of the most expressive music of his discography.

His work was both extrinsically and intrinsically valuable, and he overcame the necessity of work and was able to work with a substantial amount of freedom. What's more, having achieved this, he turned around and offered hope for people who work to live, rather than living to work, for people who try to get out of work in order to be able to live life just a little bit.

In some sense, having your work make up who you are isn't optional. The question is whether you want the identity you end up with. There's a big difference between getting saddled with an identity ('Oh, that's Sam—he cleans up all the messes we make') and constructing your own identity ('well, I mostly work in social and political philosophy'). The first verse of "Let Him Roll" gets at the way in which work can leave you without an awful lot to hang your hat on:

> Well, he was a wino, tried and true,
> Done about everything there is to do—
> He'd worked on freighters, and he'd worked in bars,
> He'd worked on farms, and he'd worked on cars.

In one sense, the wino is who he is because of his work history: he's the sort of guy who's done just about everything a body can do. In another sense, he is who he is because of something that goes beyond his work history—experiences, memories, and stories that arise from the different things he's done. Any money he might have made from these jobs has dried up, leaving the residue of a lifetime of half-remembered stories populated with half-forgotten people. It is a work history rich to the point of overflowing a Thunderbird-addled memory, a history whose only extrinsic traces are "some crumpled up stubs from the welfare checks" and "a picture of a whore in Dallas." A lifetime of physical labor, of labor spent making stuff, thus ends up as an ephemeral memory. This is a sort of labor that, if it has any value at all to the man has performed it, can have at most the intrinsic value of having shaped his personality, of having drawn lines on his face and left traces in his mind.

Work and the South

At one level, the sort of work addressed in "Southern Accents" isn't much different—it's the work of a man for whom "that drunk tank in Atlanta was just a motel room." He is a share-cropper who just might go work the orange groves down in Orlando if they don't freeze over. His labor doesn't seem to have left much in the way of the material traces of extrinsic value, either—if you go out drinking in the upscale bars of Buckhead, you don't wind up in the drunk tank—but here the intrinsic meaning of labor has been organized to give a rich sense of meaning to a life. The Yankees may call it "dumb," but "I've got my own way of working, and everything is done / With a Southern accent where I come from." Our South is the poorest part of the country, but it's also the richest. We've got our own way of talking, our own way of working, our own way of pray-ing—our own way of living. This accumulated intrinsic value is a legacy of hard work that no bank can foreclose on.

Of course, a lot of the time we aren't too sure what exactly that way of working might be. We admire hard work, but we're even more jealous of the guy next to us who always seems to be able to get out of it. If the South is the Land of Cotton, then picking cotton must be a particularly Southern form of work (the same way that you don't hear too many yankees talking about this or that "cotton pickin' thing"). Where "Southern Accents" approaches Southern labor as a question of establish-ing identity, "I Never Picked Cotton" portrays the way in which the necessity of work can be a threat to one's identity. As a child, the speaker in this song "played in the dirt while the oth-ers worked / 'til they couldn't straighten up their backs" and promised himself that he would escape the sort of life whose only content is working to ensure his continued existence for another day of work.

"I Never Picked Cotton" is at once an attack on the con-straints of work and a caution to those who would rebel against them. As he is awaiting execution, the only thing the speaker can "look back on with pride" is the fact that he never picked cotton. By escaping the constraints of work, he forged an iden-tity for himself, but that identity turned out to be a largely empty one. He gained his freedom, but was unable to do anything worthwhile—in his own eyes—with that freedom.

Getting Free from Work

There are many paths to freedom, however, besides stealing ten dollars and a pickup truck. In "Get Rhythm" and "Country Boy,"

Cash paints images of workers whose identity is largely separated from their work. They refuse the idea that their work ought to have some sort of intrinsic value, and concentrate instead on leisure—that space outside of work—in which it's possible to pursue other ways of establishing meaning.

The shoeshine boy of "Get Rhythm" doesn't get upset that he has a dirty, hard, badly paying job because he can sing as he works. Leisure for him is not the time after his work is done, but the mental space freed up as his hands move mechanically to shine shoes, separating his attention from his body. With this separation, he can carry on a sort of performance, popping his rag and singing as he works.

There's something profoundly disturbing about this image for those of us committed to building a world of good jobs. It seems to many of us that a job shouldn't end up dividing you up, leaving your head in the clouds while your hands are on the earth. In some sense this sort of separation can be enjoyable—I remember in particular a job I had for a while stuffing envelopes. It didn't take too long before I could read as I stuffed the envelopes, and I enjoyed reading. Of course, what this shows, it seems, isn't so much that we should all work as envelope stuffers. Rather, it shows that envelope-stuffing is a pretty low-down job to have someone do. The idea is that a job is better insofar as it allows me to develop skills, to carry forward projects that I actually value. That's why I like doing philosophy better than stuffing envelopes—it's nice to be able to believe that I'm getting better at it; I like to think that it's worthwhile to spend time reading the stuff I read, writing the stuff I write. I get paid for it, too, which is nice. It just seems to me that my situation shouldn't be so unusual.

My work doesn't seem to be too terribly much like that of the shoeshine boy. Cash's lyrics in this song seem to imply that anyone who is unhappy with her work conditions—or conditions of life in general—ought to simply "get rhythm," to look at exploitation and inequality and say "'I like it' with a big, wide grin." I bring this up in such pointed terms because, while the reading I'm suggesting here is indeed plausible, I don't think it's defensible against the backdrop of Cash's wider commitment to social justice. I think the implication is rather that, no matter how difficult things may look, working people are stronger than their circumstances. Not only can they survive through exploitative labor practices and an unjust world, they can do it with strength, dignity and life. This doesn't mean that we shouldn't fight against injustice; it only means that we shouldn't let the fact that we've got to fight take all the fun out of it.

At least that's what I would like to think. In fact, I even think there's some reason to take this view seriously, as in "Country Boy" and "One Piece at a Time." Both songs portray workers who respond to the necessity of work with a determination to assert their freedom and stir up just enough trouble to make it all worthwhile. The country boy works long days on the farm, but manages to end the day with enough energy left over to go fishing or hunting. It's not obvious from the song whether he's working his own fields, whether he has the ability to tell the boss to stuff it halfway through the afternoon and head on down to the creek, but he looks to be doing all right regardless. Whatever the challenges of his job, they don't seem to be any sort of effective barrier to his enjoying all the finer things in life.

To some extent this is just as true of the Kentucky assembly line worker in "One Piece at a Time." When he goes up to Detroit and gets a job putting wheels on Cadillacs, he is overwhelmed by the profound disparity between the money left over at the end of the month and the MSRP of the cars he's building. In many ways, this looks like a classic case of exploitation: a lot of us share the intuition that making an object ought to give an individual some claim to ownership over it, and it is perhaps because of these intuitions that companies sometimes have employee purchasing programs to enable the people who build the stuff to own some of it.

I take it GM lacked such a program for our hero who, realizing that they "wouldn't miss just one little piece", devised a plan to steal, one piece at a time, all of the parts needed to build that Cadillac. The song ends with the comedy of a car put together from twenty-some-odd model years, but the image proves to be tragicomic: the prospect of spending your entire working life building cars you won't ever be able to afford is a real one. All too often, labor doesn't lead to owning, but rather to "living in the hopeless, hungry side of town." If Cash tried to do his bit to carry off a little darkness on his back, maybe his hope was that the rest of us might find ourselves with a little life in us, at the end of the day, when the work is through.

Freedom in Work and a Prison in San Quentin

All things considered, Cash's work was a lot more like mine than like that of most of the people he wrote about. I like my work quite a lot and, as I said before, it seems like Cash's work was probably a good bit of fun, too. At least part of why it was so fun was because it was so free, and at least part of why it was so free was, to put it bluntly, economic. He could stick it to the people who were nominally his bosses because he made them a lot of money. Most of us probably don't make nearly as much money for our bosses as Cash made for Columbia, so when our bosses tell us to jump, we have to at least pretend to care about how high we ought to. Cash's freedom stands in stark contrast to that of most of the people who show up in his songs, perhaps at no time more clearly than at his 1969 concert at San Quentin.

Early in the set Cash and his band performed the ballad, "Wreck of the Ol' 97." The narrative of the song is straightforward: it briefly tells the story of the Southern Railroad mail train that ran between Washington and Atlanta until it crashed on September 28th, 1903. The train was the fastest to date on the Southern Railroad, and its speed was quite profitable: it operated under a federal contract worth $140,000 per annum. Deductions were made from this amount, however, for every minute of every late arrival throughout the year. The railroad, therefore, did its utmost to put the screws on the engineers to keep to time. The song records the last such instances, when thirty-three-year-old Joseph Andrew "Steve" Broady was killed trying to make up the company's time. The song by itself is a sharp indictment of the relations of force under which most of us work, but even more pointed is what Cash says following the song:

> You know, we've been on tour for about a week now, after our last recording session, and they say old Johnny Cash works good under pressure. Put the screws on me and I'll screw right out from under you, is what I'm going to do, though. I'm tired of all that shit. I tell you what—the show is being recorded and televised for . . . England, and they told me, they said you got to do this song, you got to do that song, you got to stand like this or act like this . . . they just don't get it, man, you know? I'm here to do what you want me to and what I want to do. So what do you want to hear?

Cash delivers this monologue in front of a crowd of federal prisoners, presenting himself as someone too cunning and too determined to take instructions from a group of record company stiffs. What's more, he's on the side of the prisoners. He isn't in San Quentin because anyone forced him to be, but because he freely chooses to work on behalf of the least free people in our society. By asserting his own autonomy, Cash claims his work as labor that structures his own identity, that expresses his own freedom and—perhaps—does something to expand just a little the freedom of those chained to a job or locked in a cell block.

The fact that Johnny Cash was a man who would do something like this makes me proud to have his music on when friends stop by. Popular music is always, to some extent, working class music, but I can't imagine too many popular musicians around nowadays playing concerts in a state prison, much less putting themselves in the position of angering the guards and stirring up the inmates. Cash saw their place as his place, he saw this fight as his fight.

If I Were a Carpenter

The most influential political philosopher of the twentieth century, John Rawls, was born eleven years and five days before Johnny Cash. He was born in Baltimore, at the tenuous northern outskirts of the South, as Cash was born in the western reaches of the region. He died roughly a year before Cash did. In *A Theory of Justice*, he attempted to articulate what a just society would be like by proposing that we look at a society, with all the various positions where we could end up, without knowing where we stood in that society.

For Rawls, the idea comes from eighteenth-century German philosopher Immanuel Kant. Kant argued that we always ought to act like we could want—without contradiction—everyone else to act. If everyone went around shooting people just to watch them die, there wouldn't be anyone to do the shooting or get shot—thus the contradiction. Therefore, we shouldn't shoot people just to watch them die.

Rawls figures that we ought to set up society such that everyone in society would choose that society without knowing where they were in that society. No one would agree to a society with slavery, Rawls argues, unless they already knew that they weren't a slave. Therefore slavery is unjust. Likewise, no one would agree to a society where workers end up owing their souls to the company store.

For Cash, the idea comes from Jesus. Jesus argued that we ought to do unto others as we would have others do unto us. He said that whatever we do to the worst-off people in our society—prisoners at San Quentin, say—we do to him. Jesus welcomed bartenders and prostitutes into his presence. Cash wrote songs about workers and played them for prisoners.

Cash didn't have to get into any of these fights, and certainly not on the sides he did. He was a rich man, a man who could walk away from all of them and have an easier life. His example forces us to ask questions like the following: If you didn't know whether you would be in the audience or on the stage at San Quentin, would you have any different beliefs about the way that prisoners' lives were organized? If you didn't know whether you were a carpenter or a lady, would you have any different beliefs about the relationship that ought to exist between workers and the nobility?

Cash knew he stood on the stage. He knew he wasn't a carpenter. But he also knew that he stood with the prisoners, and he knew he stood with the workers. His work gave him freedom, and he used that freedom to enter the struggle, trying to make a move to make a few things right.

5

Ring of Truth: Johnny Cash and Populism

MIKA LAVAQUE-MANTY and
ROBERT W. MICKEY

Johnny Cash was a fascinating, complex figure who inspires different interpretations by listeners and critics. One thing on which all agree is that the "Man in Black" was a populist. As such, he joins a long line of American populists that includes William Jennings Bryan, Woody Guthrie, George Wallace, Bruce Springsteen, Bill O'Reilly, Lee Greenwood, Michael Moore, Will Rogers, and President George W. Bush. A diverse list, we'd all agree. What *is* a populist, anyhow? And what is popul*ism*?

For starters, "populism" is a term of both abuse and praise. To critics, it implies a cynical, used-car-salesmanship approach to politics, an appeal to the lowest common denominator. To those proud of their populism, it implies organic grassroots democracy, mobilization of the little guy against sinister elites. When it comes to political and cultural elites—academic theorists of democracy, say—populism gives them the willies. This is no surprise. Over the years, populism has remained consistently connected with anti-elitism. So we shouldn't be surprised to discover that political elites worry about populist calls to bypass, even undermine, existing power structures. And although populists don't exactly threaten democratic theorists' jobs, they do challenge one of the shibboleths of most modern democratic theory: that political discussion needs to be thoughtful, reasonable, intellectually engaging, and nuanced. Hence the willies.

But you don't have to be elite yourself to find populism troubling. On the one hand, there's something valuable about the populist reminders of the importance of democracy: if democracy matters, the little guy should not be ignored (nor the little gal, although populists are often guilty of this themselves). Politics is too important to be left to the policy wonks. On the other hand, populist movements often mix their calls for more democracy with claims about "dirty foreigners" and "Jewish conspiracies" and the like: simplistic, often xenophobic and racist rhetoric.

These tensions can't quite be reconciled, but we can get a better understanding of them by exploring Johnny Cash's populism. Johnny Cash's version of populism was free of the more unsavory sentiments: his politics was importantly anti-racist, for example. And although some might roll their eyes at Cash's fervent patriotism or ardent religiosity, they do so at the risk of their own democratic commitments, at least in a country whose citizens are patriotic and religious. In terms of its content, in terms of the beliefs he advocates, Cash's populism ranges from the admirable to the benign. Despite this, it raises some of the same concerns people have about uglier varieties of populism.

The key positive content in populism is its insistence even— and particularly—in the face of humiliation, on equal human dignity. On this score Johnny Cash, through his person, his music and his activism, is an exemplary figure. One key worry about populism is that its main virtue is also a vice: its straight talk can make politics simplistic. Populists don't need to have simplistic beliefs—here, too, Cash's appreciation of human complexity serves as a good example—but it does turn the mobilization of citizens into a simplistic matter. The move from an emotion, however justifiable, evoked by song and dance, charisma and rousing speeches, to conclusions is so quick as to be dangerous. Populist rhetoric has a ring of truth to it, but democracy needs more than a ring. A concert, say, like a mass rally, may be a rewarding emotional collective experience, but it's not a moment of collective *thinking*. And the absence of real, public deliberation, however prevalent that absence is in modern politics in general, should trouble small-d democrats. Another virtue of populism—its healthy distrust of elites and the political institutions that they influence—can also be double-edged. For this distrust lays in tension with the diagnosis and implied cures that some populists—like Cash—offer common folk. Sometimes it's the state that will come to the little guy's rescue, as Cash himself knew.

What Is Populism?

Populism in the United States emerged in the early nineteenth century when presidential candidate Andrew Jackson's critique of ruling elites started a wave of political participation among (white and male) commoners that crashed on the shores of Washington.[1] Similar popular critiques of ruling elites had been around before, of course, but democracy and its principle of majority rule added a new ingredient—popular movements could appeal to the ideals of democracy to frame their critiques. By the end of the nineteenth century, angry farmers across the West and South launched the Populist Party. They claimed that the course of democracy had been perverted and that the interests of the little guy—the building block of popular sovereignty—had been ignored. "We assert our purposes to be identical with the purposes of the National Constitution," declared the preamble of the 1892 Populist Party platform after cataloging the many ways in which the predominant parties had perverted those purposes:

> Corruption dominates the ballot-box, the Legislatures, the Congress, and touches even the ermine of the bench. The people are demoralized; most of the States have been compelled to isolate the voters at the polling places to prevent universal intimidation and bribery. . . . The fruits of the toil of millions are boldly stolen to build up colossal fortunes for a few, unprecedented in the history of mankind; and the possessors of these, in turn, despise the Republic and endanger liberty.[2]

"The few" are unpatriotic (they "despise the Republic") and they steal the work of "the millions." There are two major critiques here, one procedural and one substantive. First, the primary advantage of the little guy in democratic politics—his numerical majority—has been undercut by procedural moves by elites that dilute his political power. Second, the 'have-nots'

---

[1] Much of the following comes from John Hicks, *The Populist Revolt: A History of the Farmers' Alliance and the People's Party* (Lincoln: University of Nebraska Press, 1961); James Turner, "Understanding the Populists," *Journal of American History* 67:2 (1980).

[2] From Henry Steele Commager, *Documents of American History*, ninth edition (New York: Appleton-Century-Crofts, 1973), pp. 592–93.

suffer from exploitation by a small number of 'haves'; they are robbed of what is rightfully theirs. The villains are the powerful elites—bankers, corporate leaders, and greedy, corrupt politicians—who only pretend to honor the ideals of democracy.

We use "the little guy" deliberately. Just like "the common man" and "the ordinary Joe," the populist framing has almost always been masculine. It isn't surprising that it was masculine in the late nineteenth century, but even after women's suffrage, populist rhetoric has tended to be masculine. It is not that populism is inherently sexist or that there couldn't be feminist populism, but populist rhetoric has tended to trade on common beliefs and prejudices—the things that have seemed self-evident and obvious for the ordinary Joe—and assumptions about gender remain important in those ideologies.

Today, the term "populism" is associated far more broadly than with the People's Party. Some famous examples: post-WWII Latin America's politics of personality around a charismatic figure, from Argentina's Juan Perón in the 1950s to today's Venezuela under Hugo Chavez; varieties of anti-immigrant and anti-foreigner movements in contemporary industrialized countries; and the politics involving issues from busing to downsizing in the contemporary United States. The term "populist" is also frequently used to chart the field of political candidates. For example, in his recent campaign for the Democratic presidential nomination, John Edwards was described as a "left populist," albeit an "accidental" one, due to his appeal to many working-class Democrats.[3] Edwards presented himself as the champion of the already (or soon-to-be) disempowered American worker against "corporate interests and the wealthy."[4] Finally, in the populist ranks too are the political masters of the media, new and old. In the last several decades, the right has been more effective at deploying this tool, particularly in the United States: conservative talk radio, Fox News and strident right-wing pundits really have only Michael Moore on the left to match that kind of populism.

---

[3] See Matt Bai, "The Poverty Platform," *New York Times Magazine* (June 10th, 2007) and Jason Zengerle, "The Accidental Populist," *The New Republic* (January 22nd, 2007).

[4] Bai, "The Poverty Platform."

So, populism has many dimensions: it can refer to a diagnosis of society's ills, a style of political communication, a mode of political mobilization, and the personal style of a populist speaker or performer. But is there a common core to populism? What does racist, anti-immigrant populism share with anti-corporate worker populism? At one level, very little; at another, quite a lot. Michael Kazin argues that the term "populism" can actually refer to several different kinds of concepts: a movement's *political beliefs* may be populist, or its *type of rhetoric* may be populist.[5] Let's call the former the content and the latter the discourse. This distinction helps us understand the commonalities between varieties of populists more easily: two apparently very different movements might be united by the discourse they use, even if their content varies radically.

What is populist discourse like, then? We can describe it in two ways, charitably and critically. The charitable description sees populist discourse as making the unnecessarily abstruse accessible to the common person. It cuts through the smoke and mirrors of elite (and elitist) politics by diagnosing what ails society using straight talk: populists won't say "abstruse"; they'll say "darned hard to understand," and they want you to suspect those who are abstruse. Populism respects the ordinary person's own understandings and feelings about an issue and wants to discuss politics in these terms. From the critical perspective, this is its problem: it means an appeal to the lowest common denominator, making the always complicated simplistic, appealing to the most unexamined knee-jerk prejudices and emotions. It risks turning politics into demagoguery. Consider, for example, the rousing end of William Jennings Bryan's famous "Cross of Gold" speech from 1896:

> If they dare to come out in the open field and defend the gold standard as a good thing, we shall fight them to the uttermost, having behind us the producing masses of the nation and the world. Having behind us the commercial interests and the laboring interests and all the toiling masses, we shall answer their demands for a gold standard by saying to them, you shall not press down upon

---

[5] Michael Kazin, "Democracy Betrayed and Redeemed: Populist Traditions in the United States," *Constellations* 5:1 (1998) and *The Populist Persuasion: An American History*, revised edition (Ithaca: Cornell University Press, 1998).

the brow of labor this crown of thorns. You shall not crucify mankind upon a cross of gold.[6]

In the critical perspective, politics *is* more complicated than Bryan implies, and to stay at the level of the feelings, basic hunches, and popular biblical imagery Bryan uses simply misses the complexities. Perspective aside, populist practices are about accessibility of the rhetoric (making things simple) and relying on emotion and the speaker's charisma to render it effective.

Different populists with very different programs have something else in common. Think back to the idea of populists defending the little guy, the common man, the everyday citizen against entrenched elite interests, and you can see it as a defense of the dignity of the individual. One way of understanding what political theorists call modernity—which coincides, roughly, with the existence of the United States as a country—is to see it as replacing hierarchical ideas about social order with one that says all people have equal dignity by virtue of their simply being human. That also means that whereas in a hierarchical society commoners were literally beneath contempt—they *could not* be humiliated or disrespected—modern citizens can now all enjoy their dignity—and fear its loss through humiliation. So where this general value serves as the backdrop for day-to-day politics, it becomes possible to criticize as unjust those policies which seem to trample upon the dignity of the common man.

The point isn't that all populists back radical equality of all humans: many populists have agitated against the equality of immigrants, for example, or of people of color. But where populists almost universally do rely on the idea about everyone's dignity is in their sensitivity to perceived slights against the common man: elite politics, you might say, is a form of disrespect. While this sentiment is noble, it doesn't always translate into noble—or equal—politics. For example, racist populism has historically taken integrationist policies as a form of disrespect. It is a violation of my dignity, the racist says, that I be asked to share a lunch counter with this person whose skin color is different from mine. Insisting on the need to respect his dignity, the racist

---

[6] William Jennings Bryan, *Speeches of William Jennings Bryan: Revised and Arranged by Himself*, Volume I (New York: Funk and Wagnalis, 1909), p. 249.

glibly ignores the idea that people with a different skin color are also people and so also deserve respect.

So populists claim to (and sometimes actually do) speak *for* and *to*. Whether at a political rally or in a concert or campaign ad, they claim to represent common folk. This claim to authenticity is more credible when it is backed up by autobiography. No effective populist fails to refer to his or her common roots, whether or not he or she has them. But besides speaking for, they also speak to their audiences—they seek to educate, criticize, mobilize, cajole, distract, and so on. In so doing, they implicitly claim to articulate our feelings and values, to hold them up to the light for us, and remind us of what we value.

They Ain't No Country Trash

Unlike many populists, Cash didn't come across as strident or angry. Because of this, he affords us a way of exploring populism without getting any of our specific political hackles raised. Born and raised in Depression-era Arkansas, Cash grew up in a region in which populist claims were frequent, especially among the South's largest group: poor, rural whites. Most had been taught that their South, proud of its culture and values, had been doubly dishonored by military defeat and by a humiliating post-war occupation by northern troops and emancipated blacks. By the early twentieth century, there were other threats to the dignity of white have-nots—especially white men. Some of these were common to the less-well-off around the country, such as the humiliation borne of losing a family farm to local bankers (which were seen as doing the bidding of "eastern" banks).

But some threats to their dignity were specific to the South. In a region of great poverty, status superiority to blacks was a consolation prize to be closely guarded. But, in the face of falling cotton prices, massive foreclosures, and the inability of many white men to fulfill their gender role as their family's breadwinner, black landownership stood as a rebuke to poorest whites' status superiority. It's no surprise, then, that when times were toughest, these whites were most likely to terrorize their black neighbors through lynching, whitecapping, and other violence.[7]

---

[7] Stewart Emory Tolnay and E.M. Beck, *A Festival of Violence: An Analysis of Southern Lynchings, 1882–1930* (Urbana: University of Illinois Press, 1995).

Prior to and during Cash's childhood, many white southern populists, whether leaders of social movements or reelection-
minded politicians, articulated populist sentiments. Many of
these men, from Mississippi's James K. Vardaman (known as
"the White Knight") to South Carolina's Cole Blease to
Louisiana's Huey Long to Georgia's Gene Talmadge, were wildly
successful in their appeals to the region's white have-nots,
despite being demonized by better-off whites as "demagogues."

  Their populist rhetoric pointed to another tension within
populism—the proposed diagnosis and the cure. These politicians articulated the standard American populist critique of procedural and substantive injustice: democratic politics was a
sham, and the sham hurt the little guy. But the possible cures
raised by other American farmers, such as those in the Populist
party,[8] were taken off the table by a profound distrust in elites.
Distrusting elites meant more than questioning the motives of
bankers and politicians; it also meant a distrust of paternalism.
In the eyes of these populists, government officials and other
would-be reformers were social engineers. As such, they raised
the threat of a different kind of humiliation—condescension.
Whether in the form of "home economics" experts telling poor
whites how to raise a family and run a household, or government bureaucrats regulating child labor, or textile mill owners
telling them how to spend their leisure time, paternalism stung.
But here was the rub: to the extent that a strong government or
other social institutions were necessary to stop the have-nots
from being mistreated, this distrust complicated the cures of the
populist diagnosis.

  Cash's own childhood reflected this tension. What saved Ray
and Carrie Cash and their children from total devastation in the
Depression was one of the New Deal's many social engineering
projects, Dyess Colony. So named after its enterprising creator
W.R. Dyess, the Arkansas state administrator for the Federal
Emergency Relief Administration, and funded by FERA, the
Colony provided housing, land, and other forms of assistance
for carefully selected white poor in Arkansas's Mississippi

---

[8] For a portrait of the role played by populist-led farmers in creating dozens
of new governmental programs and regulatory agencies during the Progressive
Era, see Elizabeth Sanders, *Roots of Reform: Farmers, Workers, and the
American State, 1877–1917* (Chicago: University of Chicago Press, 1999).

County.[9] The Colony brought together all the paradoxes that troubled southern populists. It *was* the suspect institution of the state which effected this miraculous rescue, and even rise, in people's living standard. And the treatment of families was both directly and indirectly patronizing: for example, they received lessons on home economics, and their moral standing and sobriety were under constant scrutiny. This verged on emasculating the manly breadwinners of the family by implying their women deserved information and needed help they could not provide. Indeed populist suspicions about the government's motives *were* in part well-founded: the Colony was also a get-richer-quick scheme for Dyess. What made it nevertheless borderline tolerable for Ray Cash were the rhetoric and partial reality of the place: those were all about the rugged individual. Survival still depended on the individual farmers' hard work: the state's help wasn't enough for those who didn't also help themselves.

Then Sing 'em Gospel

This was the soil out of which Cash developed his populist instincts, values, and style. His populism also departs importantly from the southern staples, but there is much that is familiar. Consider an anecdote from his second autobiography, *Cash*: Jerry Lee Lewis, Carl Perkins, and Cash are having an argument about the relationship between rock'n'roll and salvation. Lewis worries that their music will send their audiences to hell. Cash proposes a solution: "Maybe we just ought to sing whatever we sing, if they like it, and get their attention that way. Then sing them gospel."[10] Whether this discussion ever took place in the way Cash reports it doesn't matter; what matters is Cash's view, which is a nice way to illustrate a kind of populist approach to music with a message.

Now you might say that a popular artist who makes his or her art political is, almost by definition, a populist—to build a message based on accessible cultural resources just is populist. In this anecdote, what is populist, then, is the style. But Cash is

[9] Michael Streissguth, *Johnny Cash: The Biography* (Cambridge, Massachusetts: DaCapo, 2006), Chapter 1; Johnny Cash and Patrick Carr, *Cash: The Autobiography* (San Francisco: HarperCollins, 2003).
[10] *Cash*, p. 91.

populist also in substance. "Singing gospel to them" wasn't his sole or even primary, message, although Cash's Christian faith was always important for him, and that Christian faith came in familiar populist flavor, as his deep and enduring friendship with the evangelist Billy Graham suggests. Although his Christianity usually stressed themes of inclusion and redemption, there were also occasional sympathies for the parts where the fire burns hotter and brimstone smells sharper: "The Man Comes Around," for example, conjures up an Old-Testament God who is not going be kind to those who haven't walked the line.

There is also his patriotism. Love of country is a pretty easy lever to pull in almost all political communities, and it has been a populist staple, often tempering the universalism in ideas about equal dignity. At its most populist, Cash's patriotism hews so closely to a basic American flag-waving that it borders on parody. Just consider "Ragged Old Flag" or "Song of the Patriot." But they are not parodies: his love of America gets expressed in these slightly kitschy songs, but you find it also in his critical romanticism about the Old West, in his appreciation of the land, its people, and its complexities. "Ragged Old Flag" and the very project of *American Recordings* are of a piece, as far as Cash's attachment to his country goes.

Sometimes Cash also offers us the sort of anti-political politics we get in, say, "The One on the Right Is on the Left": a humorous—but ultimately pretty ambiguous—mockery of those who try to make music political. It's no news to note that criticizing someone for making things political is itself a political act; one occasionally recurring strand in populism is a frustration with "politics as usual" or politics, period. That's a version of anti-elitism: political types try to make things seem complicated—"left" and "right" and "progressive" and "liberal" and "conservative" and whatever—when a sensible person, the populist thinks, knows that things are, in the end, pretty simple. In Cash's song about "The One on the Right," part of the humor is that everyone is actually confused about their politics, yet they fight endlessly. And the lesson:

> Now this should be a lesson if you plan to start a folk group
> Don't go mixin' politics with the folk songs of our land
> Just work on harmony and diction
> Play your banjo well
> And if you have political convictions keep them to yourself.

But like many other populists, Cash is also clever, and "The One on the Right" ends up leaving things pretty complicated: the song dates from the Vietnam era, and the one musician in the dysfunctional band who claims to be non-political, well, he "got drafted."

Cash is, in short, a straight talking (though not strident), God-fearing American patriot who understands the plight of the little guy and sympathizes with him. But often, Cash's sympathy for the underdog also stands in clear contrast with other southern populists, past and present. For instance, Alabaman George Wallace, one of Cash's contemporaries, made much political hay in the South and beyond with his appeals to white supremacy and his attacks on social engineers and other bureaucrats. Against this, consider Cash's explicit support of Native American rights and his critiques of racism. Or consider his abiding "empathy," as he described it in an interview with Terry Gross, toward criminals, prisoners in particular, which opposes head-on today's "tough on crime" populism.[11] And in affirming the dignity of all varieties of oppressed and forgotten people, his "Man In Black" stands in stark contrast with those varieties of parochial populism that pit some particular "us" against some other "them."

Still, one can see even these positions as part of Cash's own populism, both in terms of discourse and substance. For example, "The Ballad of Ira Hayes" brilliantly marries a story about the rotten treatment of Native Americans with American patriotism. Although Cash didn't write the song (so you might say its brilliant politics is not Cash's), he explicitly used in an anti-racist campaign, publicly daring DJs to play it.[12] And you might say that empathy for criminals simply reflects Cash's appreciation for the difficulty of life for the ordinary man: life is hard, we all face our various demons, and some of us are just less lucky than others in resisting the temptation. In this, in fact, Cash taps into a familiar trope in American mythology: the prisoner, whether it is the unjustly imprisoned innocent man, the poor guy whom fate dealt bad cards, or the even the brilliant wrong-side-of-the-tracks

---

[11] Interview with Terry Gross. *Fresh Air*, National Public Radio, November 24th, 2005. Originally broadcast in 1997.

[12] Steve Turner, *The Man Called Cash: The Life, Love, and Faith of an American Legend* (Nashville: Nelson, 2005), pp. 107–08.

sociopath, serves as the perennial reminder of the difficulties capricious life and sinister elites can throw in everyman's way.

Now further complicate this picture with Cash's uneasy response to a threatened white supremacist boycott of his tour in the South in 1966: The racist response arose out of a newspaper photograph in which Cash's then-wife Vivian appeared black. On the one hand, Cash went to some lengths to make it clear he was not guilty of miscegenation, that Vivian was white. On the other, he did take a public stand against the supremacist rhetoric. In the end, this ambiguous response certainly succeeded in securing a successful tour.[13]

When eggheads and ivory-tower types listen to Johnny Cash or read him, they tend to dig the grassroots, the salt-of-the-earth as well as the anti-racism, but they cringe at "Ragged Old Flag" or "The Song of the Patriot," and they feel awkward when Cash describes his friendship with the evangelist Billy Graham with a straight face. But the awkward truth is that Cash doesn't see a distinction worth noticing: *we* might need to explain away the apparent inconsistency, but Cash doesn't.

Not that the man was uncomplicated, far from it. He was a veritable mess, when it came to the private morality of ordinary life: take his addictions and infidelity, on the one hand, and his faith and his commitment to family, on the other. He was also inconsistent in some of his specific political views over the years. His attention to anti-black racism, for example, evolved from a youthful blindness to a vocal condemnation in print and on *The Johnny Cash Show* in the early 1970s. But he was inconsistent in the way someone who shares the little guy's cut-through-the-crap attitude to politics will be: there are more important things in life to worry about than developing some kind of complicated political theory to live by, and every once in a while one will need to say the obvious thing about this or that political problem. If what I'm saying is not exactly what I used to say before, the problem is yours, buddy, for not understanding how things are different from the little guy's perspective.

Less glibly, we might say that what does remain consistent in Cash's thinking is a set of core commitments to keeping it sim-

---

[13] The story appears, for example, in Streissguth, *Johnny Cash*

ple, respecting ordinary people, and being able to see human worth in those who aren't valued now. And so Cash has one over the eggheads in that his appreciation of Americana, of the prisoners, of the religious believers isn't sophisticated *faux*-appreciation, but, rather, an understanding of the complexities and intelligence of the ordinary. He is not a sophisticated artist who can slum with the ordinary folks; *because* he is a sophisticated artist, he can appreciate the sophistication of the ordinary folks and convey it in ways that appeal to them.

What Is Truth?

So Cash is a complicated man, talented artist and sophisticated thinker. But will the way in which he conveys his values and politics make *other people* think in complicated and sophisticated ways? Will it make them think at all? Here is the sixty-four-thousand-dollar question for populism: how does one appreciate the intelligence of the common man? Do you do so by saying you do, or by addressing them in ways that presuppose this intelligence? Putting them in an appreciative mood and then singing gospel, one might argue, doesn't respect them. It is a form of manipulation, diametrically opposed to respectful reciprocity, as far as our hunches about the ethics of human communication go. And you might say that, indeed, any form of political rhetoric that is primarily about pumping people up emotionally disrespects their intelligence, even what philosophers call their moral autonomy. It's not that emotional appeals in and of themselves are bad; the question is whether they exploit people's immediate emotional knee jerks, as opposed to using those instincts to get them to widen their field of vision about society and think more carefully.

But Cash's anecdote about gospel isn't all we know about his attitudes toward his audiences, and not everything about his music, even his more political music, is manipulative. Rather, one might say that, at its best, it cleverly transcends its own and its audience's populist impulses and, one may hope, gets people thinking. One way it does so is by contrasting the comfortable and the easy with something that seems inconsistent with it: take American patriotism and the racist treatment of Native Americans, for example, as in "The Ballad of Ira Hayes." And things can get more complicated yet. Think of Cash's musically

unremarkable but interesting song "What Is Truth?" If one of the
hallmarks of populism is to seize on the simple, on what seems
self-evident because "it's the way things are," the generational
relativism of "What Is Truth?" departs from this radically:

> The young man speaking in the city square
> Is trying to tell somebody that he cares
> Yeah, the ones that you're calling wild
> Are going to be the leaders in a little while
> This old world's wakin' to a new born day
> And I solemnly swear that it'll be their way
> You better help the voice of youth find
> "What is truth?"

Cash's sentiment—just because kids these days believe in things
very different from what we're used to doesn't mean that they
are wrong—makes it impossible for a person to stomp his feet
and insist on his version of truth being the only, and obvious,
one.

Does Cash's music succeed in complicating matters political?
Or is it more manipulative? It's hard to say. That is, we claim,
the first inherent risk with anything popular—however
admirable or repugnant its substance—that pleases us or otherwise appeals to our emotions. The risk digs up an even deeper
tension in the very idea of democracy: on the one hand, if we
think that "the people be the judge," as John Locke put it in
1689, then the people be the judge. But, on the other hand, if
democracy is "government by discussion," as democratic theorists from Aristotle onward have believed, then democracy
requires making sure that real discussions be had. And it's not
clear whether a Johnny Cash concert—or Live Earth, or Live Aid,
or skinhead rally—are discussions. They might get someone
thinking, but they just as well only get him following because of
the charisma and appeal.

And that's the second inherent risk with populism. The more
we love Johnny Cash—or Bruce Springsteen, or Bono, or the
Dixie Chicks—the more we should worry about treating them as
our political authorities who do our thinking for us. We might
want to remember the words of another figure from America's
political history. Eugene Debs famously said, "I don't want you
to follow me or anyone else. I would not lead you into the

promised land if I could, because if I could lead you in, somebody else would lead you out." If song and dance gets you following, you aren't yet thinking.

Today, many Americans who see themselves as regular, ordinary folk—especially those in the country's alleged "heartland"—face threats to their material well-being and their dignity. Some of these threats are old—American agriculture has often been on hard times. But some are new, such as the loss of farms and jobs attributed to globalization. Small-town America seems to be sinking under the weight of outsourcing, Wal-Mart, and crystal meth. Calls to "take the country back" articulate old populist themes and flirt with old populist pitfalls. Such calls make familiar charges of the distortions of democracy caused by big money, of exploitation by the "haves." Where older versions of populism could encourage attacks on blacks and other minorities, contemporary populists—on the make during a new wave of immigration—have easy access to xenophobic appeals. Generally, the sentiment to "take back" the country is irreducibly conservative—after all, it harkens back to a time when "the people" had what belonged to them, and calls for a return to these times.

Still, rejecting many tenets of the southern populists of his childhood, Cash did point out a different way. He aimed not to return to any good-ol'-days but called on us to imagine a new, more inclusive America. But after Watergate, Whitewater, and Katrina, distrust in government—in the institutions that the have-nots can capture with their numerical advantage—hamstrings efforts by common men and women to develop a cure in line with the populist diagnosis. This is another tension between populism and democracy, one of many that await America's next Johnny Cash.

6

Johnny Cash: Philosophy as a Way of Life

GREG JOHNSON

Johnny Cash's music is not philosophy, but it is philosophical. His music is more about "philosophy as a way of life," which expresses a way of being in the world through individual and collective practices, than it is about engaging in discussions *about* philosophy.[1]

This is why Cash sings about love gone bad *and* love gone good. His gone-bad music plumbs the depth of darkness, while his gone-good music shows us that the darkness need not consume and paralyze us. As such, his autobiographical song "Man in Black" illustrates his philosophy as a way of life insofar as it highlights the interrelationship between darkness ("Till things are brighter, I'm the Man in Black") and the power of love ("the road to happiness through love and charity"). Moreover, it calls on us to defend those who cannot speak for themselves ("I wear black for the poor and beaten down") and offers us tempered hope (we can "make a move to make a few things right"). In the end Cash's music expresses a philosophy of lived existence teaching us to "try to carry off a little darkness" on our backs as we attempt to (re)engage life in all of its dimensions.

Love Gone Bad

Cash told Lisa Robinson of *The New York Post*: "I've got to remember that the black stripe is always there. Nobody's all

---

[1] Pierre Hadot, *Philosophy as a Way of Life: Spiritual Exercises from Socrates to Foucault* (Oxford: Blackwell, 1995).

good. Nobody's all bad. I guess I'm personally afraid of my dark side."[2] Much if not most of Cash's music is devoted to singing about descent into darkness. In "Cocaine Blues," for instance, he sings, "Early one mornin' while makin' the rounds / I took a shot of cocaine and I shot my woman down." Moreover, we believe him when he tells us, "I will let you down / I will make you hurt."

We normally speak of growing up and talk about going down or growing down seems awkward, at best, and wrong, at worst. James Hillman explains why this is so.

> For, in its most common usage, "down" is nothing but a downer. The soul has to drag its feet with doubts and second-guessing, if not symptoms, when pressed to accommodate itself to the upward push of career. College kids with bright promise sometimes suddenly find their "personal computer" is down. They fall off the fast track. They want to "get down." Or drinks, drugs, and depression set in like the Furies. Until the culture recognizes the legitimacy of growing down, each person in the culture struggles blindly to make sense of the darkenings and despairings that the soul requires to deepen into life.[3]

Cash's music expresses the intimate connection between the descent into darkness and all-important questions such as "Who am I? and "How should I live my life?" It honors those places in our lives that we fear most, places that are out of sight, out of bounds and places we would rather not discuss. *I shot a man in Reno / Just to watch him die.* I say "honor" intentionally to indicate how these elements *initiate* us more fully into ourselves as we struggle to live the best lives possible. It is a concerted effort to enter into certain elements or moments in our lives that hold a key to unlocking at least some of the doors to perennial questions regarding becoming human. To this end, Cash's music and life operates by the medieval principle of alchemy where "the cure is in the disease."

Cash's willingness, therefore, to take seriously the descent into darkness as essential for better self-understanding aligns

---

[2] Steve Turner, *The Man Called Cash: The Life, Love, and Faith of an American Legend* (Nashville: Nelson, 2004), p. 200.
[3] James Hillman, *The Soul's Code: In Search of Character and Calling* (New York: Warner, 1996), p. 43.

him with some of the most profound thinkers in Western philosophy. There's Socrates who, at the beginning of Plato's *Republic*, finds himself "going down" to Piraeus whereupon he discusses the importance of the just city and what it means to live life in a just way. And, then there's Friedrich Nietzsche's Zarathustra, an Odysseus- and Jesus-like figure who, in the pursuit of becoming a true self, tells us "I must descend into the depths: as you do at evening, when you go behind the sea and bring light to the underworld too, superabundant star!"[4]

The theme of descent into darkness is also found in biblical narratives. We have Jacob, the father of Israel, who will always be tied to his wrestling match with God at the river Jabbok, the encounter that took place in the dark and left Jacob permanently wounded. Jonah, who after his descent into the belly of the fish, comes to better understanding of his vocation. The Apostle Paul's story of growth (one of Cash's favorites) involves descent-as-blindness. And, finally, there's Jesus Christ who, for Cash, is paradigmatic of God's willingness to descend to the level of humans to make God's self better understood for those whose self-identity (like Cash's) is linked to this story.

Here we can ask the question, "Is the descent into darkness something we consciously choose, or is it something that is a result of the conditions in which we find ourselves?" The answer, if Cash is the model, is that it is both. When he sings "I shot a man in Reno / Just to watch him die" we get the clear sense that the principal character is someone who seeks out this kind of destructive and violent behavior, someone who appears consciously to prefer the excess of violence ("just to watch him die"). Likewise, Cash's own documented bouts with drug and alcohol addiction suggest clearly that he sought out these experiences. As he recounts in his autobiographies, when he first thought about taking amphetamines, he believed it would be good for him. More than once he knowingly chose the darkness and its ways and he never denies this.

Does Cash's life therefore suggest that we, too, should seek out such experiences in the service of living philosophically, or

---

[4] Friedrich Nietzsche, "Thus Spoke Zarathustra: A Book for Everyone and No One," in Keith Ansell-Pearson and Duncan Large, eds., *The Nietzsche Reader* (Oxford: Blackwell, 2006), p. 254.

that we cannot live philosophically without consciously choosing to do so? No.

Rather, Cash's music and life indicate something that many people already do, namely, seek out dark elements of existence (despite, or even in full knowledge of their power). That we should not seek them out is irrelevant to the import of his music. That we do face and are faced with the ways the depths of darkness demand a response from us, however, is precisely what makes his music and life more appealing than any moral treatise might otherwise be—he faces up to and honors the depths of darkness. Am I, in the end, suggesting that the descent into the depths of darkness becomes for us (as it was for Cash) an opportunity to grow into better self-understanding? Yes.

Growing down into the depths of darkness becomes for us potentially a way of learning to see the light again. For instance, Cash sings incessantly of "love gone bad" in the form of betrayal, loss or suffering. He also sings frequently about death itself. In doing so, he doesn't seem to be suggesting that we should seek out these experiences (who seeks out betrayal?); instead, he is expressing the ways that death-as-loss-and-suffering permeates our lives and, I want to add here, opens to us the possibility of *living* anew.

This is a sentiment shared by the German writer Rainer Maria Rilke who says there is "only *one* form of liberation for those who are continually submerged in suffering: to elevate suffering to the level of one's own perspective and to transform it into an aid for one's way of seeing."[5] Neither Rilke nor Cash teaches us how to learn to see by offering a program or set of moral exhortations to ensure we can control these forces and turn them into something positive. Nor does either fetishize death, suffering, or the depths of darkness or encourage us to wallow in them. To the contrary, they teach us to attend to these deathly elements so that life might again be opened to us. This view closely follows Socrates who believed that living philosophically is "training for death." We do not have to succumb to these forces, but honor them for they can (re)turn us to life. As Rilke writes,

---

[5] Rainer Maria Rilke, *The Poet's Guide to Life* (New York: Modern Library, 2005), pp. 111–12.

I do not mean to say that one should *love* death. But one should love life so unreservedly and without any calculation or deliberation that death (the half of life that is turned away from it) is at all times unwittingly included in and loved along with life" (p. 112).

These ways of understanding the growth downward illustrate two of the four modes by which the soul descends to remind us who we are and what we can become.

- First, your body: Growing down means going with the sag of gravity that accompanies aging. . . .

- Second, admitting yourself to be one among your people and a member of the family tree, included its twisted and rotten branches.

- Third, living in a place that suits your soul and that ties you down with duties and customs.

- Last, giving back what circumstances gave you by means of gestures that declare your full attachment to this world. (*The Soul's Code*, p. 62)

Cash's music expresses the ways we move toward an image of ourselves that might already be there, the "sag of gravity that accompanies aging." This movement is an acknowledgement that our lives are not just lived in the sunshine of others, but lived in the darkest parts that are often hidden (or rotten as Hillman says). By taking these parts seriously we can learn to live *with* and not *under* them. In this way, Cash's music represents a notion of philosophy as a way of life that has at its center a proper way of acting instead of affirming a set of abstract theoretical truths.

Love Gone Good

Cash's music represents more than a growing down into the depths of darkness. Not only does he sing of love gone bad, but he also sings of love gone good. Cash illustrates a notion of "turning outward" to the world that demonstrates that the darkness does not have to consume and paralyze us from living life in constructive ways. This turn outward has two trajectories in Cash's music: an ethical awareness of the power of love in our

lives, and a political awareness of responsibility for those who
cannot speak for themselves. These two ways of (re)engaging
the world, ethical and political, are Cash's way of expressing
what the twentieth-century French philosopher Gabriel Marcel
(1889–1973) called "creative fidelity."[6]

In general, "creative fidelity" indicates how we participate in
life. In particular, it indicates a way of being invested in others
in the world, or better, as Marcel describes it, the way we are at
the disposal of the other with whom we are intertwined. In
addition, it reflects a way we place our trust in others, and how
others can come to place their trust in us. Being-with-others is
a resource for learning to live with the depths of darkness. In
"Daddy Sang Bass," for instance, Cash sings about hard times
and poverty when "we'd get together in a family circle singing
loud." Not only is singing a resource, but so is the power of love
expressed in the web of relations enabling the Cash family to
approach hard times.

"Daddy Sang Bass" is an instance of "love gone good," a
power that gives us resources to learn to live with the darkness
as it is named "guilt," "murder," "cheating," "loneliness," "suffering," "death," and a whole host of other familiar terms of the
darkness. Love gone good indicates how love interrupts our
darkness and offers us the courage to move through those
moments to something potentially transformative and new in
our lives. I say "move through" because Cash's way of expressing this notion is less about overcoming the darkness and more
about living with it. This is not to deny that in his music, his
gospel music in particular, he sings of what appears to be a
denial of this life and a belief in something eternal and "more
real." Though this may certainly be the case, the point I am making here is that love is the power to help us ascend from the
descent that comes to mark our existence. Whether this is in
terms of family as with "Daddy Sang Bass," or the love of an
individual, love is way to "get rhythm when you get the blues."
It is why, in a song like "Go on Blues," he can sing "I've been
down through / That valley with you / Now I've found me /
Somebody who loves me too." Like Robert Johnson, Muddy
Waters, Hank Williams, Merle Haggard, and others who sing of

---

[6] Gabriel Marcel, *Creative Fidelity* (New York: Fordham University Press, 2002).

the constitutive element of the blues in being human, Cash does not give darkness the last word. Put in the language of "creative fidelity," love-as-participation-with-others can interrupt the potentially consuming power of the darkness.

The philosopher Paul Tillich (1886–1965) calls the darkness a "threat to nonbeing," an awareness of the possibility of total annihilation that the depths of darkness represents. Like Cash, Tillich believes that love is stronger than death and as such can give us resources for (re)entering the world anew. Tillich writes:

> Death is given power over everything finite, especially in our period of history. But death is given no power over love. Love is stronger. It creates something new out of the destruction caused by death; it bears everything and overcomes everything. It is at work where the power of death is strongest, in war and persecution and homelessness and hunger and physical death itself. It is omnipresent and here and there, in the smallest and most hidden ways as in the greatest and most visible ones, it rescues life from death. It rescues each of us, for love is stronger than death."[7]

In a way that is strikingly similar to Cash's colloquial expressions, Tillich, in the language of philosophy, describes this type of participation in life with others as an ethical act, one that gives us the courage to affirm ourselves *in spite of* those elements that threaten to paralyze or destroy us. The threat is very real, and takes the form of losing ourselves both on the individual and communal level. As Tillich explains, "We are threatened not only with losing our individual selves but also with losing participation in our world. Therefore self-affirmation as a part requires courage as much as does self-affirmation as oneself. It is *one* courage which takes a double threat of nonbeing into itself. The courage to be is essentially always the courage to be as a part and the courage to be as oneself, in interdependence."[8] In order for love to empower us, Tillich tells us that we must accept that we are accepted.

---

[7] Paul Tillich, "Love Is Stronger than Death," in F. Forrester Church, ed., *The Essential Tillich: An Anthology of the Writings of Paul Tillich* (New York: Collier Macmillan, 1987), p. 161.

[8] Paul Tillich, *The Courage to Be* (New Haven: Yale University Press, 1952), p. 89–90.

And in the light of this grace we perceive the power of grace in our relation to ourselves. We experience moments in which we accept ourselves, because we feel that we have been accepted by that which is greater than we. If only more such moments were given to us! For it is such moments that make us love our life, that make us accept ourselves, not in our goodness and self- complacency, but in our certainty of the eternal meaning of our life. We cannot force ourselves to accept ourselves. We cannot compel anyone to accept himself. But sometimes it happens that we receive the power to say "yes" to ourselves, that peace enters into us and makes us whole, that self-hate and self-contempt disappear, and that our self is reunited with itself. Then we can say that grace has come upon us.[9]

Cash, like Tillich, embraces the place of darkness in our existence, but doesn't allow it to have the last word on our lives. In Cash's music, creative fidelity includes the political responsibility to name the darkness that has and continues to destroy those who no longer are able to speak for themselves. And here Cash's music often takes on a prophetic role.

Cash's awareness of political responsibility can be summed up in the phrase "no one is free until all are free." He tells us in "All God's Children Ain't Free" that "I'd sing more about more of this land / but all God's children ain't free / I'd open up every door I can / Cause all God's children ain't free." To be sure, the sentiment "no one is free until all are free" is a difficult notion to unpack, but Cash's music suggests the following. First, in pursuing freedom we engage the world in a way that promotes a certain image of what it means to be "a free human being." This image is, as his songs about both literal and metaphorical prisons reveal, one where people are treated with dignity and respect and an image that challenges the notion that humans are simply means to the ends of society. Second, it means that not all possess the freedom they should have. Finally, the call of "freedom for all" entails a political responsibility to work for the freedom that many still do not possess.

Cash's emphasis on freedom expresses a sentiment close to that of the French philosopher Jean-Paul Sartre (1905–1980), a

---

[9] Tillich, "The Courage to Be," in *The Essential Tillich*, p. 202.

leading philosopher in the twentieth century who, in a famous essay, "Existentialism Is a Humanism," writes the following:

> When I declare that freedom in every concrete circumstance can have no other aim than to want itself, if man has once become aware that in his forlornness he imposes values, he can no longer want but one thing, and that is freedom, as the basis of all values. . . . We want freedom for freedom's sake and in every particular circumstance. And in wanting freedom we discover that it depends entirely on the freedom of others, and that the freedom of others depends on ours. Of course, freedom as the definition of man does not depend on others, but as soon as there is involvement, I am obliged to want others to have freedom at the same time that I want my own freedom. I can take freedom as my goal only if I take that of others as the goal as well.[10]

Cash and Sartre share the sentiment that "no one is free until all are free." Further, Sartre states rather explicitly what Cash does implicitly, namely, the idea that even though humans are, by *being* human free (what philosophers call an ontological notion of freedom), this does not mean that all humans possess concrete freedom(s), (what philosophers call "political freedom").[11] Finally, if "creative fidelity" suggests participation on this level, then both claim that once we are engaged in the world through this participation and awareness of freedom we have the *moral* responsibility to work for and secure the political freedom that many if not most lack. In this way, both Sartre's and Cash's insistence on freedom for all is rooted in an ethical vision of the world, which for Cash is the power of love.

In the end, Cash's music enables us to see philosophy as a way of life in two ways. On the one hand, in learning to live with the darkness that surrounds us, we can name the darkness that has silenced us and so many. On the other hand, we can learn from him and his music that our efforts at living philosophically demand a commitment to the protracted struggle that defines our "fight for freedom" as a struggle for both self-under-

---

[10] Charles Guignon and Derk Pereboom, eds., *Existentialism: Basic Writings* (Indianapolis: Hackett, 2001), p. 306.

[11] I am indebted to Robert Bernasconi for this helpful distinction. See his *How to Read Sartre* (New York: Norton, 2007).

standing and the liberation of others. This is why, to return to what I said in the introduction, his "Man in Black" encapsulates an understanding of philosophy as a way of life:

> Ah, I'd love to wear a rainbow every day
> And tell the world that everything's okay
> But I'll try to carry off a little darkness on my back
> Till things are brighter, I'm the Man In Black.

7

Of Steel Drivers and Train Whistles: Johnny Cash and Johnny Mill on the Good Life

M.J. MULNIX

> All [prisoners] have had the same things snuffed out of [their] lives. Everything that makes a man a man—women, money, a family, a job, the open road, the city, the country, ambition, power, success, failure—a million things.
>
> —JOHNNY CASH; Liner Notes from *At Folsom Prison*

According to Johnny Cash, prison life strips the prisoner of his humanity; it destroys that part of living that makes being alive something valuable. This passage highlights one of the patently clear themes that is present throughout all of Cash's body of song: a deep and reverent value for the quality of life. When all is judged together, this value takes priority over the long life.

It's not just the act of living that holds intrinsic value for Cash, but instead it's the pursuit of a happy life that yields value to existence. This is particularly apparent in his work about capital punishment and the quality of life of the prisoner. Yet, it also rings true in some of Cash's other songs. For instance, in "The Legend of John Henry's Hammer," though Henry dies prematurely, his life is still portrayed as epically valuable. This, then, is in stark contrast to the life of the prisoner, who may live longer than John Henry, but must reckon with the fact that his foolhardy actions have cut him off from all that makes for a valuable life.

John Stuart Mill (1806–1873), the famous British liberal philosopher, also maintains a deep value for the quality of life and believes that quality takes priority over quantity when it

comes to human living. Mill most directly expresses this prefer-
ence in a speech to Parliament also concerning the topic of capital punishment. It seems true, at least for Mill, that there are
situations in which the quality of a life is so poor that death is
to be preferred. To understand the views of both Cash and Mill,
we have to set out the details of what makes for a 'high-quality
life'.

For Cash, activities such as spiritual reflection, loyal friend-
ships, respect and love all contribute to living well. His hymns
and love songs express a clear embodiment of such values.
These activities all share something in common with one
another in that they engage that aspect of us that is unique to
the human individual: active self-examination and deliberative
reflection. Likewise, Mill, in *Utilitarianism*, argues that the very
definition of 'happiness' depends on drawing a distinction
between the true human pleasures and those of the beast—the
higher and the lower pleasures. Like Cash, Mill believes that
pursuit of the higher pleasures will lead to a high-quality life. Of
course, no theory of the good life is truly complete without adequate attention paid to the 'fool', and the fool makes his appearance both in the work of Cash and Mill. Many of Cash's *most*
famous lyrics can be understood as admonitions against playing
the fool.

Lessons from the Mercy Seat

In his 1868 speech given to Parliament on April 21st, John
Stuart Mill argues against a bill proposing a ban on capital punishment. Contrary to popular sentiment, Mill defends this
method of punishment, "on the very ground on which it is
commonly attacked—on that of humanity to the criminal."[1] In
other words, Mill believes that a "short pang of rapid death" is
far more merciful a punishment to inflict upon the criminal
than is "immuring him in a living tomb, there to linger out what
may be a long life . . . [but] debarred from all pleasant sights

---

[1] Mill. "Speech in Favor of Capital Punishment," I, 1. All references to the
writings of Mill are to *The Collected Works of John Stuart Mill*, 33 Volumes
(Toronto: University of Toronto Press; London: Routledge and Kegan Paul,
1963–1991). The numbers are chapter numbers followed by paragraph
numbers.

and sounds, and cut off from all earthly hope." Mill then makes explicit that it is "not human life as such that ought to be sacred to us, but human feelings. The human capacity for suffering is what we should respect, not the *mere capacity of existing*." As Mill sees it, the use of capital punishment is far more humane than is life imprisonment and this is due, in no small measure, to the conditions of prison life. Life imprisonment destroys the only part of life that makes it worth living—it destroys the quality of life.

Cash also expresses similar views on this topic in some of his songs. So, for example, in Cash's version of "I Hung My Head" the narrator gains peace when the soul of the man for whose murder he hangs, collects the narrator's soul and thus grants ultimate redemption for the crime. Or, consider "The Mercy Seat" in which Cash sings about the relief that being executed in the electric chair can bring. The title of the song evokes Mill's argument in that, at least on the surface, the instrument of execution is seen as a symbol of mercy for the condemned inmate. Moreover, in the song, the electric chair is analogous to the throne of God, bringing with it redemption and forgiveness, and so, signifying cosmic or divine mercy as well. The character of this song is happy to be getting past "all this twisting of the truth / An eye for an eye / And a tooth for a tooth." He views his execution as a welcome and merciful exit to a tortured existence.

Cash's songs often conceal a touch of irony, and so, we should not take "The Mercy Seat"[2] to be a straightforward endorsement of capital punishment. But what we can gather is that Cash truly thought that the worth of life was to be found in the quality of its activities and that this was more morally significant than the fact of life alone. In this way, then, both Cash and Mill appear to agree that, at least sometimes, capital punishment mercifully mitigates the suffering of particular prisoners. Since both Mill and Cash sincerely express the belief that what makes a life worth living is the quality of that life, we need to know what makes for a good, high-quality life. What criteria can we list that would pick out all and only high quality pursuits?

---

[2] N. Cave and Mark Harvey. 2000. "The Mercy Seat" [recorded by J.R. Cash] on *American III: Solitary Man* [CD]. Nashville: American Recordings.

Higher and Lower Pleasures

Part of what it means for something to be of high quality is that it is especially valuable to our happiness. Happiness, claims Mill, is the ultimate moral good. As a utilitarian, all human actions are to be judged according to the consequences they engender, and specifically how much happiness they bring about. As such, claims Mill, "actions are right in proportion as they tend to promote happiness; wrong as they tend to produce the reverse of happiness" (*Utilitarianism*, II, 2).

Three things need to be said by way of clarifying this principle, which Mill called "The Greatest Happiness Principle." First, by happiness, Mill states he means pleasure. Second, we should not mistake this principle to mean that the right action is that action which yields the most happiness for the agent engaged in the activity. No, the right action is the one that, on balance, maximizes the happiness of all those affected.

Lastly, when we are confronted with a true moral dilemma, a situation where every possible course of action open to us will lead to bad consequences, the Greatest Happiness Principle will require that the right action is the one that minimizes suffering. This then applies to Mill's argument in favor of capital punishment. It is not as though Mill thought that executing someone would make them happier! Rather, he believed that such punishment would minimize the suffering that certain criminals would be forced to endure at the hands of a retributive judicial institution. This also seems to apply well enough to Cash's "Mercy Seat." In the "Mercy Seat" the narrator seems to have decided for himself that his life is no longer worthwhile, and that ending his current anguish seems a merciful retreat.

It is not the mere capacity to exist that should be considered, but the pain or happiness that falls upon a life that should guide our moral decisions. If the ultimate moral value is happiness, then we are right to ask: In what does happiness consist? How do we achieve it? Where is it to be found? Mill thought that answering these questions requires drawing a distinction between two types of pleasure: higher and lower kinds. This, however, begs for further explanation if we are going to understand what the ingredients of happiness are.

Even though we can measure the quantity of pleasures—seeing that some activities give us *more pleasure* than others—Mill is careful to state that pleasures do not differ only with respect to their relative quantity. Pleasures can also differ in relative quality. Given this, a smaller quantity of a higher-quality pleasure may be preferred to a larger quantity of a lower-quality pleasure. An analogy might make this more clear. Suppose I am a diamond dealer and I have an excess in supply. In order to drum up business I hold a raffle and the winning ticket will entitle its holder to a prize. As it turns out, you are the holder of the winning ticket. When you come to collect your prize, I tell you that you have a choice. On the one hand, you can take this pile of diamonds. In total, there are one hundred carats worth of diamonds. Still, they are, all of them, small diamond chips and larger diamonds of poor quality. On the other hand, you can also choose to accept this single diamond, which weighs in at a mere five carats. However, it is flawless in terms of cut, clarity, and color. The question is: which choice would be preferable? Most (hopefully all) of us would decide to take the single five-carat diamond. After all, even though you would receive far less in terms of *quantity*, it is a worthwhile trade-off, since the *quality* of the five-carat diamond is so superior to the hundred-carat pile of flawed diamonds. Pleasures, according to Mill, like diamonds, can be evaluated both in terms of quantity and quality, and sometimes we will sacrifice a huge quantity of a low-quality pleasure, for a much smaller quantity of a high-quality pleasure.

The Verdict of the Competent Judges

Supposing Mill is correct in thinking there are two types of pleasure, we still need a reliable method for determining which pleasures are superior in quality. With respect to how it is that we can come to know the relative quality between two pleasures, Mill recommends a competent judge approach. He writes:

> Of two pleasures, if there be one to which all or almost all who have experience of both give a decided preference . . . that is the more desirable pleasure. (*Utilitarianism*, II, 5)

Mill believes not only that this is the *most credible* method for discerning among the distinct qualities of pleasures, but it is also the *only method* available. He believes that desiring an object and its being pleasurable are identical, and so the only possible way to distinguish between the quality of pleasures is to verify empirically that some pleasures are actually more desired than others. The only people capable of making an informed judgment about such matters are those who have experienced both types.

Though there may be some measure of disagreement among competent judges, when there is relative unanimity regarding the higher quality of a particular pleasure compared to others, we are right to conclude that that pleasure is superior. Moreover, there are some pleasures so resoundingly preferred as to allow their sacrifice only in the rarest of cases, regardless of the quantity to be traded for another lesser pleasure. Some examples of these highest of pleasures might include liberty and security, both of which are so important to human happiness that one cannot, according to Mill, imagine a person being happy without them.

Here Cash again appears to agree with Mill. He consistently places individual freedom as a central value in his songs. One need only recall some classic Cash songs to be reminded of the critical role that liberty occupied in Cash's vision of a truly happy life. Take, for instance, "I Never Picked Cotton." Cotton workers (as well as miners, such as the narrator's father) were trapped in a sort of wage-slavery. They were paid enough to survive, but were kept destitute enough by their pittance that they had no real choice but to remain cotton pickers, unless like the saga's narrator they opt for a life of crime. Or, consider "The Wall," in which a prisoner decides to try to escape by scaling a wall. No one had ever succeeded and everyone who had tried was no longer alive. Yet, this prisoner decides that his freedom is so valuable that he would rather risk near certain death than remain imprisoned.

But then, we should ask, when I actually prefer a pleasure which has been universally tagged as lower in its quality to another superior pleasure, am I wrong to pursue the pleasure I desire more? Mill answers that, "It is better to be a human being dissatisfied than a pig satisfied; better to be a Socrates dissatisfied than a fool satisfied" (*Utilitarianism*, II, 6). He intends the life of the pig and the life of the human to represent "two modes of existence," and furthermore, "those who are acquainted with and equally capable of enjoying both do give a marked prefer-ence to the manner of existence which employs their higher fac-ulties" (*Utilitarianism*, II, 6 and 8).

It's not that the life of a dissatisfied Socrates will be more full of pleasure, in the sense that there will be a greater quantity of pleasure in his life than in the satiated pig's life, but rather that such a life is itself judged by us to be more intrinsically valu-able—it's more worth living. A pig is not actively and con-sciously involved in the living of its own life, but appears to be a passive responder to his environment. As such, the pig's notion of happiness cannot satisfy the human conception, since part of what it is *to be happy*, is that we are involved in the cir-cumstances that lead to our pleasure—that they come to us as a result of our own deliberative life choices.

The Ingredients of Happiness

The key to being a happy human being amounts to actively engaging oneself in the living of one's life—actively pursuing and evaluating the ends that each of us, as individuals, find value in. At the foundation of this process is the ability for an individual to be self-directed—the ability to express and develop one's individuality, since without that, we could not hope to be involved in our lives in the way necessary for us to enjoy the higher order pleasures that are open to us in virtue of our natural capacities:

> Having said that Individuality is the same thing with development, and that it is only the cultivation of individuality which produces, or can produce, well-developed human beings, I might here close the argument: for what more or better can be said of any condition of human affairs, than that it brings human beings themselves nearer to the best thing they can be? (*On Liberty*, III, 10)

According to Mill, a strong relation holds between individual-ity and happiness. Notice, however, what it is to express one's individuality *through* activity is not an activity itself, but instead, is a *mode of activity*. Performing a certain type of action is not enough to guarantee that we are expressing indi-viduality through our conduct. Instead, it is the case that two people (or even the same person) can engage in similar acts, and yet one is an expression of individuality, while the other is not.

So, for example, two different people could end up deciding to continue their education after high school by attending college. But, one may do so unreflectively—maybe because his parents demand that he do so, or maybe because it just seems to be a social expectation that everyone will or should go to college. Another person may also decide to go to college, though for reasons that were her own. Her decision was the result of careful consideration in which she examined whether this future course made sense against the background of her life goals and her present desires. Hence, while each person reaches the same point about what to do with their life, one has done so in such a way as to express her individuality, while the other has acted like little more than a machine, following a plan or design that was laid on him from the outside. So, individuality is about the way an action was chosen by the actor, and not something having to do with the type of action performed.

According to Mill, people should value liberty and the ability to express their individuality because "freedom is the first and strongest want of human nature," and it is "an element of happiness" for any individual.[3] Cash, too, seems to suggest that freedom is crucial to a worthwhile existence. Again, in his liner notes for his *At Folsom Prison* album he writes about the experience of being in prison:

> You sit on your cold, steel, mattressless bunk and watch a cockroach crawl out from under the filthy commode, and you don't kill it. You envy the roach as you watch it crawl out under the cell door.[4]

The prisoner envies the cockroach simply because this creature, for all of its other limitations, is free to leave. Being free seems to be the first and most important ingredient of the happy life. Despite this, the liberty to be self-directed—or being given the ability to express our individuality—is not good in itself. It's only good insofar as it is backed up by proper training of our higher

---

[3] Mill. *The Subjection of Women*, IV, 19–20.
[4] J.R. Cash, 1968. Liner Notes on *At Folsom Prison* [CD]. New York: Sony Music Entertainment.

mental faculties. Mill states that among the reasons to value individual activity is that it requires a person to 'flex' their mental muscles and that it makes them more distinctly human. This underscores Mill's idea that what will or will not fit into each individual's subjective construction of happiness is unique to that person. Additionally, however, it reveals that we must deliberate for ourselves to determine which choice makes sense on this given occasion—whether there are any salient differences obtaining between this circumstance and other circumstances that might lead us to behave in ways different from what we have done before. This requires the use of "the human faculties of perception, judgment, discriminative feeling, and even moral preference," all of which "are exercised *only* in making a choice" (*On Liberty*, III, 3). In the end, this act of deliberation is an expression of our individuality, such that even if we do decide to follow the custom, we have *chosen* to do so, not because it is customary, but because we reason that it will make our chances of being happy more likely.

John Henry: Man or Machine?

For all the emphasis on the value of individuality, both Cash and Mill recognize that freedom to choose for oneself the direction one's life will take is only as good as the rational abilities of the person who enjoys such freedom. So, in such songs as "Don't Take Your Guns to Town" or "Devil's Right Hand" or "Delia's Gone" or "Cocaine Blues" we are introduced to characters whose desire for freedom is undermined by their own irrationality—each allows their desire to be total individuals to trump the wise advice of their parents, elders and society with the results being disastrous. That is, just as we should not *accept* custom for the reason that it is the custom, so too, we should not *reject* custom just because it is the custom. Sometimes, the desire to be free, not to be 'tied down', leads to a sort of irrational rebellion that is not reflective, but is instead, foolish.

The characters in the above songs fail to achieve happiness precisely because they are fools, in the sense that they do not make use of their higher human capacities in judging what is right for their unique situation. These individuals do not actively deliberate about and choose the path their lives will take. Instead they reject advice merely because it comes from others;

they are "rebels without causes" and rebels without causes are foolish. In fact, both Mill and Cash place a strong emphasis on the advice given to us by our elders, especially our mothers. Mill argues in *The Subjection of Women,* that mothers occupy a privileged position when it comes to the moral education of society (IV, 22). If only the antagonists of "Folsom Prison Blues," "Don't Take Your Guns to Town," and "The Devil's Right Hand," had listened to the good advice of their mothers instead of rejecting it out of hand, then they might not have suffered their respective fates.

In "The Legend of John Henry's Hammer," Cash's testament to the human spirit, the hero rhetorically asks, "Did the Lord say that machines ought to take the place of livin'?"[5] Obviously, the answer is that machines cannot replace the human side of life. And, in *On Liberty*, Mill stressed the importance of the engaged human spirit.

> He who lets the world, or his own portion of it, choose his plan of life for him, has no need of any other faculty than the ape-like one of imitation. . . . Human nature is not a machine to be built after a model, and set to do exactly the work prescribed for it. . . . One whose desires and impulses are not his own has no character, no more than a steam engine has a character. (*On Liberty,* III, 4–5)

Beasts and machines operate according to instinct or design. But this does not require the exercise of higher faculties. John Henry boasts that he can do anything the line boss asks him to. On the other hand, the steam-engine cannot even respond to a simple "How's you?" The human spirit is active, malleable, adaptable, responsive, un-caged—free. When the human spirit is literally caged by a prison cell, or figuratively caged by foolish neglect of the impact a present choice has on future happiness, the result is devastating: we lose all that makes living valuable. In order to engage individually in the pursuit of happiness we must deliberately choose for ourselves our own direction in life; we must be self-directed individuals in order to facilitate the enjoyment of certain pleasures associated with

---

[5] J.R. Cash and J. Carter. 1962. "The Legend of John Henry's Hammer" on *At Folsom Prison.*

our nature; we must be actively and consciously involved in our own living.

Some might argue that John Henry really was just a contented fool—that he did not, in fact, pursue the higher pleasures—since, after all, he gave up life just to beat a machine at driving rail spikes. So long as the course our life takes is something that we have been actively involved in, and so long as we actually succeed in achieving some measure of conscious pleasure from our activities, then we are experiencing higher-order pleasures, pleasures that are distinctly human. Understood as such, there is no question that John Henry was a happy individual. He fully engaged his human energies in the pursuit of what he took to be valuable. He was far from a fool—he is a shining example of the best of the human spirit.

The upshot is that according to both Cash and Mill freedom in-and-of-itself is not the goal. Rather, to enjoy *rational freedom* is the quest of the true individual. If freedom alone was the goal (and not a tool to be used in pursuit of our other goals), then the life with more freedoms would always be better than the life with fewer freedoms. But this just does not seem true. Most of us would prefer to live in a society that guarantees the freedom to meet together in a temple or church or mosque to practice our religious beliefs, and yet, also limits our freedoms with respect to driving through extensive traffic laws, over a society which is set up in the reverse—allowing us to drive however we want, but restricting our ability to practice our religion collectively. But if freedom were the goal, then you would think the opposite would be true, since in the society without traffic laws, we have more freedoms (just in terms of sheer number) than in the society that only safeguards religious freedom. What this example seems to reveal is that it is not the quantity of freedoms we value, but what those freedoms allow us to do. As such, we prioritize particular freedoms according to the value of the ends each opens to our pursuit: we value freedom as a means and not as an end.

Do Fools Harm Others Through Their Bad Example?

Unlike the pig, whose natural cognitive limitations prevent him from recognizing the value of the higher pleasures, the fool suffers

from a different problem. He has the ability to use his higher
human faculties to pursue the higher pleasures, but instead, the
fool sacrifices his chance at such pleasures for immediate short-
term gain in lower pleasures. Cash believes fools are made, not
born. So what makes a person a fool? There are two possible
causes for the making of a fool: external (society-based) causes,
and internal (character-based) causes, or a combination of both.
Sometimes we make fools of ourselves because of personal,
moral and psychological shortcomings; whereas, on other occasions we are made fools of by social circumstance. The fool gets
himself into trouble by either not thinking carefully about the
way his action will affect his future interests, or by not being
allowed to pursue his own interests due to social shortcomings
and prejudice.

Nowhere does Cash express his vision of the good life and
the dangers of playing the fool better than in his monumental
"Folsom Prison Blues."[6] In this song we get the antithesis of a
moral exemplar: the *anti-exemplar*. A quick examination of the
lyrics of this song will reveal just how critical freedom is to one's
happiness, and just how quickly one can undermine his future
happiness through foolhardy use of that freedom. To start, we
are immediately reminded of the lost freedom suffered by the
narrator who hears the train "comin' round the bend," from his
prison cell. Of course, the train symbolizes the freedom that is
no longer part of the anti-exemplar's life. As it slides past
Folsom Prison, it serves as a painful reminder of what has been
lost. And the Man in Black sings, "I know I had it comin' / I
know I can't be free / But those people keep a movin' / and
that's what tortures me."

Cash's prisoner consciously chose to forgo his long-term
happiness when he shot his victim. He claims to know and
accept the consequences of his action—that he will never again
enjoy the freedom that is so critical to human well-being.
Moreover, his candid acknowledgement of these facts seems to
suggest that if he had just actively considered his choice before
he shot the man down, he could have predicted how poorly it
would end for him. What is more, he did not even have a strong
motive that might have explained why he was compelled to
consciously forgo his future happiness, like revenge or jealous

---

[6] J.R. Cash. 1955. "Folsom Prison Blues" on *At Folsom Prison*.

rage. The motive he gave was that he was curious, he just wanted to watch a man die. Accordingly, his current situation seems as though it were entirely and easily preventable. If only he had made better use of his human capacity for rational deliberation, he might actually be on that train.

This is the paradigm of irrational action: to know that what you are doing will end poorly for you, and yet to do it anyhow; to consciously sacrifice your long-term happiness for short-term amusement and pleasure; to knowingly pursue the lower pleasures at the expense of the higher—that is a fool's game. We can forgive the murderer in "I Hung My Head" (as does the victim in the song) because it was an unintentional mistake. To be sure, negligence is not morally insignificant, and so those who live in a careless way should not be immune to moral judgment. But to destroy your hopes at future happiness the way the anti-exemplar of "Folsom Prison Blues" does—in a knowing way—is truly foolish. For such fools, perhaps their life *will* be better if it is controlled by some other system: perhaps by a prison system.

John Henry, the Steam-Engine, and Folsom Prisoners

We know that John Henry died a happy human. However, as the anti-exemplar in "Folsom Prison Blues" shows, the same human capacity that opens the door to higher order pleasures in human experience, also brings with it the ability to suffer more acutely. Mill, too, recognized that this was a feature of being human, and yet, he also rejoices in this risk:

> A being of higher faculties requires more to make him happy, is capable probably of more acute suffering, and certainly accessible to it at more points, than one of an inferior type; but in spite of these liabilities, he can never really wish to sink into what he feels to be a lower grade of existence. (*Utilitarianism*, II, 6)

Whether Mill is correct in believing that we can never wish to sink into a lower grade of existence is certainly dubious—after all, Cash suggests that, at least sometimes, we envy cockroaches. Still, Mill does seem right in the sentiment that possessing the higher faculties is at once both the blessing and the curse of humanity: to be human is to possibly be happy, but probably to suffer the fate of fools. Through his songs, Cash frequently explores, with an honesty and sympathy that are beyond reproach, the many points at which suffering can enter our lives. He gives voice to a life that is, unfortunately, a more common human experience than that of the noble moral saint.

PART III

Love

8

A Line Worth Walking: June Carter Cash and the Power of Love

JAMES F. SENNETT

> She said we were soul mates, she and I, and that she would fight
> for me with all her might.
> —Johnny Cash, *Cash: The Autobiography*

Johnny Cash's last hit song was a heart-wrenching cover of Trent
Reznor's anthem to despondency, titled simply "Hurt." Steve
Turner, Cash's official biographer, reports, "Although written
about the pain of heroin addiction, Cash had appropriated the
song's gritty imagery, masterfully turning it into a melancholy
meditation upon his own mortality."[1]

Mark Romanek's award winning video of the song offers a
sympathetic though honest picture of Cash in his last days: fee-
ble, sad, contemplative, and even regretful. The video's most
touching moment comes as Cash sings the haunting lyrics,

> What have I become, my sweetest friend?
> Everyone I know goes away in the end.

"As he delivers these lines," says Turner, "the view cuts to June,
standing at the foot of the staircase watching him with conflicting emotions of admiration and pity, wonderment and sorrow
etched across her face" (p. 3).

It is an excruciatingly intimate scene, and we are self-con-
sciously aware of intruding where we do not belong, eaves-

---

[1] Steve Turner, *The Man Called Cash: The Life, Love, and Faith of an American
Legend* (Nashville: W Publishing Group, 2004), p. 2.

dropping on a moment that should be shared only by these
enduring lovers. Yet we also feel privileged, for we sense that in
these few seconds we have drunk deeply of everything the two
had meant to each other for the past thirty-five years. And it sad-
dens us to know that, within a year of this shooting, we will
have lost both of these great icons of country music and
American folklore.

    In his second autobiography Johnny Cash spoke candidly of
the role June played during those critical years when alcohol
abuse and drug addiction threatened to destroy everything he
made of his life.

> The publicity in the 1960s was that June saved my life, and I some-
> times still hear it said that she's the reason I'm alive today. That
> may be true, but knowing what I do about addiction and survival,
> I'm fully aware that the only human being who can save you is
> yourself. What June did for me was post signs along the way, lift
> me when I was weak, encourage me when I was discouraged, and
> love me when I was alone and felt unlovable.[2]

The legend of John and June, bathed in more than enough fact
to legitimate the myth, is one of the power of love to resurrect
the human soul, regardless of the depths to which it has sunk.

    Long before he met June, John[3] wrote and recorded the song
that launched his career:

> I keep a close watch on this heart of mine;
> I keep my eyes wide open all the time.
> I keep the ends out for the tie that binds;
> Because you're mine, I walk the line. ("I Walk the Line,"
>   1956)

Though originally written as a pledge concerning his first marriage to Vivian Liberto, John's signature song stands today as a
tribute to the love that lifted and encouraged him when he was
at his most unlovable.

---

[2] Johnny Cash, *Cash: The Autobiography,* with Patrick Carr (San Francisco:
Harper Paperbacks, 1997), p. 314.

[3] Since all principals referred to in this chapter share the last name "Cash," I
will refer to them primarily by their first name only: John, June, John Carter,
and Roseanne.

June Loves John

The most cursory glance at the mountain of literature concerning the Cash family that has sprung up in recent years reveals one undeniable fact—John and June were in love. Says Marshall Grant, bass player for the *Tennessee Three* and family friend for fifty years, "John and June were so much in love it was almost unbelievable."[4] Their son John Carter has testified, "Through all the years ahead, the successes and failures, triumphs and heartaches, their love lasted."[5] At June's funeral Roseanne Cash said of her father and stepmother,[6] "Her love filled every room he was in, lighted every path he walked, and her devotion created a sacred, exhilarating place for them to live out their married life" (*Anchored*, p. 53). Years before they would become husband and wife, June herself (together with good friend Merle Kilgore) penned lines about John that would soon constitute one of her future husband's biggest hits:

> The taste of love is sweet
> When hearts like ours meet.
> I fell for you like a child,
> Oh, but the fire went wild. ("Ring of Fire," 1963)

But just as clear from that same literature is the fact that the solid foundation that kept their love in place was largely June's doing. It was first and foremost her emotional stability, spiritual strength, and unswerving commitment that kept them together—through John's repeated addictive episodes and periodic unfaithfulness, through the agonizing strains that a show business lifestyle invariably heaps on a relationship, through the inescapable pain and dreariness of senior years wracked with the inevitable physical and emotional scars of two lives lived hard and fast. Her lifelong friend Joyce Trayweek described her

---

[4] Marshall Grant, *I Was There When It Happened: My Life with Johnny Cash,* with Chris Zar (Nashville: Cumberland House, 2006), p. 184.
[5] John Carter Cash, *Anchored in Love: An Intimate Portrait of June Carter Cash* (Nashville: Thomas Nelson, 2007), p. 58.
[6] I use this term advisedly, and purely as a conventional convenience. In the same eulogy in which Roseanne described June's special form of love, she also noted that June had banned the word "stepchildren" and its kin from her house (*Man Called Cash*, p. 10).

as "like a steady ship holding course, no matter how the wind blew. She never went off into hysteria or showed great fear. She was gentle and kind, always" (*Anchored,* p. 93) And John Carter remembers, "Mom especially had the ability to heal and to forget the scars. That was her grace, her great gift to him. That is how they stayed together for thirty-five years" (p. 71).

Perhaps most telling is the fact that, from all accounts, the selfless and attentive love June showered on her husband was different in degree, but not in kind, from her general habits of life. June was a woman for whom love, concern and self-sacrifice were standard operating procedures. Her son's biography is replete with testimonies to this effect:

- "June was . . . universal love made incarnate in a pretty, talented, frisky package" (Lisa Kristofferson) (*Anchored,* p. 16).

- "[She] had a unique way of making everyone feel like her very favorite friend and the most amazing person she'd ever known" (Lisa Kristofferson) (p. 57).

- "She was the most accepting person I've ever known" (John Carter) (p. 95).

- "June Carter Cash loved as deeply as anyone I have ever known, and she was the most forgiving person I have ever known." (John Carter) (p. 128)

Of the many eulogies delivered at her funeral, the most powerful came from Roseanne Cash, John's oldest daughter and the only family member to speak. In June's eyes, Roseanne recalled, "there were two kinds of people in the world: those she knew and loved and those she didn't know—and loved." She went on to describe the very special brand of love that characterized June's life and spilled over in a unique way in her relationship with Roseanne's father.

> She looked for the best in everyone. It was a way of life for her. If you pointed out that a particular person was perhaps not totally deserving of her love . . . she would say, 'Well, honey, *we just have to lift him up.'* . . . It took a long time for me to understand that what she did when she lifted you up was *to mirror the very best part of you back to yourself.* She was like a spiritual detective: she

saw into all your dark corners and deep recesses, *saw your potential and your possible future and the gifts you didn't even know you possessed*, and she 'lifted them up' for you to see. (Turner, pp. 10–11, emphasis added).

This language of lifting up echoes her father's words, quoted earlier, "What June did was . . . lift me when I was weak. . . ." Earlier in his autobiography John spoke of the time when June first joined the Johnny Cash Show tour: "I was enthralled. Here was this vivacious, exuberant, funny, happy girl, as talented and spirited and strong-willed as they come, bringing out the best in me. It felt wonderful. We all liked it, in fact; she was a tonic for the whole crew. Life on the road improved immensely" (*Cash*, p. 215).

By all accounts, June was a woman with extraordinary capacities for love, encouragement, and blessing. She showered these on all around her, and especially on her husband. In so doing she played a vital role in saving Cash from himself and preserving the gift he was to American music and culture.

The Philosophy of Love

Philosophers debate over the proper analysis of what Bennett Helm has called "the complex phenomenology of love."[7] Of course the term *love* is ambiguous—it can be used to denote everything from the general respect and consideration that is due everyone we meet to the unique passion and devotion typically reserved for our "one and only." While philosophers of love address issues all along this continuum, analyses are generally aimed at a brand of love that is discriminating and privileging. That is, philosophers of love seek an understanding of the kind of love that (i) portions off specific people as its objects (i.e., it is not, indeed *cannot* be, applied to everyone); and (ii) warrants or sanctions a privileged station for those so chosen—

---

[7] Bennett Helm, "Love," in the *Stanford Encyclopedia of Philosophy*, available online at http://plato.stanford.edu/entries/love/, first published April 2005. Much of the forthcoming discussion owes its inception and conception to Helm's extremely helpful article, which also contains expositions and critiques of many aspects of the philosophy of love that we cannot mention or discuss here.

the love justifies certain kinds of preferential treatment for its objects which is not owed to or legitimately expected by others. Such love is applicable to varying degrees to friends, family members, and romantic intimates, among others. It is this brand of love that we are concerned with in this chapter.

Philosophers of love are sharply divided over the best way to think of this discriminating and privileging form of love. One debate which we can only mention concerns whether love is best thought of as an emotional phenomenon (involving feelings and attitudes) or a volitional one (involving choices and actions). Noted ethicist Harry Frankfurt, for example, argues for a volitional approach: "That a person cares about or that he loves something has less to do with how things make him feel . . . than with the more or less stable motivational structures that shape his preferences and that guide and limit his conduct."[8] In other words, the values and priorities that guide a person's actions also influence who and what that person will love— much more so than feelings. Other philosophers insist on an emotive analysis, seeing love either as an emotion proper or as a complex of emotions.

A third school of thought holds great insight for our exploration of June's capacity for love, and is, therefore, the one on which we will focus. This school understands love as a kind of valuing. So, for example, June loves John just in case June *values* John or *judges* John *worthy* in a certain way. Valuational theories are divided over the nature of the valuation. Is there something about John, independent of his relationship with June, that June rightly appraises as valuable, or does June *bestow* or *impute* value on John, which then becomes the focus of her love? We can call these two interpretations the *appraisal* theory and the *bestowal* theory.

Following eighteenth-century philosopher Immanuel Kant, appraisal theorist J.D. Velleman grounds the value of the beloved in the notion of human dignity.[9] Such dignity morally demands from us a respect that prevents us from using people as means to our ends. We may, however, go further and respond

---

[8] Harry Frankfurt, "Autonomy, Necessity, and Love," in his *Necessity, Volition, and Love* (Cambridge: Cambridge University Press, 1999), p. 129.

[9] J.D. Velleman, "Love as a Moral Emotion," *Ethics* 109 (1999), pp. 338–374.

to the dignity in certain persons with a willingness to open our-selves up to intimacy and vulnerability. In so doing we move from respect to love. Velleman explains why we come to love some people and not others in terms of what Helm calls "the contingent fit" between the different ways inherent dignity is behaviorally expressed by different people and the different ways people respond to those expressions. We are morally obligated to respect all people. We are not morally obligated to love all people. And the difference between the two is more or less a result of the accidents of culture, personality, and other exigencies of life.

By contrast, bestowal theorists such as Irving Singer argue that we find value in those we love for the simple reason that we put it there.[10] The lover confers an intrinsic worth on the beloved that stems strictly from the psychology of the lover, and not from any characteristics or qualities of the beloved that can be objectively judged as lovable. The beloved may, of course, possess admirable qualities, but the lover's love cannot be explained in light of them. Explanation for the love lies solely in the projected worth originating in the mind and heart of the lover. This projection need not be voluntary or even con-scious—indeed, bestowal theorists typically eschew any voli-tional dimensions. Nonetheless, on this view June loves John primarily because of who June is (or, at the most, because of who John is as a result of his relationship with June), never sim-ply because of who John is.

To many this theory seems at first glance completely wrong-headed, appearing to argue that love is manufactured from psy-chological whole cloth, without reference to any objective qualities of the beloved. But it is in fact a quite plausible approach. Bestowal theory bears a striking resemblance to the so-called *agapē* conception of love espoused by Christian the-ology (*agapē* is the most common word for "love" in the Greek New Testament, especially in theological contexts). Such love is typically characterized as stemming from the lover's Christian commitment and gratitude to Christ and completely unaffected

---

[10] Irving Singer, "From *The Nature of Love*," in *The Philosophy of (Erotic) Love*, edited by Robert C. Solomon and Kathleen Higgins (Lawrence: University Press of Kansas, 1991), pp. 259–278.

by the inherent qualities of the beloved. The Christian is under obligation to love even (and especially) the unlovable.[11]

In my days in Christian ministry, as part of my regimen of premarital counseling, I would ask each bride-to-be why she loved her fiancé (so also for the groom-to-be). I would routinely receive a litany of accolades, after which I would point out that any number of people—including others she knows personally, bear those same qualities. So why does she love her partner rather than those people? This question invariably stumped my parishioners and made it clear that what was motivating their love was something more than—perhaps even distinct from—a mere catalog of lovable attributes. A most plausible candidate for that "something more" is a psychological projection on the part of the lover.

Appraisal and bestowal theories differ in at least two important ways. First, appraisal theories are *objective*, grounding themselves in facts about the beloved, while bestowal theories are *subjective*, grounding themselves in the personal endowment of the lover. Second, appraisal theories are *passive* in that love is understood as a response to a pre-existing condition—whatever it is about the beloved that the lover appraises as lovable. Bestowal theories, on the other hand, are *active* in that love is understood as an original enterprise, motivated by the predisposition of the lover. Part of the difficulty with the dichotomy forced on us by these opposing approaches is that a full analysis of love seems to require both active and passive elements, both objective and subjective dimensions. We will return to this difficulty in the next section.

While there is much about both the appraisal and bestowal theories that rings true, they share a common problem. Both seem incapable of accounting for the *justification* of love—for the fact that we can give reasons for why we love the people we do. For example, while Velleman's appraisal theory *explains* why, for example, June loves John rather than someone else, it does not *justify* June's loving John rather than someone else.

---

[11] Because love is considered an obligation, Christian theologians and philosophers are much more likely to analyze it as a volition than a valuation. Nonetheless, the end result of loving because of who the lover is rather than who the beloved is reveals a strong semblance to the bestowal theory. Helm notes that Singer's theory bears a similar likeness to volitional theories.

According to Velleman, the justification of June's love for John just is John's inherent dignity—a trait shared by anyone else June might love. Were June to love someone other than John, that love would be justified on exactly the same grounds. Hence there is no justification for June loving John *rather than* some other person. However, I am quite certain (as, I believe, most people are) that my love for my spouse to the exclusion of others is not merely explainable but justifiable. There are reasons why I love her and not someone else that gives my love for her rational foundation. It is not simply arbitrary or a happy accident. Yet it is difficult to see how Velleman—or any other appraisal theorist—can make room for such justification.[12]

The situation for bestowal theory is even more dismal. Since the valuation originates in the psychology of the lover rather than the qualities of the beloved, there seem to be no grounds for justification *at all*. While appraisal theory cannot justify June's loving John rather than someone else, it can give a reason for June's loving John rather than *not* loving John—namely, John's inherent human dignity. Bestowal theory cannot offer even this much. The observation above that bestowal theories are inherently subjective helps illuminate why this problem arises. With no objective basis, our love for others becomes nothing more than autobiography—a reporting of what is psychologically the case with no basis for judgment concerning whether or not it should be, or whether or not it makes sense.

The bestowal theorist might simply bite the bullet here—as Singer seems to do in places—and concede that love is not justifiable. However, contemporary philosophy typically seeks what is called a *descriptive* analysis of concepts—one that captures all dimensions understood in ordinary speech as essential to the concept under investigation. To insist that love on a certain account is not justifiable is to concede that the account is, so far forth, not a descriptive one. We do typically consider love to be justifiable—we can give reasons that provide some sort of rational defense for our loving one person rather than another. For many philosophers rejection of this one conceptual feature alone would be enough to reject any theory.

---

[12] See Helm for a discussion of how problems for Velleman's theory apply to appraisal theories in general.

So the two sides of the love-as-valuation coin leave us with something of a dilemma. While each offers us helpful insights into the workings of love, both hit a conceptual snag on the crucial issue of justifying the love we have. Furthermore, as presented, the appraisal and bestowal approaches are mutually exclusive—they cannot both be true. As helpful as they both appear, we cannot embrace both.

June Love

I believe that June's special form of love, as described by her stepdaughter and exemplified throughout her life, offers us a fresh way to think about love as valuation—a way that navigates between the horns of the appraisal-bestowal dilemma noted above. Furthermore, this approach provides helpful insights into the nature of discriminating and privileging love. While I do not pretend to offer here anything approaching a full analysis or theory of love, I do nonetheless believe that many of the problems facing ethicists concerned with the philosophy of love can be addressed significantly with the example of "the Angel of Appalachia" (*Anchored*, p. 1).

Rosanne pointed out two essential planks in June's form of love. First, June "looked for the best in everyone." Second, she responded to those who appeared to lack a "best" by resolving, "we just have to lift him up." Let us call this approach *June Love*. Rosanne explained how the two strategies of June Love—seeking the best in the beloved and lifting the beloved up—worked in tandem: "She saw into all your dark corners and deep recesses, saw your potential and your possible future and the gifts you didn't even know you possessed, and she 'lifted them up' for you to see." If a person's "best" was not readily apparent in actuality, June found it in potentiality. In other words, June Love does not simply involve a judgment of who a person is, but primarily an estimation and precognition of who that person can be.

Such an approach bridges the gap between appraisal and bestowal, utilizing the best and avoiding the worst of each approach. Recall that we identified two crucial distinctions between appraisal and bestowal theories: (a) appraisal theories are *objective* while bestowal theories are *subjective*; and (b) appraisal theories are *passive* while bestowal theories are *active*.

We noted also that a full analysis of love would need to be both active and passive, both subjective and objective. By uniting appraisal and bestowal approaches, June Love moves us much closer to such a full analysis.

In lifting the beloved up, June Love does not simply recognize the current state of the person and judge that state lovable (mere passive appraisal), nor does it simply project lovability on a person completely irrespective of that person's qualities and characteristic distinctions (mere active bestowal). Rather, the June Lover deems persons lovable based as much (or even more so) on who they *can be* as on what they *are*. June Love contains an essential passive element: one cannot discover who a person can become without understanding and responding appropriately to who that person currently is (strengths, weaknesses, hopes, fears).[13] June Love likewise contains an essential active element: appropriate response to the beloved includes not simply an understanding of the beloved's current state but imaginative predictions of what that state could develop into—given proper encouragement and guidance—as well as initiative in providing such encouragement and guidance.

Furthermore, June Love is objective. It is grounded in the person of the beloved and is not simply an arbitrary bestowal that takes no account of the character of the beloved. What one *can be* is a function of what one *is*. Nonetheless June Love also contains an essential subjective element. Since it is grounded in the beloved's *potential,* it requires the imaginative projection of the lover, going well beyond the characteristics the beloved currently displays and involving active participation by the lover (rather than simple acknowledgment of objective reality). Such participation includes projection of possible future states and commitment to the beloved based on that projection.

June Love also supplies a way to account for the justification of love—a problem that plagues valuational theorists, as we saw. Since June Love is objective, it contains a grounding in fact that bestowal theory lacks, and thus escapes the mere descriptive, autobiographical quality that afflicts analyses like Singer's.

---

[13] Singer attempts a similar move (pp. 272–73), but Helm points out that such a maneuver belies the moniker "bestowal theory." However, since June Love does not aspire to this label, it inherits no analogous problem.

Furthermore, since different people come with different sets of qualities and potentialities, there is room to provide justification for loving one person *rather than* another—the problem that troubles Velleman and other appraisal theorists. For instance, one might wish to argue that June's love for John rather than someone else is justified in the fact that John's set of qualities and potentialities is more suitable than someone else's when matched up with John's gifts and abilities and June's inclination to utilize those gifts and abilities in encouraging someone to realize his potential, or some such thing. However such an account might work, my point is that June Love provides a basis on which to distinguish the beloved from others in such a way as to provide grounding for the rationality or appropriateness of the lover's loving the beloved rather than anyone else.[14]

June Love and Codependence

June Love contributes to the philosophical study of love in at least one other way that we have heretofore not mentioned, but which is quite germane to the subject of this book. June Love gives us a basis for distinguishing genuine, healthy love from the relational pathology known as "codependence." Codependent behavior typically occurs under the guise of support for or

---

[14] The editors of this volume have raised an important and thought-provoking question concerning June Love for which I can here offer no more than a preliminary response. They ask, "Does June Love require supplementation in some cases? Might there be cases in which there is, comparatively speaking, little or no potential, but in which love should still be given?" So, for example in the case of a severely mentally challenged child, one might see very little potential, but might nonetheless display tremendous love. Two points come to mind in response. First, June Love is as much about actuality as potentiality, and the proper balance between the two will be a case-by-case issue. In the case described, one may very well find most if not all motivation for love in the actuality of the person – innocence and helplessness, for example, are certainly powerful inducements for love. Second, "potential" almost certainly needs to be broadly construed. The child may have little potential for productivity or accomplishment pragmatically conceived, but nonetheless hold great promise for bringing joy and fulfillment to the lives of those with whom she interacts. Again, these are no more than thoughts and would require much fleshing out in order to expand June Love to a full-fledged theory of discriminating and privileging love.

encouragement of a person caught in addictive, obsessive-compulsive, or other self-destructive lifestyles. Codependent persons often justify their behavior by appeal to their love for the addict. But far from being healthy for the codependent or beneficial for the addict, codependent behavior is enabling and relationally detrimental. For instance, a battered woman may return time and again to the physical and emotional environs that license her partner's abusive behavior, insisting that she does so because she loves him and he needs her.

Codependents do not engage in June Love. While they may claim to recognize and encourage the potential for good they see in their partners, their enabling behavior is not conducive to the realization of that potential or to anything other than reoccurrence and entrenchment of the destructive behaviors. While June Love can and should be directed toward victims of self-destructive behavior—the original June Lover herself did so for many years—it will not enable or excuse such behavior. June Love will instead battle it constantly by ensuring that the beloved is incessantly confronted with the damaging results of his behavior, the realization that such behavior is neither inevitable nor unconquerable, and the auspicious promise of overcoming grounded in the potential of the beloved that is the heart and soul of June Love.

Johnny Cash's self-destructive behavior patterns are well known to anyone who knows anything about his life, as is June's constant struggle to get or keep him out of those patterns. Marshall Grant recalls, "John actually did more damage to himself than he did to anyone else. He was destroying himself little by little, and June and I worried about that a lot. We did everything we could to help him, to keep him straight, to get him from town to town, and to get him to go home—but that was something he just would not do" (p. 133).

The real story, of course, is not nearly as storybook as the modern myths would have it. In fact, it appears that June herself suffered from addictions late in life (*Anchored*, p. 130). But the fact remains that a high-profile celebrity couple with three failed marriages between them managed to build and maintain a life of strong commitment and deepest devotion for over a third of a century. And there can be no doubt that the foundation for that success was unwavering June Love applied steadfastly by its namesake.

In his biography of June, John Carter confesses his own problems with addiction and witnesses to his mother's practiced administration of June Love for him as well. In language reminiscent of his stepsister's memorable eulogy, he testifies,

> Dad's and my addictions never stopped my mother from loving us and believing in us. . . . Mom was loving and generous, thoughtful and caring, and she could always find a reason to look up, to believe that *the best in a person would eventually come out*. . . . Although the spirit of disease might torment her loved ones, sometimes making us hard and vicious, she saw beyond that ugliness into the heart of her child or husband, *finding the beauty within us*. That's what she continually focused on, the goodness in us rather than the darkness . . . (p. 125, emphasis added).

Conclusion: June Love Beyond the Jordan

One of the many songs sung at June's funeral was Terry Smith's inspiring country ballad, "The Far Side Banks of Jordan," which John and June had first recorded in 1976 and again on June's 1999 album *Press On*. The song records the testimony of a couple so deeply in love they can hardly bear the thought of being parted by death. In a move haunting for its foreshadowing of events, it was decided that June should solo on the second verse:

> If it proves to be His will that I am first to cross,
> And somehow I've a feeling it will be,
> When it comes your turn to travel likewise, don't feel lost,
> For I will be the first one that you see.

The refrain that follows echoes through eternity with a reminiscence of the June Love that saved her beloved from his fears, from his addictions, from himself.

> And I'll be waiting on the far side banks of Jordan.
> I'll be sitting drawing pictures in the sand.
> And when I see you coming I will rise up with a shout,
> And come running through the shallow water reaching for
>   your hand.

The line June chose to walk was hard, frustrating, at times debilitating and maddening. But it was a Line Worth Walking. It was a line worth walking because of who June was, and because of who she knew John could be—who he in fact proved to be. Herein lies the power of love—a power to call people to transformation while allowing them to stay true to themselves. It is June Love. It gave the world John R. Cash—and it also gave us June Carter Cash.

9

Guess Things Happen that Way: Johnny Cash and the Frailty of Human Nature

GORDON BARNES

In 1956, Johnny Cash pledged his enduring love and commitment to his wife, Vivian, in the classic hit, "I Walk the Line."

> I keep a close watch on this heart of mine
> I keep my eyes wide open all the time
> I keep the ends out for the tie that binds
> Because you're mine
> I walk the line

However, despite his profession of love and commitment, Johnny Cash would soon be unfaithful to Vivian. He cheated on her with several women. Why did Johnny Cash say one thing, and then do another? Was his profession of love insincere? Was he just lying or deceiving himself? Or was he simply a hypocrite? These are the explanations that come to mind; however, they are not the only possible explanations. There is another possibility, which is suggested in another song that Cash sang. The song is entitled "Guess Things Happen that Way."

> Well, you ask me if I'll forget my baby
> I guess I will some day
> I don't like it, but I guess things happen that way
>
> You ask me if I'll get along
> I guess I will some way
> I don't like it, but I guess things happen that way.

The speaker says that he doesn't like it that he will fail, but "things happen that way." What does this mean? It means that a good will is not always sufficient to produce good actions, because the will is weak. And notice: the speaker doesn't say that this is only true of him. When he says "things happen that way," he seems to be saying that things can happen that way to anyone. This suggests a very disturbing view of human nature. Human beings are not as stable or dependable as we would like to think. Human nature is extremely frail, even in the best of us.

Decades of research in what is called *the situationist tradition* in social psychology support this thesis. Investigation shows that human behavior is extraordinarily sensitive to variations in circumstance. How people act is more strongly influenced by their circumstances than by their character as individuals.

This disturbing truth about human nature was manifested in the life and music of Johnny Cash. In songs like "Don't Take Your Guns to Town," Cash sings about people who are overcome by circumstance. Of course, as that song also reveals, these same people are sometimes responsible for putting themselves in those circumstances. This ultimately leads Cash to two moral lessons. First, we should be charitable toward those who act badly, because if we had been placed in the same circumstances, we might have acted the same way ourselves. Second, we should be cautious, and avoid circumstances that might lead us to act wrongly. We should not "bring our guns to town." This is real moral wisdom. There is a lot to be learned from the life and music of Johnny Cash.

The Beast in Me . . .

Imagine this situation. A person has just made a phone call from a pay phone in a shopping plaza. As she leaves the pay phone, a passerby drops a folder full of papers, which scatter all over the ground in the caller's path. Will the caller stop to help this person in distress, or will she just walk on by?

Now here is a wrinkle. For some of the callers, a dime was planted in the pay phone's coin return slot, while for others, the slot is empty. Therefore some of the callers will find a dime before they leave the pay phone, while other callers find nothing (either because there is no dime, or because they do not look). Will this minor difference in the situation affect the behavior of the callers toward the person in distress? This experiment was conducted by A.M. Isen and P.F. Levin in the early 1970s, with striking results. Eighty-seven percent of the callers who found a dime in the coin slot stopped to help the person in distress. By contrast, ninety-six percent of the callers who did *not* find a dime in the coin slot did *not* stop to help the person in distress. Whether or not the caller stopped to help was largely determined by whether or not the caller found a dime in the coin slot.[1] This slight difference in the situation played the largest role in determining these people's behavior.

In the early 1970s, researchers invited students from Princeton Theological Seminary to participate in a study of "education and vocation." Unbeknownst to the seminary students, they were actually the subjects of an experiment. The students began by filling out questionnaires in one building, and then they were asked to walk to another building, where they would make an oral presentation. Before leaving the first building, the students were told one of three things: either (a) they were running late, (b) they were right on time, or (c) they were running a little early. Then, on the walk between the two buildings, the experimenters placed a person, slumped in a doorway, apparently in some sort of distress. Would the seminary students stop to help the person in distress, or would they walk on by? And would their belief about the time affect their behavior? Sixty-three percent of those who were running early stopped to help the person in distress, whereas ninety percent of those who were running late did not stop to help the person in distress.[2] Here again, the nature of the situation played the largest role in determining behavior.

What these experiments show is that whether or not people help someone in need is more strongly influenced by the nature of the situation than by their character as individuals. Numerous other experiments support the same thesis. For example, recent experiments have found that subjects near a fragrant bakery or

---

[1] Isen and Levin 1972, cited in John Doris's book, *Lack of Character: Personality and Moral Behavior* (Cambridge: Cambridge University Press, 2002), pp. 30–31.

[2] Reported in Darley and Batson 1973, and cited in Doris, *Lack of Character*, pp. 33–34.

coffee shop are more likely to change a dollar bill than subjects who are in a neutral-smelling place.[3]

We might be unimpressed by these results, because they involve relatively minor, insignificant actions. While the subjects in these experiments are sometimes neglectful, we might doubt whether they have done anything seriously immoral. So all that these experiments show is that human nature is frail when it comes to minor, insignificant actions. If these were the only experimental results, then this conclusion would be warranted, but these are not the only experimental results. It is time to look at the two most shocking experiments in the situationist research tradition.

From 1960 to 1963, Stanley Milgram conducted a series of experiments that later became known as "the obedience experiments." The experiments involved approximately a thousand subjects from all walks of life, including high school teachers, postal clerks, salesmen and engineers. In each case, the experiment proceeded as follows. The subject is brought into a room by the experimenter, who is dressed in a white lab coat. The experimenter instructs the subject to sit down across from another person. Unbeknownst to the subject, this other person is a trained participant in the experiment. The subject is then designated "the teacher," and the person across from him is designated "the learner." The subject is given a list of words, and is instructed to ask the learner for the meaning of each word. Every time the learner gives an incorrect answer, the subject is instructed to give the learner an electric shock. The subject is informed that the voltage of the shock will increase with each wrong answer. Unbeknownst to the subject, there are no electric shocks. Rather, the learner has been trained to act as if he is being shocked. As the experiment proceeds, the voltage of the shocks increases, until the learner begins to scream. The learner eventually pleads to end the experiment, saying that he has a heart condition, and that he wants to stop now. After each new question, and each new shock, the experimenter tells the subject that the experiment requires the subject to continue. The subject is never threatened or coerced in any way.

[3] *Lack of Character*, pp. 30–31.

What Milgram discovered was astonishing. Sixty-five percent of the subjects obeyed the instruction to keep giving electric shocks, even after the learner screamed and begged to end the experiment. In the years since Milgram's original experiment, the experiment has been repeated many times, and the results are always roughly the same: two-thirds of the subjects are obedient, no matter how much the learner screams and pleads.[4]

One of the most striking facts about the obedience experiments is that none of the subjects whom Milgram surveyed predicted that they would be fully obedient. So it seems that the subjects themselves, prior to the experiment, would have regarded their behavior as contrary to their character.[5] Moreover, when the subjects were allowed to choose the shock levels for themselves, only three percent of them ever delivered the maximum shock. Thus, the level of shock that the subjects were willing to deliver depended on whether or not they were instructed to deliver the maximum shock. Once again, the nature of the situation seems to have been the strongest influence on the subjects' behavior. Whether or not they gave a maximum shock was strongly influenced by whether or not they were given an instruction to continue the experiment.

I now turn to what is perhaps the most shocking experiment of all. In the early 1970s, researchers at Stanford University created a simulation of an American prison in the basement of the psychology building. They recruited male college students, none of whom had any history of crime, emotional instability, or intellectual or social disadvantage. From a pool of seventy-five applicants, the researchers chose those who were judged to be the most stable, and the most mature. These twenty-one participants were then randomly divided into two groups. The members of one group were assigned the role of 'prisoners', while the members of the other group were assigned the role of 'guards'. The prisoners were confined in this simulated prison, complete with barred cells. A closet served as a solitary confinement for misbehaving prisoners.

The results were astonishing. Within the limitations imposed on them by the researchers, the guards enacted every kind of

---

[4] Milgram 1974, cited in *Lack of Character*, pp. 39–49.
[5] *Lack of Character*, p. 49.

sadistic punishment they could imagine, such as requiring the prisoners to clean out toilets with their bare hands. One student's story is especially striking. Prior to the experiment, this student said: "As I am a pacifist and non-aggressive individual, I cannot see a time when I might maltreat another living thing." However, on Day 5 of the experiment, here is what this same student entered into his log.

> This new prisoner, 416, refuses to eat. That is a violation of Rule Two... and we are not going to have any of that shit. . . . Obviously we have a troublemaker on our hands. If that's the way he wants it, that's the way he gets it. We throw him into the Hole, ordering him to hold greasy sausages in each hand. After an hour he still refuses. . . . I decide to force feed him, but he won't eat. I let the food slide down his face. I don't believe it is me doing it.[6]

This is a snapshot of what happened to stable, mature, well-adjusted college students when they were placed in a prison simulation. The situation transformed a non-aggressive pacifist into an abusive prison guard. Once again, the nature of the situation strongly influenced the subjects' behavior, regardless of their character as individuals before they entered the experiment.

. . . Is Caged by Frail and Fragile Bars

Our natural inclination is to deny that these experiments really tell us anything about ourselves. We want to say that we would never act in the way that these people acted. There must have been something wrong with *them*, something that is not wrong with *us*. But do we have any reason to think that we are so different from the people in these experiments? Remember that Stanley Milgram's subjects came from all walks of life—schoolteachers, engineers, postal workers. The subjects in the Stanford prison experiment were college students at one of the best universities in the country, and all of them were chosen precisely because they were mature, stable, well-adjusted individuals. So what reason do we have to think that we are significantly different from these people? It's very hard to admit that human nature is frail in all of us. It is hard to admit that we, ourselves,

---

[6] Quoted in Haney and Zimbardo 1977, cited in *Lack of Character*, p. 51.

might be capable of doing things that we disapprove of so strongly. However, that is exactly what the evidence suggests.

These experiments tell us that the way human beings act is more often determined by their situation than by who they are as people. Minor differences in the situation often determine how we act. Did we just find a dime in the coin slot, or not? Do we smell the pleasant aroma of a nearby bakery, or not? Are we running late for an appointment, or not? More strikingly, we seem to be capable of horrendous actions in certain situations. If we feel the pressure of an instruction from an authority figure, then we will give an electric shock to someone who screams and pleads with us to stop. If we are placed in an environment that looks and feels like a prison, then we will throw someone into a closet and force-feed them when they refuse to eat.

In all these cases, our behavior is dictated by the situation that we find ourselves in. Our intentions, however good, are overcome by the situation. I might intend to help people in need, but whether I will depends on my situation. I might intend never to harm or abuse another person, but whether I will depends on my situation. As hard as it is to accept, this is what the evidence tells us about ourselves as human beings. Our will is weak. Our nature is frail. Johnny Cash was aware of this, having learned it in his own life. Based on this realization, he offered two moral lessons that we would all do well to learn.

So Hear the Kneeling Drunkard's Plea

Johnny Cash's life experience taught him this deep truth—that human nature is frail. Cash's songs are filled with stories of people whose situations determine their fate. In the song, "I Never Picked Cotton," the protagonist leaves his rural, southern hometown, where his parents and his siblings all pick cotton. He explores life in the city, and thrives in his own way, until one night in Memphis, when he is accosted by a bigot.

> It was Saturday night in Memphis
> When a redneck grabbed my shirt
> When he said go back to your cotton sack
> I left him dying in the dirt

> They'll take me in the morning
> To the gallows just outside
> And in the time I got
> There ain't a hell of a lot
> That I can look back on with pride.

The protagonist in this story never intended to kill anyone, but when he was suddenly accosted, he reacted violently, and that sealed his fate. The situation, which he did nothing to bring about, was his undoing. This brings me to the first moral lesson that Cash draws from the frailty of human nature. Since the situation plays such a large role in shaping people's behavior, we should be charitable toward those who act badly, because if we were placed in a similar situation, we might have acted just as badly ourselves.

This is not to say that people are not responsible for their actions. Cash never denies that people are responsible for their actions. The point is just that every one of us is capable of doing something wrong if we are placed in the wrong situation. Even good people can do very bad things. So the fact that a person acts badly does not automatically imply that he is an unusually bad person. In fact, as the evidence shows, a person who does something very bad could be very similar to you or me. Therefore we should be more charitable, and less judgmental, toward those who act badly. We should hold them responsible for their actions, but we should not automatically condemn them as people. They might be people much like us, who found themselves in a bad situation, and acted badly out of human weakness.

No song expresses this attitude of charity and forgiveness better than "Kneeling Drunkard's Plea." In that song, an old drunkard staggers into the graveyard of a country church, to kneel at his mother's grave. He asks God for mercy, over and over again, and then Cash tells us that he knows that God, in heaven, is listening. The message is clear. Just as God listens and forgives the drunkard for his wrongdoing, so should we. In light of Cash's understanding of the frailty of human nature, we can understand even better why he takes this attitude of charity and forgiveness. Since Cash was right, and human nature is frail in all of us, we should do likewise.

And Beware of the Beast in Me

This brings me to the second moral lesson that Cash draws, which is well expressed in the song "Don't Take Your Guns to Town." A young cowboy named Billy Joe grows restless with his life on the farm, and so he decides to go into town. Billy Joe means no one any harm. He just wants to go experience life in the town. His mother, fearing for his safety, tells him not to bring his guns to town, but the young cowboy rejects her advice. He tells her that she has nothing to worry about, because he can take care of himself. So Billy Joe takes his guns, and rides into town, where he goes into a saloon to have a drink. After he has had a drink, an old cowboy at the bar begins to make fun of Billy Joe. Angered, Billy Joe reaches for his gun, but the stranger is quicker, and he shoots Billy Joe. As Billy Joe dies, he realizes that his mother was right. He should not have brought his guns to town. Billy Joe thought that his character and his intentions were strong enough to secure his fate, but when he is belittled by the cowpoke in the bar, he reaches for his gun, and that is his undoing. He did not intend for this to happen, but the situation proved too much for him.

Here is the second moral lesson that Cash can teach us. One of the most important skills in living the moral life is the ability to avoid compromising situations. Since human nature is frail, we are all capable of acting badly in certain situations. So in order to avoid acting badly, we must try to avoid such situations. We must be aware of our own limitations, and act in light of that awareness. If we overestimate ourselves, as Billy Joe did, then we will find ourselves in a situation that overcomes us. In order to prevent this from happening, we must accept our own vulnerability, and take care to avoid situations that would exploit that vulnerability. Human vulnerabilities vary from person to person. So in order to avoid compromising situations, each of us will have to examine our own vulnerabilities, and then use that knowledge to avoid compromising situations. If we take the time and effort to do this, then we might be able to avoid a tragic fate like Billy Joe's.

Johnny Cash's life experience taught him that human nature is frail, even in the best of us. Life can throw a person into a situation that brings out the worst in him. No one is completely invulnerable to this. It can happen to anyone. Once we realize this, as Cash did, we should be more charitable toward those who act badly. This does not mean that we do not hold people responsible for their actions, but we should realize that we are all susceptible of serious wrongdoing, especially if we find ourselves in a situation that brings out the worst in us. Moreover, we should be very careful to avoid compromising situations. We should not bring our guns to town. And then, with a little luck, maybe things won't happen that way.[7]

---

[7] The evidence I have presented in this chapter, and its significance for moral philosophy, are discussed at length in Doris's *Lack of Character*. I am heavily indebted to Doris's discussion, though my application of his work in this context is my own.

10

'Til Things Get Better: Hope and Redemption in Black

JACOB M. HELD

In his *Confessions*, St. Augustine asks, "What is it in men that makes them rejoice more when a soul that has been despaired of and is in very great danger is saved than when there has always been hope and the danger has not been so serious?"

He answers: "the more pain there is first, the more joy there is after." [1] We appreciate the story of someone being pulled back from the brink of destruction, and revel in their success because it speaks to their strength, and it conveys a message of hope. We even seem to praise these fallen and saved individuals more than those whom we may deeply respect but who have always kept on the straight and narrow. There's satisfaction in the drama. Perhaps this is why Johnny Cash's music and life touch his fans so deeply. His life is this story of the struggle for redemption and his music chronicles his journey.

My inspiration for this chapter came while watching *Walk the Line*. In 1968, when Johnny Cash is looking to make a comeback he proposes recording a live album from Folsom Prison, the now monumental, *Johnny Cash at Folsom Prison*. But the record label is not sold on the idea. One of those present at the meeting remarks, "Your fans are church folk, Johnny. Christians. They don't want to hear you singing to a bunch of murderers and rapists tryin' to cheer them up." Cash responds, "Well, they're not Christians then." This seems simple enough.

---

[1] St. Augustine, *The Confessions of St. Augustine* (New York: Penguin, 1963), pp. 164, 166.

Christians forgive, right? But should they always forgive? What are the limits to forgiveness and does Cash's statement reflect a more basic moral ideal, namely, humility?

I think Cash was expressing the notion that barring omniscience we ought to withhold full-scale condemnation of our fellow human beings out of the recognition that there but for the grace of God, or perhaps in his own case June Carter, go I.

We're all morally flawed in some way; some more than others obviously, but being flawed we ought to be humble in our judgments. And who better to communicate this lesson than one who had fallen and was saved, several times, through the grace and goodwill of those closest to him? Cash approaches this issue—redemption—from a Christian perspective, but the message is universal. In fact, Christian ethics probably resonates with so many because it speaks to fundamental ethical truths.

Through the Fire and the Flood . . . Redeemed by the Blood

Most often references to redemption are made in religious contexts. Johnny Cash's own song, "Redemption," is a good example. In this song, he discusses being redeemed by "the blood," that is, through Jesus Christ. Redemption in this context is part and parcel of a retributive notion of justice. Wrongs, in this case sin, must be repaid and the price is blood. And what could be more personal, more signifying of a personal debt than blood; that which gives one life, that which is essential for life? Classical theories of justice often revolve around blood debts; an eye for an eye and so on.[2] The language of wrongs and punishment is spoken in terms of exchange, and blood is currency. The only way to pay for a past wrong is through one's own blood or suffering. Christ redeems us, that is, he revalues us and restores our worth through his own blood thus satisfying our cosmic debt as sinners.[3]

As one scholar notes, the message of the crucifixion and our atonement is that Jesus Christ makes an objective transaction

---

[2] See William Ian Miller, *Eye for an Eye* (Cambridge: Cambridge University Press, 2006).

[3] See Romans 3:24,26; 5:11

substituting his blood for ours and paying off our debt.[4] Redemption, as a redeeming, is a buying back of our self from sin. That is, it is a total revaluation effected through Christ's sacrifice. But this idea of redemption as a revaluation of one's self from one of low estimation to one of greater value is not unique to Christianity. People often speak of a change of heart or a change of character as though it were a total self-overhauling, the end result of which is a new person. In the Christian narrative this can only be done through our blood debt being paid by Christ.

The message of Christian redemption is expressed well in the Sermon on the Mount, as well as throughout the Gospel of St. Matthew: "Blessed are the merciful; for they shall obtain mercy" (5:7); "Love your enemies, bless them that curse you, do good to them that hate you, and pray for them which despitefully use you, and persecute you" (5:44); "Judge not, that ye not be judged" (7:1); and finally, "Then came Peter to him, and said, Lord, how oft shall my brother sin against me, and I forgive him? Till seven times? Jesus saith unto him, I say not unto thee, Until seven times: but, Until seventy times seven times" (18:21–22). The message here is one of forgiveness. But not forgiveness as simply forgiving wrongful acts once the wrongdoer has repented, but rather humility in the face of wrongdoing. One is not supposed to judge harshly or condemn another not because we are supposed to be pushovers, but because we can't know somebody's deep character, that is, their true self.

The Gospel of St. Matthew presents two issues. First, there's the claim that we should not condemn others since we are sinful also, that is, the charge of hypocrisy. Secondly, there is the epistemic problem that to condemn another person demands a kind of knowledge we can't obtain, one about another's essential self. Thus it is only God who can judge since it is only God who can know a person to her core.[5] God is the one who is gonna cut you down, or save you; not your neighbor. Thus, one message of the Fall is humility. Since we are all sinful, tainted,

---

[4] Thomas Williams, "Sin, Grace, and Redemption," in *The Cambridge Companion to Abelard*, edited by Jeffrey E. Brower and Kevin Guilfoy (Cambridge: Cambridge University Press, 2004) p. 260.

[5] See Jeffrie G. Murphy, *Getting Even: Forgiveness and Its Limits* (New York: Oxford University Press, 2003) Chapter 8.

or otherwise corrupt we lack the moral authority to condemn another, and since we can't know someone's deep character, full scale assessments are unwarranted.

But most of us readily condemn others and even execute them if we deem the wrong heinous enough. With twenty-five minutes to go we're all waiting to hear the convict yell and we all want to watch him die. But even in the most extreme cases the Christian message of redemption demands humility. "For he maketh his sun to rise on the evil and on the good, and sendeth rain on the just and unjust" (Matthew 5:45). Most importantly this attitude of humility demands that we remain hopeful in the capacity of even the most rotten to effect moral transformation, or redemption. Cash's first marriage presents a good case in point. In his autobiography he recounts his problems in that marriage and says, "these days I don't carry any guilt about those days."[6] He isn't guilty now not because he didn't do bad things, and not even because he has made payment for them, but because he is a different person than he was when he did those things; he has been redeemed, or revalued through a substantial character transformation.

As frail, flawed, or "fallen" all troubled people need to be redeemed. Perhaps as fallen himself, Johnny Cash felt so deeply for convicts, addicts, and the lowliest among us out of a sense of camaraderie. "The convicts [are] all brothers of mine," he noted.[7] And as he sings in "Man in Black," he wears the black for the beaten down, the prisoner who has paid for his crime, the reckless one whose bad trip left him cold, and those who haven't listened to or read the words that Jesus said. There is solidarity among the fallen. And the demand for humility in our moral judgments stems from the acknowledgment of our own imperfections, that is, our own capacity to fall.

But redemption can't happen without grace. Grace demands that the moral transformation be facilitated by an outside force, that is, redemption is a communal effort, and this makes sense. If redemption is about a substantial character transformation, then it's probably unreasonable to expect the fallen to save themselves. If your flaw is one of deep character you can't rely

---

[6] Johnny Cash with Patrick Carr, *Cash: The Autobiography* (New York: HarperCollins, 1997), p. 144.
[7] Johnny Cash, Liner Notes, *Johnny Cash at Folsom Prison.*

on yourself to make good judgments that will lead to moral improvement; you'll most likely need assistance. This need for help seemingly denies the ideal of autonomy or individual freedom, self-control, and personal responsibility and instead makes the claim that someone can only be saved through intervention.[8] And I think my use of the word "intervention" is fitting. Just as we don't demand of the addict that they straighten themselves out without assistance, so the morally corrupt can't be expected to go it alone.

Cash needed June and the Carters. He couldn't have done it alone. Interdependence may deny an ideal of autonomy and self-reliance, but it affirms a fact of human existence. There is no such thing as a self-made person; we are all interconnected. The fallen need help in order to realign their moral compass. But it is not and it should not be as simple as forgive and forget. Sometimes people need to be judged harshly and sometimes they ought not to be forgiven, and some people do seem rotten and never make the change no matter how much help they are given.

It Ain't Me Babe: Forgiveness, Acts, and Character

When we usually speak of wrongdoing and wrongdoers, we speak of somebody having done something wrong. They are supposed to be apologetic, make some sort of restitution and then the wrong is put behind them, that is, we forgive them. Only the most heinous of acts are described as unforgivable, and this is because we think the act itself is demonstrative of the kind of person somebody is. But when we usually speak of forgiveness we assume that somebody can be forgiven because a particular indiscretion is not constitutive of who they are. We separate the person from the act, so although we disapprove of the act, we accept the person.[9]

Forgiveness begins by assuming you can sever the action from the agent. That is, it is possible for a good person to do a

---

[8] See Stephen Mulhall, *Philosophical Myths of the Fall* (Princeton: Princeton University Press, 2005), Introduction.
[9] See Jeffrie G. Murphy and Jean Hampton, *Forgiveness and Mercy* (New York: Cambridge University Press, 1988), p. 24.

bad thing, so in assessing the wrong we are more concerned with the action than a full assessment of the person. We forgive somebody because we believe them to be a good person who merely made a mistake. Forgiveness of an act only makes sense in reference to an assessment of the person as basically good, and their repentance verifies this judgment. If I repent and I am forgiven the act is removed from my record and I begin with a clean slate. My repentance demonstrates that I wish to dissociate myself from the act; it is not reflective of the kind of person I am.

Consider the example of somebody setting fire to Los Padres National Wildlife Refuge. If during the trial he responded that the endangered condors are yellow buzzards which he cares nothing for and that he didn't even start the fire, his truck did and it's dead, then it is clear he is not repentant. He doesn't care about the impact he has on others and at this moment he is displaying the characteristics of a heartless and despicable fellow. He should not be forgiven. In fact, anger would be the appropriate response to him. One shouldn't be a doormat. If forgiveness is a virtue it is only so in contexts supportive of self-respect.[10] But if someone is truly repentant, then to withhold forgiveness is to be unreasonably vindictive. But the assessment of acceptable forgiveness hinges on a character assessment.

It seems to be a prerequisite of forgiveness that the goodness of my character be acknowledged. I am only forgiven once I am contrite, and contrition is important because it shows a change in disposition, namely, that I no longer wish to be associated with the type of wrongdoing I had done. So what happens when someone is not contrite and shows no signs of remorse? What do we do with the wicked?

The message of redemption, namely, humility and hope, is that we cannot cast the wicked aside. Condemnation is unwarranted since it relies on problematic knowledge of deep character and forecloses the possibility of salvation, something which can't be predicted with certainty. Redemption is about hope and transformation.[11] It allows us to deal morally with those who don't seem to be forgivable, but who remain human beings.

I could rephrase the above account in terms of an exchange relation. Through your wrong action you have bought a share

---

[10] See Murphy, *Getting Even*, pp. 18–19.
[11] Murphy and Hampton, *Forgiveness and Mercy*, p. 32

of guilt and the only way to pay it off or make good on your debt is to atone in a sufficient manner. Your character functions as your creditor such that any action is potentially forgivable so long as your character remains solvent, that is, so long as you are not a morally bankrupt or a rotten human being. So long as your character is good it can potentially pay off your guilt or debt. To stretch the analogy even further, redemption or offering hope of a moral transformation would be equivalent to giving a loan. When your character is bankrupt you need a hand up. Others grant you this by recognizing your capacity as a moral agent to change, or redeem yourself even if currently you have nothing and no obvious promise. That is, based on a risk assessment you are seen to be a viable human being who could very well make good on a loan. In moral terms, forgiveness only makes sense in the broader context of a theory of redemption. We can only forgive the decent and this requires a character assessment the limits of which are set by a theory of redemption. Yet some are hostile to the idea of being judged according to external standards and requiring help in order to become a decent person as defined by these standards.

Nietzsche and Redemption: He Wants the Kingdom, But He Doesn't Want God in It

According to Friedrich Nietzsche (1844–1900), the message of Christian redemption is a denial of life. In order to give the idea of redeeming the fallen credence one must first admit that we are fallen, that this life is lacking, unappealing, and in need of saving, and that salvation can only come from without, that is, by giving to another the power to make our lives valuable. The result of seeing ourselves as fallen and in need of redemption is to view ourselves as dependent and weak, that is, with humble hearts and on bended knees, begging for help. "Here is *sickness*, beyond any doubt, the most terrible sickness that has ever raged in man; and whoever can still bear to hear . . . how in this night of torment and absurdity there has resounded the cry of *love* . . . or redemption through love, will turn away, seized by invincible horror."[12] Herein lies the problem with redemption; it is only

---

[12] Friedrich Nietzsche, "On the Genealogy of Morals," in *Basic Writings of Nietzsche* (New York: Modern Library, 1992), p. 529.

needed if we begin from the presumption that we are fallen, that we perceive our life as worthless and only salvageable once redeemed by a transcendent force who proffers redemption through grace.[13] And perhaps Nietzsche is onto something if redemption is only a metaphysical concept about our relation to a transcendent order. But in terms of moral theory redemption is about humility, hope, and transformation.

Nietzsche sees in Christianity a masochistic self-hatred of our drive to exercise power or domination, our will to power. He believes we have infused society with a perverse admiration for slave morality, namely, values that favor the weak like humility, altruism, forgiveness, and dependence, and thus we deny our drive to be assertive and strong. We hate ourselves when we find we desire whatever contradicts this slave morality. Thus, we hate ourselves and see in ourselves a fallen nature that must be purified, an assertiveness that must be pacified.[14] Nietzsche objects to the idea of reliance and instead praises the ideal of self-mastery. He doesn't like the idea of somebody telling him he is not good enough and only through their help can he hope to become better.

Yet Nietzsche does believe that redemption as revaluation is a praiseworthy goal. He thinks it is crucial that one revalue instances of one's life in order to restore their meaning. Our failures gain value when they are reintegrated into a narrative of a successful, complete life. This idea is expressed most fully through the notion of the eternal recurrence of the same, wherein each instance of life is seen as worthy insofar as it constitutes a necessary moment in a now praiseworthy existence. "I taught you, 'The will is a creator.' All 'it was' is a fragment, a riddle, a dreadful accident—until the creative will says to it, 'But thus I willed it.' Until the creative will says to it, 'But thus I will it; thus shall I will it.'"[15] Each troublesome or problematic event in our lives is redeemed, or revalued from being lamentable to laudable if our life as a whole is lived well, that is, if we perceive

---

[13] For commentary see R. Lanier Anderson, "Nietzsche on Truth, Illusion, and Redemption," *European Journal of Philosophy* 13:2.

[14] The First Essay of Nietzsche's *On the Genealogy of Morals* covers this material well.

[15] Friedrich Nietzsche, "Thus Spoke Zarathustra," in *The Portable Nietzsche* (New York: Penguin, 1976), p. 253.

it to be lived well. Thus, the person is not fallen, they as a human being do not need to be redeemed. Instead, it is certain aspects of their life that need to be seen in perspective as elements of a great life. It is only fitting that in preaching his own message of redemption Nietzsche adopts the standpoint of savior or Christ figure in Zarathustra and even composes the book like a gospel.

But can we redeem ourselves? Can we buy ourselves back from ourselves? Is a self-revaluation worth anything? Consider Saul/Paul as depicted in Cash's *Man in White*. Before his conversion on the road to Damascus he believes his violence and hatred fully justified according to his own fanaticism. Each instance is redeemed for him according to his own set of values. Do we want to allow him the right to claim his life valuable because he finds value in persecution and destruction?

The problem with a Nietzschean account is that redemption as a total revaluation wherein what was once found lacking is now seen to be of value ought to be beyond one's own power. If we redeem our own lives through telling a story where our past indiscretions are revalued as good insofar as they are moments on the path to a life we now value for whatever reason, what is to prevent us from slipping into self-delusion and merely rationalizing our past mistakes and deluding ourselves that our pathetic life is desirable? This seems to be the sad state of most peoples' lives where each self-help manual, life coach, and erstwhile guru preaches acceptance of errors and acquiescence in profligacy and rejects the idea of being judged by an external, absolute standard; you're okay the way you are. But what legitimates our redemption is external verification affirming that our revaluation is genuine. If redemption is like a creditor, we can't coin our own money. If we insinuate that redemption is a subjective matter, one of individual self-transformation, then we remove its promise of true moral change. Change of perspective is not moral transformation.[16] Redemption is a powerful concept because it is a character judgment imposed by another; somebody whose judgment is respected and binding. Of course being judged can be quite painful, and we experience negative assessments as shame.

---

[16] Nietzsche's view is more complex than presented here, but the above account is sufficient to communicate the problem of saving one's self.

On Being "Reduced," Not Wasted

Shame is a powerful emotion, one that is felt so deeply because it is a complete negative assessment of who one is. Whereas guilt is merely a statement that you did a bad thing, shame is the assessment that you are a bad person.[17] The woman in "Long Black Veil" actually lets her lover go to his death rather than admit to an extramarital affair. The moral condemnation she would face is so unbearable that she would let an innocent man die, and he would rather be thought guilty of murder than despised as an adulterer.

Shame is felt for many reasons. Some make the distinction between natural and moral shame.[18] If we're discussing shame in the context of moral philosophy, then we should focus on moral failings and moral shame, not natural shame and our ashamedness for those things of which we aren't blameworthy such as appearance, slow-wittedness, or being a boy named "Sue." As natural shame, shame is unfair and useless. In cases where it is felt due to natural, involuntary, and non-moral factors it serves no purpose. But moral shame is different.

Being morally ashamed is when one is assessed to be lacking in relevant moral ways. It demands an objectively determined set of values and a way to determine when one has fallen short of these. In instances of moral shame the effect can be positive. One can learn about important shortcomings and be motivated to correct them thus becoming a better person. Sometimes one ought to feel ashamed, and a truly shameless person, one who could never believe oneself to be morally lacking is incredibly arrogant, lacking in any standards of behavior whatsoever, or both.

Redemption as a full character reassessment functions in relation to shame just as forgiveness does with respect to guilt. We are guilty of a bad act, we repent and are forgiven. We are shameful of a faulty character; we are redeemed and then set

---

[17] See Johann A. Klaassen, "The Taint of Shame: Failure, Self-Distress, and Moral Worth," *Journal of Social Philosophy* 32:2 (Summer 2001), pp. 174–196; John Sabini and Maury Silver, "In Defense of Shame: Shame in the Context of Guilt and Embarrassment," *Journal for the Theory of Social Behavior* 27:1, pp. 1–15.

[18] For example, John Rawls, *A Theory of Justice*, revised edition (Cambridge, Massachusetts: Harvard University Press, 1999), Chapter VII, Section 67.

back on the right path. The values against which one is judged will determine when one ought to feel shame. To redeem oneself is to reconnect to these moral values through change in one's character, to see oneself through the gaze of the other, the judge, whether real or imagined and assess who one is as a person.[19]

As a social evaluation or the application of external criteria we can see why external assistance would be required in order to be redeemed. We both need the help of the other, and her verification that we have made the change. The transformation must be effected by the other; only she can remove the taint since it is only through her recognition and bringing of me back into the fold that I am reaffirmed as a respectable human being. I can only walk the line with some help, that is, because you are mine, because we are interdependent I need you to help me walk that line and to let me know when I slip.

Understanding redemption in this way explains why humility in our moral judgments is so important. Since we are dealing with deep character, an aspect of us nobody has full access to, we must be cautious in our assessments. In fact, we ought to operate on the faith that another person can change and the hope that what appears to be change actually is so. This optimism may be the catalyst needed to facilitate the very transformation our hope presupposes. Redemption, as one scholar put it, functions at the level of the "future perfect." [20]

Once I am redeemed, my past self is seen as one that was necessary on the journey towards becoming this newly redeemed and worthy human being. Thus, after my redemption I will retrospectively have always been the kind of person who could have been redeemed. I am only able to become that new person if I believe it possible to redeem those past acts, that is, if I believe that I can become the kind of person who, when seen in hindsight, was always capable of being redeemed. I have to believe myself to be a certain kind of person before I can actually become that kind of person. I, and most importantly others, have to view me as redeemable.

---

[19] See Christopher Bennett, "Personal and Redemptive Forgiveness," *European Journal of Philosophy* 11:2, p. 133.

[20] See R. Lanier Anderson, "Nietzsche on Truth, Illusion, and Redemption," *European Journal of Philosophy* 13:2, p. 210. Anderson uses the idea to clarify Nietzsche's notion of redemption in terms of the eternal recurrence, but it is also relevant to my account.

This is the problem Cash wrestles with when considering his father and himself. He asks, "Was I evil, but then made a change, walked the line, and was a godly man, but then slipped and fell and became evil again?" Or with respect to his father, "Was he redeemed? . . . Was Daddy's conversion real, and if it was, why didn't I see it all the time . . .?"[21] With respect to Cash and his father, the redemption of each is never certain but always possible; there is always the faith and the hope that it is so. Our knowledge will be imperfect, but the possibility remains open.

The Doors Are Never Locked

The idea of redemption acknowledges a fact about human beings: we are fallible and capable of moral progress. We ought to afford people the opportunity to redeem or revalue themselves, but this is difficult to do. We don't know when somebody has actually made a substantive character transformation; we often don't know if we ourselves have. Redemption affirms the hope that things and people can and will get better; better times will come, or at least they might. This hope can even facilitate change by affording the benefit of the doubt, even when the possibility of change may be doubtful. Nobody is beyond hope, nobody is irredeemable. Whether it is a penitent convict who wishes nothing more than to give his love to his kid and his wife Rose or a despicable murderer who kills a man in Reno just to watch him die, we must withhold ultimate condemnation. It's beyond us to make a definitive judgment of moral worth, which is what an execution, or even life in prison without the possibility of parole, does to the likes of Joe Bean and others. We see into others through a glass darkly, and so we must remain humble in our blindness. Unlike the Masons who rejected Cash's application on "moral grounds." He notes, "Evidently the progress I'd made . . . didn't count for much" (p. 222).

Perhaps Johnny Cash's music and life are felt so deeply by so many because we do believe in the infinite possibility of moral change and Cash himself proves the lesson. So up front there ought to be the man in black, so we don't forget the simple lesson of redemption.

---

[21] Johnny Cash, *Cash: The Autobiography*, p. 239.

11

Cash, Kant, and the Kingdom of Ends

YOLANDA ESTES

You might well ask:

- What inspires a person who spends her days and nights preoccupied by the nearly incomprehensible theories of Immanuel Kant to write about Johnny Cash?

- Why should I bother with Kant's philosophy, since Estes says Kant is so much like Cash anyway—and since listening to Cash is so much more amusing?

When I was a young child, I did not while away my time reading Kant but lying on my grandparents' bed listening to my grandfather play his guitar. He played "Wildwood Flower," "I Love My Rooster," and (along with those old-timey favorites) songs of Johnny Cash. So, I love Cash, because I loved my grandfather and his guitar.

"Wildwood Flower" and "I Love My Rooster" are traditional songs. "Wildwood Flower" was originally a parlor song, "I'll Twine 'mid the Ringlets," written by Maud Irving and Joseph Philbrick in 1860, and was often performed by the Carter Family. It was my grandfather's warm-up and "I Love My Rooster" (silly song) was a concession to his first-born grandchild.

Cash was a popular singer for the first time in those days. Today, he's popular again and I would say—from the depths of my own musical ignorance, so forgive me, Cash fans—rather overvalued; but I will always enjoy his music and empathize with his attempt to walk a very thin line with unsteady feet.

My grandfather, as grandfathers are wont to do, instilled many values (and perhaps, a little of the beast) in me. When I grew older—whilst still a child—I discovered that many of my grandfather's values (and hence my own), like Cash's, rested on the authority of revealed texts and religious dogma. For a while, I feared it was necessary to either relinquish my moral values or my rational consistency; but eventually, I discovered that certain people, like Kant, had already wrestled with that terrifying false dichotomy, so I turned to philosophy.

Regardless of one's religious or moral commitments, "The preacher said, 'Jesus said'" is simply not a good reason for accepting anything—religious, moral, or otherwise—as true. Cash expressed many commendable sentiments and perceptive observations, but he offered nothing in the way of a considered reflection about the rational origin or grounds for those moral notions. Kant did. Anyone who admires the essence of Cash, would do well to take a look at the substance of Kant.

Cries for Justice—the Man in Black and the Sage of Königsberg

There's no true moral justice on earth. The undeniably vicious perpetuate evil due to the corruption of their hearts; and the essentially virtuous succumb to evil due to the weakness of their wills. The wicked prosper while the good suffer. So it was; so it remains; so it will be. Humanity cries out for justice, but no earthly jury, judgment, or sentence balances the moral scale.

In the eighteenth century, the German philosopher Immanuel Kant (1724–1804) proposed an ideal of ultimate justice, or a kingdom of ends, wherein the inequities of natural and human law would be remedied. In the twentieth century, the singer-songwriter Johnny Cash offered a similar ideal of final judgment, or a kingdom of God. His poignant illustrations of human striving and frailty—of human hope and despair—complement Kant's abstract moral theory.

Kant and Cash were vastly different in their characters and ways of life. Cash was no philosopher, and Kant was surely no singer-songwriter. Although he never offered a declaration of atheism (or any other theological perspective), Kant's religious views were heterodox. Cash was a Christian. Before he found a measure of peace in his marriage to June Carter, the Man in

Black's sensuous passions led him on a nation-wide journey of law-breaking, drug abuse, and illicit sexual relations. The Sage of Königsberg never left his hometown, rarely crossed authorities, and most probably died a virgin. Despite a forgivable penchant for French fashion, he abided by a fastidious regimen, serving as a model of decorum, parsimony, and honor.

Rarely hampered by propriety or thrift, Cash's reckless conduct disappointed his fans and harmed his friends and family. Nonetheless, his songs touched millions, addressing the concerns of ordinary people at home, at work, or in prison. Kant's abstruse transcendental idealism proved challenging even to his peers, and although he was an inspiring and dynamic teacher, he took no pains to reach the uncultivated masses.

Despite their differences, Kant and Cash accepted comparable ethical codes, each devoting his life's work to expounding similar visions of moral duty, responsibility and justice. Although they might be accused of imposing overly stringent demands on themselves and others, they grasped the infirmities that deflect our moral quests. Each perceived human beings as intelligent, sensitive creatures with spiritual aspirations, whose desires and duties generally collide and whose happiness and righteousness rarely coincide. Moreover, they grasped that this world stifles virtue, cultivating the basest inclinations, but insisted that hardship and temptation relieve none of us of our duty. Finally, they recognized that moral justice demands a reconciliation of nature and reason.

The Preacher Said (On the Moral Law and the Golden Rule)

Now I say that man, and in general every rational being, *exists* as an end in himself, *not merely as a means* for arbitrary use by this or that will: he must in all his actions whether they are directed to himself or to other rational beings, always be viewed *at the same time as an end.* (Immanuel Kant)[1]

Well, we can see that the world is full of greed. There's so much hate yet there's so much need. What should we do when no one seems to care? What can we do when there is no love there? And

---

[1] *Groundwork of the Metaphysic of Morals* (New York: Harper and Row, 1953), p. 95.

then, the preacher said, "Of love, Jesus said, Love thy neighbor as thyself" (Johnny Cash)[2]

Kant and Cash subscribed to duty-based, or deontological,
moralities. Deontologists believe moral obligations derive from
principles—laws or rules—but neither the validity of those principles nor the value of the actions they generate can be determined by their consequences. Kant based moral duty on the
categorical imperative, or moral law, which commands that
actions respect humanity in ourselves and others whereas Cash
based duty on the Golden Rule, which commands that we treat
others as we would be treated by them.

Kant's moral law states "Act in such a way that you always
treat humanity, whether in your own person or in the person
of any other, never simply as a means, but always at the same
time as an end" (*Groundwork*, p. 96). According to this principle, human nature consists in rational freedom or our capacity
to choose goals that we have conceived for ourselves. Our
highest goal is to realize our own humanity by becoming completely rational and free—autonomous—so humanity is an end-
in-itself, requiring no justification or objective. Treating
humanity as an end entails permitting others to determine their
own ends or goals rather than just using them as means—tools
or things—to accomplish our aims; likewise, it requires embracing our own dignity and freedom rather than regarding our
lives as expendable or determined by the vagaries of nature or
fate. Ultimately, the moral law commands us to respect and foster human autonomy.

Kantian morality uses the moral law to determine particular
moral duties toward ourselves and others. Since lying and other
mendacious conduct, including self-deceit, subvert rational free
decision, the moral law forbids it; and likewise, the moral law
encourages behavior that promotes human development such as
charity, education, and compassion. Obviously, deeds intended
to harm or destroy human beings physically, such as rape, suicide, or murder, constitute particularly egregious crimes under

---

[2] "The Preacher Said, 'Jesus Said'." In this chapter I refer to songs either written or performed by Cash—each might be said to express Cash's views insofar as he decided to present them to the public—using tight paraphrases rather
than exact quotations.

the moral law, as do those meant to own, barter, or demean human bodies, such as slavery, prostitution, or careless sexual intercourse. Although Kant found it difficult to imagine a world without war, he found it equally difficult to conceive of war as anything other than state-sanctioned violence and murder.

In "The Man in Black," Cash urged his listeners to 'live as Jesus did'. Like other Christians, he regarded Jesus as a moral exemplar, whose behavior and teachings—as portrayed in the Bible—could provide a practical guide for living. Broadly and generously construed, Christianity may be regarded as providing the basis for a morality of love. Jesus told his followers to love their neighbors as they loved themselves or to treat others as they would be treated. This is often called the golden rule.

Only a very crude interpretation of the golden rule would suggest that we should treat others specifically as we wish to be treated, because our individual preferences are unique and thus, rarely applicable to others. Nonetheless, most of us would allow that we do not want to be manipulated, coerced, or otherwise used for another's purposes, however benign, but rather that we want the opportunity to satisfy our needs and pursue our goals without interference from others. Moreover, most of us hope to receive and expect to give a measure of compassion. So interpreted, the golden rule calls for mutual respect and compassion.

Cash's songs depict the lives of ordinary, flawed human beings, taking up the part of the poor and downtrodden, the confused and deceived, and the victims of injustice, violence, and war. Cash obviously regarded these issues—his perennial themes—as among the most serious assaults on humanity. The purpose of his work was not merely to illuminate the plight of his fellows but to incite his listeners to address it by showing compassion and respect to others and, if necessary, demanding compassion and respect for everyone.

The Wanderer (On the Good Will and the Good Heart)

For if any action is to be morally good, it is not enough that it should *conform* to the moral law—it must also be done *for the sake of the moral law*: where this is not so, the conformity is only too contingent and precarious, since the non-moral ground at work will now and then produce actions that accord with the law, but

very often actions which transgress it. (Kant, *Groundwork*, pp
57–58)

I went walking, looking for one good man, a spirit who would not
break or bend. (Cash, "The Wanderer")

Kant and Cash would have agreed that our deeds must not
only agree with a moral principle but also be inspired by rever-
ence for the spirit of morality. Kant called such an attitude the
good will. Cash had his own notion of the good will—a heart
motivated by love—which we might call the good heart. The
Kantian idea of a good will involves choosing to do what is right
simply because it is right without regard for desires or consequences.

A good will is motivated solely by respect for the moral law,
or the idea of right. It transcends or supersedes the natural inclinations that normally govern human activity and that occasionally accord with morality. Ordinarily, we sustain and develop
ourselves because doing so satisfies our physical or psychological needs while producing feelings of pleasure. Likewise, we
show consideration for others because we are social creatures,
enjoying the companionship and empathizing with the condition of our kind, or because we are politic beasts, soliciting the
assistance and fearing the retaliation of our peers. Deeds stimu-
lated by nature may coincide with those demanded by duty, but
chance often disrupts this uneasy agreement between happiness
and morality. So it is, a sick or depressed individual loses interest in self-preservation and self-development. So also, a threatened or wounded person protects his own interests rather than
promoting those of others. When morality fails to secure our
well-being, we become disinclined to virtue, but our reluctance
need not preclude dutiful action, because the good will coun-
termands natural inclination, choosing the good to the detriment
of the prudent.

Kant said, "It is impossible to conceive of anything at all in
this world, or even out of it, which can be taken as good without qualification, except a good will" (*Groundwork*, p. 61).
The good will is good in itself, because the spirit of morality
animates it, allowing it to withstand any perversion of good
traits (virtues or talents) for evil deeds and to avert any performance of evil deeds for good results (our own or another's
happiness). Its moral effort always succeeds despite the vicis-

situdes of circumstance because it always performs its duty, which consists in striving to obey the moral law without regard for consequences.

For Cash, following the golden rule meant embracing the spirit of love underpinning it, which involves not merely an emotion but also a solemn intention and fervent effort to satisfy moral necessity. Although many of the protagonists in his songs—and Cash himself—often fell short of demonstrating either consistently firm intentions or efforts, he revealed the importance of looking beneath the surface of moral action. In "God's Gonna Cut You Down," he claimed that many people 'throw their rocks and hide their hands, working in the dark against their fellow man'.

Cash's protagonists insinuate that the motives of their deeds carried greater moral weight than the results. The ruffian Sam of "Sam Hall," offers some grim humor at his own hanging, advising the witnesses that their secret iniquities match his public offenses. Likewise, the convict in "Folsom Prison Blues," who shot a man "just to watch him die," suggests that his gratuitous motive amplifies the reprehensibility of his crime. In contrast, the penitent boy in "I Hung my Head" arouses sympathy not only because he regrets his thoughtless act of manslaughter but also because he never designed to harm the victim.

The Beast in Me (On the Conscience and the Demand for Justice)

> In a theory that is based on the concept of duty, concern about the empty ideality of this concept quite disappears. For it would not be a duty to aim at a certain effect of our will if this effect were not also possible in experience. (Kant, "On the Common Saying,"[3] p. 280)

> The beast in me is caged by frail and fragile bars: Restless by day and by night, rants and rages at the stars. God help the beast in me. The beast in me has had to learn to live with pain and how to shelter from the rain; and in the twinkling of an eye might have to be restrained. (Cash, "The Beast in Me")

---

[3] "On the Common Saying: That May Be Correct in Theory but It Is of No Use in Practice," in *Practical Philosophy* (Cambridge: Cambridge University Press, 1996).

Kant and Cash believed that their moral principles applied to everyone at every time and in every place, admitting neither exception nor excuse. Nonetheless, they allowed that the frailty of the human will and the opacity of the human conscience prevent us from fairly judging ourselves or others. Moreover, since human law fails to recompense moral wrong while natural law fails to reward moral goodness, and neither system engenders moral reform or progress, they would have agreed that perfect justice surpasses any earthly law.

For Kant, 'ought implied can'. Insofar as we are human, we recognize our duties; and insofar as they are duties, we can fulfill them. The moral law never exacts too high a tribute, since it only demands that we try our best to fulfill the obligations revealed by conscience. Nonetheless, the will is weak and the conscience easily misled by caprice, desire, and pretext. When forced before the naive tribunal of our own heart, we tender elaborate sophistries. In brief, "Innocence is a splendid thing, only it has the misfortune not to keep very well and to be easily misled" (*Groundwork*, p. 72). Only the most self-deceived reprobates among us would vouch for their innocence, but only the blindest could believe in the justice of natural or human law. Natural law does not distribute good or ill according to moral merit and human justice does not remediate these natural inequities. Moreover, neither system compensates those who suffer evil, reforms those who commit it, or sustains those who would eschew it.

Cash's impulsive delinquents dimly glimpse their own motives, but they offer no excuses for their wicked deeds or appeals to their mitigating circumstances. The Folsom Prison murderer says that he knew the difference between right and wrong and thus, he 'had it coming' and 'can't be free'. Sam grants his actions were bad, accepting death and damnation as his rightful lot. In "I Hung My Head," the condemned youth willingly forfeits his life, only aspiring to reconcile with his victim in eternity. Cash's protagonists are not essentially evil but rather impetuous men who—like Cash himself—reflect belatedly on their intentions. Nonetheless, in "God's Gonna Cut You Down" and "When the Man Comes Around," he suggested that even the most assiduous self-examination might fail to measure the human heart, which could only be weighed on a scale unskewed by man.

Cash, like Kant, recognized the travesty of human justice. His listeners understand that no inmates reformed in Folsom Prison, no hangings settled the moral score, and no war avoided collateral damage. On the contrary, many evil-doers escaped punishment, many victims went uncompensated, and many upright men died to quiet the scruples of the elite or the fears of the masses. Although most of Cash's characters harbor no hopes for earthly redemption, many express desires to apply their delayed moral maturity to a future grown suddenly short. In "I Hung My Head" and "Hurt," each protagonist discovers that he can neither recover what he lost nor replace what he stole within the constraints of time. Cash insists that the need for true reformation, recompense, and justice exceeds worldly powers.

When the Man Comes Around (On the Kingdom of Ends and the Kingdom of God)

To view ourselves, therefore, as in the world of grace, where all happiness awaits us, except insofar as we ourselves limit our share in it by being unworthy of happiness, is, from the practical standpoint, a necessary idea of reason. (Kant, *Critique*,[4] p. 640)

I know dark clouds will hang round me. I know my way is rough and steep, yet beauteous fields lie just before me where God's redeemed their vigils keep. ("Wayfaring Stranger")

Kant and Cash envisioned a better world wherein an all-knowing judge would distribute just deserts in exact proportion to virtue and wherein everyone could strive eternally toward moral harmony and transformation. For Kant, this world was the kingdom of ends implied by rational morality. For Cash, it was the kingdom of God described by scriptural prophecy. For both, it was an object of faith that human beings should espouse by living as if perfect justice already prevailed.

Kant postulates the kingdom of ends as the only possible reconciliation of man's natural sensible needs with his rational moral demands. As sensuous beings, we want a sensible happiness, but nature treats us inequitably and morality often requires

---

[4] *Critique of Pure Reason* (New York: St. Martin's Press, 1965).

us to sacrifice our desires. As moral beings, we demand that virtuous deeds (while not performed for the sake of consequences) generate the good results intended by their authors,
but nature rarely conforms itself to our wills. Human law cannot
amend these injustices deriving from the conflict between nature
and reason, because it must be administered by imperfect people with limited natural and rational capacities. Moral law
demands that human beings ameliorate their deficiencies, but
because their task is infinite, they cannot accomplish it within
the limitations of space and time.

True justice, for Kant, presumes an impartial judge with
unlimited natural power and unlimited rational insight. Such a
sovereign authority could fulfill sensible need in exact proportion to moral merit, reading the secrets of the human heart and
requiting them in kind, thus ensuring that moral goals led to
rational results in a kingdom of ends. We cannot demonstrate
the existence of such a realm, but according to Kant, belief in a
kingdom of ends is reasonable, because the rational law of
morality requires it. Ought implies can: morality demands justice, so it entails no contradiction within human nature without
providing for its mediation, commands no deed of human will
without securing its rational conclusion, and imposes no obligation on human conscience without allowing for its realization
in eternity. The ideal of the kingdom of ends allows moral subjects to embrace their moral obligations without regrets or fears,
secure that they are transforming the present, imperfect world in
the image of a future, better one.

In "When the Man Comes Around" and "God's Gonna Cut
You Down," Cash proposes a similar kingdom wherein the
needs of nature and of spirit coincide, an unimpeachable
authority distributes moral deserts, and people rise above the
moral frailties that afflicted their mortal lives. His sovereign
also 'decides who to free and who to blame,' and unlike
earthly authorities, measures every soul to the 'penny weight
and hundred pound.' However, Cash's image of perfect justice
is the kingdom of God, which follows Armageddon and the
Day of Judgment. Until Armageddon, he says, 'no shalam, no
shalom' is possible, because recompense and peace require
justice; but after 'what's done in the dark is brought to the
light', respite and forgiveness can exist alongside retribution
and condemnation. Just as many of his wayward characters

aspired to redemption, so Cash hoped to 'start again a million miles away'.

Although Cash believed in the kingdom of God, and most probably in the biblical prediction of Armageddon, he did not design to prove his beliefs. For Cash, as for Kant, the realm of perfect justice was an object of faith, which he derived from scriptural authority rather than from the rational implications of the moral law. Nonetheless, he suggested that the kingdom of God, like the kingdom of ends, begins here in space and time. The moral subject's task is not to bide the time until securing better options in a future world, but to strive for improvement in the present world. Even if 'things will never be right,' we must live as if the kingdom of God (or of ends) is come.

From Cash to Kant—and Back Again

Although convergent in essence, Kant and Cash diverged in substance. Unlike Kant, who developed a well-conceived theory of morality, Cash gave no rational justification for his moral notions, which are rooted in scriptural authority and religious conviction. Nonetheless, his vivid imagery certainly adds some human warmth to Kant's chilly abstractions. Kant and Cash show that a rigorous moral code need not ignore the complexities of human life. Each in his fashion acknowledges that our moral effort, while fraught with confusion and discouragement, is ultimately guided by an ideal of justice.

My grandfather died while I was writing this chapter. He had lost the ability to play the guitar and to express his values coherently, but I think that he would have been pleased to know that his grand-daughter wrote something about Cash (and that his name appeared in a philosophy book), so I dedicate this chapter to Marion Edward Wells, who played the best "Wildwood Flower" of all time.

PART IV

Justice

12

Johnny Cash, Prison Reform, and Capital Punishment

DAVID KYLE JOHNSON and LANCE SCHMITZ

At the age of five, little Johnny Cash was working in the cotton fields, singing along with his family as they worked as share-croppers.[1] His family's economic and personal struggles during the Depression shaped his worldview; that's why so many of his songs reach out to—and touch—the poor and the outcasts of society. It also might help explain how he came to take on the persona of the "Man in Black." As the song of that title says,

> I wear black for the poor and the beaten down
> Livin' in the hopeless, hungry side of town
> I wear it for the prisoner who has long paid for his crime,
> But is there because he's a victim of the times. . . .
>
> Oh, I'd love to wear a rainbow every day,
> And tell the world that everything's okay.
> But I'll try to carry off a little darkness on my back.
> Till things are brighter, I'm the Man in Black.

Cash didn't merely pity such people; he identified himself with them in hopes of setting things right.

Although he never served hard time himself, Cash was most famously known for his sympathy regarding the plight of the imprisoned. Many of his recordings—"I'm Just Here to Get My

---

[1] For more on Cash's life see *Johnny Cash: The Biography* by Michael Streissguth or *Cash: The Autobiography.*

Baby Out of Jail," "Columbus Stockade Blues," "The Wall," "Give My Love to Rose," "I Got Stripes," "Send a Picture of Mother," and most notably "San Quentin" and "Folsom Prison Blues"— were written from the point of view of a prisoner and clearly indicate his compassion for the common criminal. Consider the plight of the prisoner in "Folsom Prison Blues":

> I'm stuck in Folsom Prison
> And time keeps draggin' on
> But that train keeps a rollin'
> On down to-San-An-Tone

> When I was just a baby
> My mama told me, "Son,
> Always be a good boy;
> Don't ever play with guns."
> But I shot a man in Reno
> Just to watch him die.
> When I hear the whistle blowin'
> I hang my head and cry.

Even though the prisoner shot a man in Reno just to watch him die, Cash still pities his situation. In real life, Cash's pity took the form of exchanging letters with the incarcerated and helping many of them in their return to life outside the prison walls. Cash's empathy was most visibly demonstrated when he performed concerts for the inmates of Folsom Prison and later San Quentin.[2] And if you listen to these recordings, you will see that he clearly thinks the prisoners are mistreated. At the least, prisoners are forced to drink water that tastes like it "ran off of Luther's boots."

But if something's wrong with the prison system, how should it be reformed? Through his life and lyrics, Cash argued for reforming the prison system from a retributive system to a reha-

---

[2] He did perform at other prisons in different venues. For instance, his first such concert was at a prison rodeo in Huntsville, Texas, in 1956. However, his concerts at Folsom Prison and San Quentin were his most famous. (See "Columbia Records Radio Hour—Johnny Cash: The Solitary Man Interview with Tim Robbins, Parts 1 and 2", broadcast on Progressive Torch and Twang on WDBM-FM, East Lansing on September 16th, 2003.

bilitative one and for the abolition of capital punishment. And although there is much philosophical disagreement surrounding these issues, a strong case can be made that Cash was right.

Retribution and Rehabilitation

Cash certainly didn't think that the prison system should be abolished. Consider the lyrics of "Man in Black."

> I wear the black for the prisoner
> Who has long paid for his crime,
> But is there because he's a victim of the times.

Cash doesn't deny that the criminal needs to serve his time; he objects to the prisoner serving "overtime." But overtime was not the only mistreatment prisoners suffered. Consider the lyrics of "Jacob Green."

> Jacob Green got busted for possession.
> Next morning early he appeared in court.
> But he was sent to jail to wait,
> To be tried at some later date . . .

> At the jail they took away his clothes to shame him
> And to make sure Jacob Green had no pride left.
> They cut of all his hair.
> Today they found him hanging there.
> Afraid to face the day he killed himself.

> [Chorus:]
> It happened yesterday,
> And if you turn your head away
> Somewhere in some dirty hole the scene will be rerun.
> Not only Jacob Green, but many more you've never seen.
> It could be someone that you love gets done like Jacob
> Green got done . . .

Again, it's not that Jacob shouldn't serve time if guilty. But being imprisoned shouldn't drive him to suicide. The system needs not to be abolished but reformed before there are more Jacob Greens.

Because the prison system hasn't been reformed many Cash recordings, such as "Folsom Prison Blues" "San Quentin," "The

Beast in Me" and "The Man Who Couldn't Cry"—all written from
the point of view of a criminal—take pity on the plight of the
criminal. But Cash not only fought for reform in concert and
lyric; he crusaded for prison reform in "real life." He was an out-
spoken critic who often used his fame to further the cause. He
even knew several presidents and, on more than one occasion,
used his social visits to address with the president the need for
American prison reform.[3]

But how did Cash think the prison system should be
reformed? To answer this, it will be helpful to look at the philosophical debate regarding the justified punishment of criminals.
There's a fundamental dispute over what justifies the punishment that criminals receive. After all, one of the main purposes
of government is the protection of its citizens; thus, normally,
the government cannot justifiably harm one of its citizens. Since
punishment certainly harms, if the government is going punish
its criminals, it must have a justifying excuse to do so.

The most commonly cited justification for criminal punishment is the guilt of criminals. Their crime, it is argued, entails
that they deserve punishment. In fact, a guilty criminal's action
may even create a moral duty on the part of others to ensure
that the criminal is punished. Thus, according to "the retributive
theory," since guilty criminals have done wrong the government
is justified—in fact obligated—to punish them accordingly.

The most common alternate punishment theory is the utilitarian one. Utility suggests that the moral good is found in what
ensures the greatest amount of happiness for the greatest number of people—that is, "the greatest societal happiness."
Utilitarians suggest that the government is obligated to do that
(and only that) which ensures the greatest societal happiness.
They thus suggest that the only way the punishment of a criminal can be justified is if the punishment generates more happiness (in society) than the absence of the punishment would.
When comparing two kinds of punishments, the one that generates the greatest overall "societal happiness" should be preferred.

The two theories often agree about when punishment should
be administered. Jailing, for instance, keeps violent criminals—

---

[3] Most notably, in July 1972, Cash spoke with President Nixon about the need
for reform in the American prison system.

like Willy Lee from "Cocaine Blues"—from immediately repeating their crime and deters others from committing similar crimes.[4] Since the prevention of crime makes for a happier society, the utilitarian theory suggests that violent criminals should be imprisoned. The retributive theory suggests the same and thus the two theories agree that violent criminals should be jailed.

Where the two theories disagree, however, is concerning the purpose of punishment; thus they differ significantly in their recommendations for what kind of, and how, criminal punishment should be administered. The retributivist thinks that the purpose of such punishment is to ensure that the criminal gets his due. Commonly what is known as *lex talionis*—the moral code summarized in "Mercy Seat" as "an eye for an eye and a tooth for a tooth"—is assumed by the retributivist and thus they think that the severity of a criminal's punishment should reflect his crime. The utilitarian, on the other hand, thinks that the purpose of such punishment is to ensure greater social happiness. Consequently—since the crime, once done, can't be undone—the punishment should be designed to deter future criminal behavior. This includes deterring others from committing similar crimes (which the punishment of the criminal should do) but also includes deterring the criminal himself. The criminal will be kept from criminal behavior while incarcerated but the utilitarian will also want to ensure that the criminal will not repeat the crime once released. This will most effectively ensure greater societal happiness.

So, say you are guilty of robbing the Santa Fe like Joe Bean in the song "Joe Bean." The retributivist will say that your punishment should reflect your crime: an appropriate fine and appropriate prison time. But what you do in prison is of little consequence; as long as it is unpleasant enough to count as punishment, the prison term serves its purpose. The utilitarian will suggest otherwise. You should serve time; even though it makes you unhappy it will ensure that you don't just turn

---

[4] Encouraging deterrence though fear of prison sentences is actually the purpose of "Cocaine Blues." The song tells the tale of Willy Lee who kills "his woman" with a .44 in a cocaine-induced rage over the fact that she had five other boyfriends; Willy Lee gets a ninety-nine-year sentence and the song ends with the plea, "Come on you've gotta listen unto me, lay off that whiskey and let that cocaine be."

around and rob again. It will also discourage others from copying your crime. But, to promote even greater societal happiness, your time in prison should be spent in endeavors to ensure that, once you get out, you will never do such a thing again. This "rehabilitation" will promote an even greater social happiness than your mere punishment since you will be much less likely to repeat your crime once freed and since you yourself will lead a happier life. This is why the utilitarian theory is often called the "rehabilitative theory."

Rehabilitation could take many forms and would be modified as new, more successful methods are developed. The experience *does* need to be unpleasant—we can't rehabilitate our criminals in luxury resorts because the punishment won't act as a deterrent—but whether or not the punishment "fits" the crime is irrelevant according to the utilitarian. Even if you deserve heinous punishment, it's not the government's job to dish it out. The government is only supposed to do that which best ensures the greatest societal happiness possible (from available alternatives) and rehabilitation is just that.

Cash and Rehabilitation

So now we can return to our question: How did Cash think the prison system should be reformed? He clearly favored the rehabilitative approach. The evidence for this can be found in many places, but the clearest evidence is found in the lyrics of "San Quentin."

> San Quentin, you've been livin' hell to me. . . .

> You've cut me and have scarred me through an' through.
> And I'll walk out a wiser weaker man;
> Mister Congressman why can't you understand.

> San Quentin, what good do you think you do?
> Do you think I'll be different when you're through?
> You bent my heart and mind and you warped my soul . . .

> San Quentin, . . .
> may all the world regret you did no good.

Clearly Cash detested the fact that San Quentin doesn't change the inhabitants in a positive way. What it should be doing is *benefiting its inhabitants* and in turn society; but instead it just cuts and scars them, bending their heart, mind, and soul and making them—perhaps wiser but—ultimately weaker. If only the lawmakers, the Congressmen, could understand this and make a change!

Cash believed criminals could be rehabilitated; Cash even had direct experience with it. Glen Shirley, who was a prisoner at the first Folsom Prison concert and wrote (among others) "Greystone Chapel" (first performed that night), was paroled three years into his life sentence and went on to lead a "good productive life" for many years until he committed suicide in 1978.[5] Merle Haggard, who had lived a life of criminal behavior before he sat in the front row at the first two San Quentin concerts, was later released, gave up his criminal life, and became a famous country music star himself. He even recorded a duet with Cash in Nashville: "I'm Leaving Now." The problem is that it wasn't the prison system that rehabilitated them. Cash attributed Shirley's parole and rehabilitation to his musical contributions.[6] Haggard attributes his rehabilitation to a conversation he had with Caryl Chessman, an author and death row inmate, while in isolation.[7]

But in his beliefs, Cash was the exception; the retributive approach to criminal punishment is most commonly assumed. However, we think Cash was right. So the burden is now on us to object to the retributive theory and defend Cash's rehabilitative one. There are two main claims behind retributivism. The first is that guilty criminals morally deserve to be punished in proportion to their crime. The second is that it is the government's responsibility to ensure that people receive what they morally deserve. Both claims are dubious.

Do Criminals Deserve to Be Punished?

Most retributivists defend the first claim based on moral sentiments they believe others share. Michael S. Moore claims that

---

[5] Glen Shirley's rehabilitation is called into question by Marshal Grant. See *I Was There When It Happened: My Life with Johnny Cash* (Cumberland House, 2006), pp. 153–54.

[6] See the Cash-Robbins Interview

[7] See http://www.cmt.com/artists/az/haggard_merle/bio.jhtml.

our moral reactions to stories of criminal behavior include the belief that criminals deserve to be punished in a way that reflects their crime. We might even feel a desire to carry out the punishment ourselves but certainly we feel they shouldn't simply *get away with it*.[8] But there are number of things wrong this kind of reasoning.

First, the fact that our natural moral reaction to criminals is to believe that they deserve to be punished in proportion to their crime does not entail that they do. Such reactions are most often rooted in a desire for revenge—to return harm for harm—and many philosophers think that the desire for revenge is barbaric and unethical. Socrates, for instance, suggested that desires for vengeance and harming one's enemies are immoral. "True moral goodness," says Socrates, "is incapable of doing intentional injury to others . . ."[9] If he's right, our vengeful sentiments are immoral, and thus they cannot be used to supply a moral obligation to carry out retribution.

Second, even if having that moral reaction is ethical, it is not a solid basis for legal punishments. If it were, since it approves of *"eye for an eye,"* it would be acceptable to—as legal punishment—rape rapists, torture those who torture, and kill murders in the same way that they killed their victims. But this just doesn't seem right; we outlawed cruel and unusual punishment a long time ago.

So it seems that first claim—guilty criminals morally deserve to be punished in proportion to their crime—is not well supported. To save it, some suggest that criminal punishment shouldn't reflect the crime *exactly* but criminals still deserve to be punished to some degree (perhaps even the criminal feels this way). To defend this, some argue that what criminals are morally deserving of is the punishment that the law dictates for their crime. They knew they would be punished if they were caught. Doesn't the fact that they knowingly risked the punishment entail that they deserve to be punished?

At first glace this seems right but after careful reflection one sees the argument's flaws. First, knowingly doing an action that

---

[8] See Michael S. Moore, "The Moral Worth of Retribution" in Joel Feinberg and Jules Coleman's *Philosophy of Law, Sixth Edition* (Wadsworth, 2000).
[9] Gregory Vlastos, *Socrates: Ironist and Moral Philosopher* (Ithaca: Cornell University Press, 1991), p. 196.

risks punishments hardly makes one deserve the punishment. Consider the protagonist of "Long Black Veil" who refused to give the police his alibi even though he knew it "meant his life"; he was "in the arms of his best friend's wife" and wanted to protect her. He knows the consequences of his action are death, but he hardly deserves to die. Additionally, the law doesn't seem to dictate moral deserts in the way suggested. Even if one knew that Nazi German law prescribed the death penalty for harboring Jews, it hardly follows that one is morally deserving of death for knowingly doing so.

But most people's moral sentiments run pretty deep; so you, the reader, might not be convinced. So let's assume—for the sake of argument—that, normally, people who perform criminal acts are morally deserving of punishment—maybe not because of our moral reaction and maybe not punishment that precisely reflects the crime, but punishment all the same. We will now turn to criticizing the second claim: "It is the government's responsibility to ensure that people receive their moral deserts."

What's the Government's Responsibility?

Moore admits that most retributivists think that ensuring moral desert is the government's responsibility. Since vengeance belongs to God—"vengeance is mine, saith the Lord,"[10] "sooner or later God's gonna cut you down"[11]—but since God doesn't exist, he argues, vengeance must be the responsibility of the state. However, this argument is quite weak. Even if God doesn't exist (which many deny), it is hardly obvious that God's duties should be deferred to the state. I doubt many think that the government needs to be in the business of answering prayers and forgiving sins.

In addition, even though most will admit that lust, greed, envy, and pride (and their variants) are immoral, not many think that such things should be punishable by law. Many think that adultery is immoral and that adulterers are morally deserving of punishment; but not many think it is the government's role to punish adulterers for their adultery. That the government should

---

[10] Romans 12:19 (KJV).
[11] "God's Gonna Cut You Down."

not be in the business of enforcing moral deserts seems to be commonly assumed, if not simply commonly acknowledged.

John Stuart Mill (1806–1873), one of the most well known utilitarians, even offers up an argument for this. As a utilitarian, Mill concludes that a government is obligated solely to ensure *the greatest societal happiness* for its citizens. Ensuring that its citizens have the liberty to pursue what makes them happy is the best and only way to do so. Realizing that harming others is what makes some people happy—and if they are allowed to do so the greatest societal happiness will not be accomplished— Mill realized that sometimes citizen's liberties must be restricted. But, he concluded, "the only purpose for which power can be rightfully exercised over any member of a civilized community, against his will, is to prevent harm to others."[12] Since merely ensuring reception of moral deserts doesn't prevent harm to others, Mill suggests that ensuring the reception of moral deserts is not the government's responsibility.

> If any one thinks that there is justice in the infliction of purpose-less suffering; that there is a natural affinity between the two ideas of guilt and punishment, which makes it intrinsically fitting that wherever there has been guilt, pain should be inflicted by way of retribution; I acknowledge I can find no argument to justify punishment inflicted on this principle. . . . The merely retributive view of punishment derives no justification from the doctrine I support.[12]

This doesn't mean that Mill is against punishment. Deterring would-be criminals is necessary for overall societal happiness, and criminal punishment does just that. As Mill suggests himself, "to deter by suffering [the infliction] of suffering is not only possible, but the very purpose of penal justice."[14] But it does mean that retribution is not the government's job.

So, it seems, the two central claims of the retributivist—criminals deserve punishment and it is the government's responsibility to make sure they get it—are false. Additionally, both Cash

---

[12] See John Stuart Mill, *On Liberty* (Indianapolis: Hackett, 1978), p. 9.

[13] *The Collected Works of John Stuart Mill* (Toronto: University of Toronto Press; London: Routledge) IX, p. 462.

[14] This is from *Mill's Parliament Speech*. You can find a manuscript of this speech here: http://humanum.arts.cuhk.edu.hk/~hkshp/wclassic/mill-punishment.htm.

and Mill were right. "Punishment regards the future alone. Safety, not vengeance, is its object. The only fit end of punishment is the prevention of crime."[15] Since rehabilitation is clearly the best way to accomplish the prevention of crime, the prison system should be revised according to the rehabilitative theory.

Cash and Mill on Capital Punishment

Capital punishment is, quite simply, *the Death Penalty*. Cash wanted capital punishment abolished. He was one of many artists who wrote a song for the soundtrack of "Dead Man Walking." That song ("In Your Mind") and many other recordings—such as "Twenty-five Minutes to Go," and "I Hung my Head."—take pity on the plight of death row inmates. Some—such as "Joe Bean," "Mercy Seat," and "The Long Black Veil"—make an argument for its abolishment. But the best argument is rooted in Cash's (and Mill's) rehabilitative theory of punishment.

Mill actually used this theory to *support* capital punishment; he even gave a speech in front of Parliament on April 21st, 1869, defending it. But an examination of Mill's speech will reveal why, today, the theory entails that capital punishment should be abolished—and why, today, Cash and Mill would agree.[16]

First, Mill suggested that the death penalty should be reserved for "atrocious cases"—where the criminal's very character is murderous making him "unworthy" to live among mankind. This is like Cash, who—in utilitarian fashion—admits that execution of certain particularly evil criminals has made the world a better place.[17] Obviously, for both Mill and Cash, if rehabilitation is an option, rehabilitation should be favored. But more importantly, since the current system doesn't save capital punishment for only "atrocious cases," but usually minorities

---

[15] *The Collected Works of John Stuart Mill* IX, p. 165

[16] For a great article that shows Mill is not a retributivist, even though he very occasionally sounds like one, see "Mill on Capital Punishment: Retributive Overtones?" by Michael Clark in *Journal of the History of Philosophy* 42:3 (2004), pp. 327–332.

[17] Cash however also suggested that he didn't know that "death was the answer" for ridding the earth of such criminals—he then proposed "a spacecraft to another planet or something." See the Cash-Robbins Interview.

and the poor who can't afford adequate legal representation, both Mill and Cash would agree that the current capital punishment system should be abandoned (or, at the least, revised).

Second, even though most people are more afraid of death, Mill thought life imprisonment was more cruel. In Mill's time, a life sentence would include a lifetime of hard labor. Since even the criminal's happiness must be considered when calculating society's overall happiness, making a guilty criminal suffer needlessly at the hands of lifetime of hard labor should not be tolerated. However, since life imprisonment no longer includes a lifetime of hard labor, Mill would no longer defend capital punishment on these grounds.

Third, Mill supported the death penalty because he thought it the most effective criminal deterrent and thus that it ensured the greatest societal happiness. However, since the case for capital punishment's deterrent effects is now known to be weak, Mill would have to abandon this line of argumentation.

Agnes Heller, for example, argues that there are three motivations for murder—compulsion, passion, and profit—and that a threat of capital punishment cannot deter anyone with such motivations. Those who murder compulsively—like Charles Manson, John Wayne Gacy, or Jeffrey Dahmer—are mentally ill individuals who kill because they're compelled to. They know the consequences of their actions (they try to hide their crimes), but kill anyway because something inside their broken minds drives them to. Those who kill in the throes of passion—for example, those who kill their husband for having an affair—are similar; they are compelled by their emotions and don't even consider their action's consequences. Those who seek profit—such as mobsters—are purely rational. They murder for personal gain and thus only murder when they believe they won't get caught; and since they don't believe they will be punished, the threat of capital punishment can't deter them.[18]

The numbers weaken the *deterrent argument* as well. California's murder rate actually dropped after it abolished the death penalty in 1968 and historically, states with the death penalty have, on average, a much higher murder rate than those

---

[18] Although Heller is a very well known and respected philosopher, the easiest place to find Heller making this argument is, ironically, on The Showtime Network: Season 4, Episode 3 of *Penn and Teller's Bullshit!*

without. This even holds true for neighboring states; the murder rate in Missouri, which has the death penalty, is more than three times higher than its neighbor Iowa, which does not.[19] Of course these statistics don't *prove* that capital punishment increases murder rates or that its absence decreases them; the mere correlation of two things does not prove a causal connection between them.[20] But what this does show is that convincing evidence for capital punishment's deterrent effect doesn't exist. Mill couldn't defend it on those grounds.

Lastly, Mill was convinced that, if the death penalty led to the excessive taking of innocent lives, the death penalty should be abolished.

> . . . if by an error of justice an innocent person is put to death, the mistake can never be corrected; all compensation, all reparation for the wrong is impossible. This would be indeed a serious objection if these miserable mistakes—among the most tragical occurrences in the whole round of human affairs—could not be made extremely rare. The argument is invincible where the mode of criminal procedure is dangerous to the innocent.[21]

Mill still supported capital punishment because he was convinced that the criminal system's presumption of innocence would prevent the taking of innocent lives. However, given the now known number of convicted innocents, Mill would be forced to admit that capital punishment should be abolished. Since only 1973, 123 people have been exonerated after being wrongfully convicted of murder[22] and new DNA testing recently freed its two-hundredth innocent criminal.[23] Granted, none of these innocents were executed, but these statistics make the likelihood of undiscovered wrongful convictions (and executions) very high. Mill's faith that our legal system's presumption of

---

[19] See www.deathpenaltyinfo.org.

[20] After all, the murder rate might be higher in Missouri than in Iowa because Missouri has more and bigger cities than Iowa—Kansas City [444,000] and St. Louis [355,000] versus Des Moines [194000] see: http://en.wikipedia.org/wiki/List_of_United_States_cities_by_population.

[21] Mill's Parliament Speech.

[22] http://www.deathpenaltyinfo.org/article.php?scid=6&did=110.

[23] http://www.deathpenaltyinfo.org/article.php?did=2314&scid=64.

innocence is sufficient *to avoid* the conviction of innocents seems misplaced.

This latter worry clearly played a large role in Cash's argument against the death penalty. Joe Bean was innocent of the crime for which he was convicted and sentenced to death[24] and so was the protagonist of "Long Black Veil." But it is "The Mercy Seat"[25] that most clearly articulates the plight of the convicted innocent.

> It all began when they took me from my home and put me on Death Row; a crime for which I am totally innocent, you know . . . And the mercy seat is waiting, and I think my head is burning, and in a way I'm yearning to be done with all this weighing of the truth . . . And anyway I told the truth and I'm not afraid to die. . . . Into the mercy seat I climb, my head is shaved, my head is wired . . . the mercy seat is smoking, and I think my head is melting and in a way that's helping to be done with all this twisting of the truth . . . And anyway I told the truth, but I'm afraid I told a lie.[26]

Cash himself said that his remaking of this song was his way of "striking out" against the death penalty. Specifically, he was angry at (then Texas governor) George W. Bush who said, according to Cash, even in the face of DNA's ability to clear innocent criminals, "if anyone was sentenced to death, on death row, he needed to die."[27] Clearly, because of the risk of executed innocents, Cash called for capital punishment's abolishment.

------

[24] Joe Bean wasn't exactly innocent. He was innocent of that particular crime; but he had killed twenty people by the time he was ten. As the song suggests, "they're hanging Joe Bean for the one shooting that Joe Bean never did."

[25] Originally written by Nick Cave but performed by Cash on *American III: Solitary Man*.

[26] The original Nick Cave version of "The Mercy Seat" is not as obviously about a convicted innocent. The song's tone and last line—"I'm afraid I told a lie"—leaves one with the impression that the criminal in the mercy seat is actually guilty. But that's not how Cash viewed the song. And—as he made clear in *The Cash-Robbins Interview*—when Cash remade songs, he never worried about the song's "original meaning" but only about the meaning that he ascribed to it. According to Cash (and Robbins), what the criminal in the mercy seat was lying about was *not being afraid to die*—not about *being innocent*.

[27] See the Cash-Robbins Interview.

The Good, The Bad, and The Ugly

There are a number of objections to consider on Cash's behalf; some good, some bad, and some ugly. Anti-capital punishment activists may actually take objection to our argument. "Capital punishment," they might argue, "is impermissible because it is hypocritical, not because it violates some utilitarian rule. We punish the murder by doing to him the same thing that was his crime: we murder him." However, this argument is BAD. When a guilty murderer is capitally punished, the circumstances are considerably different than a murder. The murderer (in most cases) killed an innocent person, the murderer, however, is guilty. The criminal has been found guilty by a jury of his peers; the murderer's victim had no trial. Capital punishment is still wrong, but not because it is murder.

Others will object to utility. "If the majority," they argue, "takes delight in capital punishment (like in an old west town that loved public hangings), utility couldn't be used against it." But Mill pointed out that this argument is BAD too. The majority crushing a minority (like its criminals) for its own benefit Mill called "the tyranny of the majority." He argued that utility rules it out. Even if the majority would be made happier in specific matters (like getting to watch a "good old-fashioned hanging"), the restrictions of liberty such things would entail ultimately work against the greatest societal happiness.

Others argue that that utility is not the correct *gauge* for governmental action. "The government should act to protect our rights," some argue, "not ensure the greatest societal happiness. Since criminals guilty of murder have no right to life—they gave it up by violating the right to life of their victim—their execution is permissible." But this argument is UGLY. Even if protecting rights should be the goal of government action, it does not follow that execution is permissible. According to the constitution, our right to life is inalienable and that means it cannot be forfeited by any action, even murder.

Of course, the government can't protect everyone's rights. If protecting your inalienable right to liberty means not protecting the liberty rights of many others, then your right to liberty should not be protected; that is why it is permissible to violate the inalienable right to liberty of criminals by locking them away. But only when one's rights are in conflict with the rights of others is it permissible to violate one's rights. Since the government can protect our right to life without violating the incorrigible murderer's right to life—by locking him away instead of executing him—violating his right to life with execution isn't permissible.

One argument that is GOOD, however, is this. "The fact that we call them 'inalienable rights' does not necessarily entail that they are." That's correct and maybe our rights aren't inalienable. John Locke (1632–1704), for example, argued that our "natural right" to life can be forfeited by violating the life rights of others. Immanuel Kant (1727–1804) even argued that we respect the right to life of the murderer when we capitally punish him because we treat him how he apparently believes people with the right to life should be treated. Cesare Beccaria (1738–1794) disagrees and suggests that rights cannot be lost. We encourage you to do your own research.

But whether it be for utilitarian reasons or for the protection of rights, Cash clearly favored the rehabilitative view and the abolition of capital punishment. This is why he performed at San Quentin and Folsom for free, even though others may have called it *celebrity suicide*. Because of Cash's humanity, he was determined to put a human face on the American criminal and shed light on the American prison system to suggest that even criminals should be treated humanely.[28]

---

[28] A very special thanks go out to Douglas Neal, host of "Progressive Touch and Twang" on WDBM, 88.9 FM, East Lansing, who went to extraordinary lengths to get us the Cash-Robbins Interview

13

Inspired Anger: Closed to the Public

DAN HAGGERTY

I remember my first impression of the Man in Black. I was seven. It was a cold, wet Saturday afternoon in late winter. There was nothing to do. No friends around to play with and my mother, brothers, and sisters were out of the house. But my father was home. He was sitting at the kitchen table with a beer. He brought the record player into the dining room, which was open to the kitchen. He played what he called "Cowboy Music."

My father really wanted to raise his four sons and two daughters on a ranch out West, but instead he made a living selling heating and air conditioning out of his shop on Torresdale Avenue in Philadelphia. He did install swinging saloon doors in the entrance to our "rec-room," though. I was lying on the carpet by the fireplace. A second vinyl album dropped and spun. The automatic arm placed the needle down in the first groove. After a few familiar whooshing sounds I heard, "Hello. I'm Johnny Cash."

The album was *Johnny Cash at Folsom Prison*, live. The song was "Folsom Prison Blues." I liked it. My father gave no indication of what he felt. But I could tell. He liked it too. Mr. Cash's voice made me feel good, like a sure shooter, like a cowboy. And then that line. "I shot a man in Reno / Just to watch him die." Whew. Did I overhear something that I wasn't supposed to hear? I stole a quick glance at my dad. He gave no sign of disapproval. And I was hooked.

"Hurt": Music and Philosophy

Eleven months before he died, Johnny Cash and producer Rick
Rubin released *American IV: The Man Comes Around*. Those of
you familiar with the album know that it covers a number of
songs, including "Hurt" by Trent Reznor of Nine Inch Nails. In
addition to the album, Cash and director Mark Romanek filmed
a music video for "Hurt" that earned seven nominations at the
2003 MTV Music Awards. It won the award for Best Cinematog-
raphy. Nearing death and looking like it, Johnny Cash offered
viewers a haunting performance of a dark song.

As you may know, the Man in Black turned out many dark
songs over his career, beginning with "Folsom Prison Blues" and
its famous, laconic lyric about having shot a man in Reno *just
to watch him die*. Cash left a legacy of songs about trouble,
strife, crime, punishment, and loss. But, we notice a different
kind of darkness in his rendition of "Hurt." The video begins
with a series of images: a man struggling under the weight of
the world, a frightening horse rider, an elaborate display of fruit.
Then, we watch and listen to Cash's acoustic guitar and grave
voice. "I hurt myself today / To see if I still feel / I focus on the
pain / The only thing that's real."

The images in the video and the emotion in the music and
vocals move us in profound and unsettling ways. We can hear
a kind of sorrow that walks the line between fury and madness.
At times in the video, Cash sits at his white piano, looking old,
sad, angry, and in pain. With his thick bent finger, he pounds
the same key over and over and over again, as we hear, "And
you can have it all / My empire of dirt / I will let you down / I
will make you hurt."

Cash's "Hurt" expresses and represents powerful emotions.
The video struck me directly. I was moved to wonder, what is
he feeling? Who did he see when he sang those words? I first
conceived of *inspired anger* while wondering over these questions and the images in the video. Slowly I came to understand
inspired anger, which we may provisionally describe as a collection of sorrow, regret, forlornness, and wrath, stirred with
futile desire. In order to differentiate inspired anger from other
kinds of anger, we will turn to contemporary music and
philosophy.

"Flushed From the Bathroom of Your Heart": Emotion and Pop Culture

In a scene from *Walk the Line*, Cash tells music executives that he wants to record a live album at Folsom prison. The letters, stories, and emotions of prisoners reach Cash through fan mail, just as Cash reaches the prisoners through his music. The executives hate the idea, giving him all their reasons why they think the album will not sell. Cash records anyway.

On the live album *Johnny Cash at San Quentin*, we hear Cash speak to the inmates. Before he begins "I Walk the Line," he tells them the performance is being recorded and televised. He says, "They said, 'You gotta sing this song. You gotta sing that song. You know. You gotta stand like this and act like that.' I just don't get it, man. You know. I'm here to do what you want me to do and what I want to do." If we understand pop music as mass-marketed entertainment created precisely for the sake of commercial success and profit, Johnny Cash played to the wrong crowd. Although the man and his music have enjoyed popularity from generations of fans, including most recently the MTV generation, Cash wrote many of his songs for the poor, the oppressed, the unlucky, and the imprisoned. This is a far cry from pop music icons such as The Monkees, Spice Girls, and Britney Spears.

What is the difference between popular music like Cash's and pop music? In a word, we might say, *heart*. The music of Johnny Cash has heart. This is what distinguishes it from pop music. Pop music is entertainment, not art. Cash made an indelible impression on popular culture *as an artist*. In order to distinguish popular art, like Cash's music, from entertainment, like pop music, we can consider the differences in how and why we produce music. Unlike pop musicians, Cash does not produce in ways predetermined by commercialism or industrial music. This is obvious in his words from the recording at San Quentin. How does he produce, then? He produces *as an artist*. Cash's music is a work of art because it arises from human emotion, as opposed to pop music which arises from and is produced for the sake of human consumption.

Now, pop psychology misunderstands human emotion. It either leads us to think that emotions are neither good nor bad, or that all painful emotions are bad because they are painful and all pleasant emotions are good because they are pleasant. Unfortunately, pop psychology forgets the wisdom of the great philosophical tradition from Plato (427–347 B.C.E.) and Aristotle (384–322 B.C.E.) through Thomas Aquinas (1225–1274), Thomas Hobbes (1588–1679), René Descartes (1596–1650), Baruch Spinoza (1632–1677), and David Hume (1711–1776). All of these philosophers provide robust accounts of human emotions and their significance, meanings, and values in our lives.

Pop psychology seems to confuse emotion with feelings and sensations, and with moods. Philosophers distinguish between these by what we call "intentionality." Here, we do not use the word "intention" in its ordinary sense, namely, a person's aim or purpose in performing some action. Instead, in philosophy, intentionality means our minds' power to represent aspects of the world to the self in consciousness. It refers to those states of human consciousness that have the power to be *about something*. Feelings and sensations are different from emotions insofar as they lack intentionality.

Let's take an example of a feeling and a sensation, and distinguish them from emotions. Fatigue is a feeling of weariness or lassitude. An itch is a (usually) unpleasant sensation. Now, my itches and fatigue at the end of the day are not *about* anything. Sure, I feel them. They register in my consciousness. But as mental phenomena they are not *directed towards* any object, real or imaginary. Our emotions, on the other hand, are directed upon features of the world. Our anger is about something, even if we do not know what it is about. We might not know what we are angry about, or even that we feel anger, but if we are angry, there is something we are angry about. Often, people seek out psychoanalysts for help in understanding their anger. But we do not go to therapists to figure out what our itches are about, usually. This is because, like our fatigue at the end of the day, itches (usually) aren't about anything.

Moods, such as crankiness or giddiness, on the other hand, are different from emotions because they tend to be about everything or nothing at all. If we become giddy, say in school or at church, there comes a point when there really is no answer to the question, what are you laughing about? The best we could say is either everything or nothing at all.

We now understand the differences between emotions, on the one hand, and feeling, sensations, and moods on the other.

With this in mind, let us turn to the different kinds of anger as understood by philosophy and as expressed in the music of Johnny Cash.

"Trouble in Mind": Anger, Just Anger, and the Music of Johnny Cash

In the *Rhetoric*, Aristotle (384–322 B.C.E.) defines anger as "a desire accompanied by pain, for a conspicuous revenge for a conspicuous slight at the hands of men who have no call to slight oneself or one's friends" (II.2, 1378a31ff.). Although anger is an emotion accompanied by pain, in *Nicomachean Ethics* Aristotle contends that a good person, a *phronimos*, must be capable of getting angry. For, not to get angry and "to endure being insulted and put up with insults to one's friends is slavish" (IV.5, 1126a8). Instead, it is praiseworthy and virtuous for a good person to be "angry at the right things and towards the right people, and also in the right way, at the right time and for the right length of time." With Aristotle, we understand that though not all anger is good, there are some kinds of anger that are justified and praiseworthy.

Aristotle helps us see that, contrary to pop psychology, we should not regard all anger as pathology or unwanted "stress." Anger is *about* real or supposed slights or injuries. We can feel anger about personal injury, and about injury to other people we care about. Though feeling angry is painful, we should not reject all anger as nothing better than an unwanted source of stress. Painful emotions are not always bad. What's more, though anger is accompanied by pain it is not only or entirely painful. It can also be accompanied by pleasure. (We'll discuss the pleasures of anger later.) How can we distinguish good anger from bad anger? Following Aristotle, we can distinguish between justified anger, which is a good emotion felt by virtuous people, from unjustified anger, which is a bad emotion that leads to vice.

Just anger is directed at perceived injustices. It is a desire, accompanied by pain, to correct injustices, or to see them corrected. It's an entirely appropriate emotion. In fact, Aristotle thinks it's the duty of good and excellent people to feel just anger when they perceive injustice. It is anger that aims at and is about correcting injustices.

Cultivating and feeling just anger takes practice and reflection. It's a habit developed gradually. Children should be taught not only how to control their anger, but also how to feel and express justified anger, which is to say anger towards the right people, in the right amount, at the right time, and for the right length of time. For, as Aristotle says, "it is not easy to determine how and with whom and in what circumstances and for how much time one ought to be angry, and at what point one does so rightly or goes astray" (NE 1126a33 ff.). Although it's difficult to achieve, just anger signifies virtue and is a mark of good and excellent people. It signifies maturity. Unjustified anger, on the other hand, is either excessive or deficient. When a person becomes habitually excessive or deficient in their anger, the bad habit hardens into a character trait, becoming a vice. We must consider these two forms of unjustified anger, namely, deficient anger and excessive anger, separately.

We should get angry at perceived injustices. If we do not, this shows a moral emotional deficiency. Habitual deficiency of just anger constitutes and reveals significantly flawed characters. As Thomas Aquinas says, following Aristotle, "excellence makes people prone to anger" (ST I-II. Question 46, article 3). People of excellent character are prone to just anger directed at perceived injustices, while deficiency of just anger falls short of the virtue of good and excellent people.

From the point of view of pop psychology it may seem strange to connect feeling or not feeling emotions with being or failing to be a good or excellent person. Pop psychology seems to suggest that emotions and feelings are never good or bad. Pop culture might lead us to think that people can and should feel whatever they do with impunity, as it were. Philosophy teaches us otherwise. To feel or not to feel certain emotions can be ethically bad in two related ways. First, when we do not feel just anger, this impugns our character. Why should we care? We should care because what assails and corrupts our character impedes our flourishing as human beings. This stunts our growth and limits our ability to feel in the world. Second, when we neglect to feel justified anger we fail to live up to our moral duty. For we neglect the people we should care about, including ourselves. So, we should feel justified anger because we should care for justice and we should want to make right.

Those of you familiar with the popular 2005 film *Walk the Line* know that it portrays a lot of unjustified anger in the life of Johnny Cash. Like many of us, Johnny Cash moves back and forth between feelings of justified anger and unjustified anger— or anger that is deficient or excessive. When we listen to the music of Johnny Cash, however, we often hear songs that express just anger. This is not to suggest in any way that all of Cash's music is angry, or that anger is the only or even the primary emotion that comes through his music. There is a good deal of humor in his music as well. But Cash seems to get justified anger right. Unlike some other contemporary artists who seem distinctively sullen, or who rage, rage, rage at everything and nothing at all, much of the music of Johnny Cash expresses a mature, measured anger.

Also, Cash's music represents and expresses just anger precisely insofar as much of it is about perceived injustices and the desire to see them corrected. Many of his songs are about the poor, the imprisoned, and the marginalized of society. Cash sings about everyday wrongs and harms committed against human dignity and love, such as disloyalty, forgetfulness, neglect, and failures of recognition. Some of Cash's songs about injustices and other serious harms that give cause for justified anger include, "San Quentin," "Ira Hayes," "Oney," "The Man in Black," "Hard Times," "Country Trash," "Five Feet High and Rising," "Born to Lose," "I Guess Things Happen That Way," "Tear Stained Letter," and "I Still Miss Someone."

With these songs in mind, we may notice that, while anger is accompanied by pain or sorrow at perceived injustices, anger is also accompanied by pleasure. People who are excessively angry, for example, may enjoy the pleasures of feeling powerful, intimidating, or dangerous. People who are deficiently angry may enjoy the pleasures of feeling unaffected, detached, or in control. Yet, pleasure also accompanies just and virtuous anger. Thomas Aquinas notes that justified anger is always accompanied by hope, which gives pleasure. We feel pleasure as we hope for vengeance, for the satisfaction obtained by a repayment of injuries or slights, and for seeing wrongs made right. We feel this pleasure in much of Cash's music.

In particular, let's consider the song "Oney." Cash dedicated "Oney" to "the working-man." In this song, Oney is a shop supervisor who hounds a certain working-man all day on the

job, and all night in his dreams. As supervisor, he stands at the
gate in the morning and "rants and raves like I committed murder / Clocking in five minutes late." But, over the course of
twenty-nine long years:

> I've been workin', buildin' muscles
> Oney's just been standin' round a gettin' soft.
> And today about four-thirty
> I'll make up for every good night's sleep I've lost
> When I'm gone I'll be remembered
> As the workin' man that put his point across
> With a right hand full of knuckles
> 'Cause today I show old Oney, who's the boss.

Finally, justified anger may be accompanied by pleasure as
well as pain when we hope, not for vengeance, but for repentance, forgiveness, and reconciliation. In "The Kneeling
Drunkard's Plea" and the moving "Spiritual," both from his 1996
Unchained, Cash sings about being justly angry with oneself
while hoping for mercy, forgiveness, and salvation.

Pop culture and pop psychology need to move beyond the
blanket rejection of all anger as flawed, and come to an understanding of justified anger. Much of the music of Johnny Cash
represents and expresses just anger, while philosophy helps us
understand the nature of just anger and how to distinguish it
from unjustified anger. This is important for the development of
good and excellent people who come to challenge and correct
perceived injustices.

"I See a Darkness": Cash and Inspired Anger

There's another kind of anger to be found in the music of
Johnny Cash. We can see, and hear, and feel a different kind of
anger in Cash's rendition of "Hurt." This anger does not fit the
analysis of justified anger, since it does not aim at correcting perceived injustices. Nor is it inappropriate or unjustified anger,
being neither deficient nor excessive. It is what I call *inspired
anger*. By this I mean desire, accompanied by pain and sorrow
without hope, for justice, restitution, or restoration *that can
never be*. Inspired anger is without hope precisely because there
is nothing to be done about what is wrong, no way of correct-

ing the perceived injustices, no way of restoring what has been lost.

Why call this "inspired anger?" What is the role of inspiration here? We can take our cue from Plato (427–347 B.C.E.), Aristotle's teacher. In his little known dialogue, the *Ion,* Plato has Socrates (470–399 B.C.E.) say that good poets and artists create not from knowledge of their subject matter, but from inspiration: "All good . . . poets recite all their fine poems not from skill but because they are inspired and possessed" (533e–534a). The Greek word for "being inspired," *enthusiasmata,* implies being *not in one's right mind,* which for Plato means having one's reason overtaken by emotions and desire. It is not a pejorative term, however. Plato includes falling in love as a kind of inspiration or possession, a way of being happily not in one's right mind.

The Greek meaning carries over to some extent into English, where the word 'inspiration' means, literally, the act of blowing on or blowing into, and, figuratively, a breathing or infusion into the mind or soul. Putting these meanings together, artistic inspiration is a way of being not in one's right mind, such as to be moved, transported, or *blown away* by emotion and desire.

What's the source of artistic inspiration? Plato thought good artists were blown away by "the god or Muse." The source of artistic inspiration must be powerful. It must take possession of the artist, of her mind, of her soul. We may attribute such a force not only to the god or Muse, but to the world. Lived experience is itself a profound source of artistic inspiration and inspired anger. And good artists, as I think Plato might agree, are sometimes blown away by human life.

Possible worlds of inspiration include stories in rich detail about relations to self and others, relations to time, suffering, longing, and death, relations to birth, and to the quickening and dying of seasons, to name just a few. And inspired anger, in particular, is told in stories of great futile desire. It is represented in stories about aspects of human life, accompanied by pain and sorrow without hope. But such aspects of being-human-in-the-world are, for the most part, secluded, cloistered out of sight. It is as if we conspire to shut up and hide the truth about human loss, regret, and futility. And yet, seeing the concealment only intensifies feelings of inspired anger.

Inspired anger hurts. But it is also tragic and beautiful. It is tragic because we desire justice, restitution, or restoration without hope. We know that what is desired can never be, and that what is wrong can not be made right. Perhaps the most painful, poignant, futile human desire is our wanting somehow to make death right. The make-up, the flowers . . .

Though tragic, inspired anger is also beautiful. Its beauty is in its revelation. Such anger reveals and expresses hidden, painful truths about human life. Inspired anger is beautiful to the extent to which real human life is beautiful. And while inspired anger is accompanied by pain and sorrow, while it hurts, there are pleasures in it yet. For all the pain and sorrow, there is pleasure in seeing and feeling, *so this is the world*. Such is the pleasure of revelation, of being blown away by the striking disclosure of truths previously hidden, unknown, unfelt, or not realized. And when such desire reaches language, poetry happens.

Good artists and poets are sometimes blown away by inspired anger, by the howling desire for what can never be. And their art and poetry reveals and expresses dark and hidden truths about human life. This is what the music video for Cash's rendition of "Hurt" does so well:

Oh death . . . Oh time . . .
I see . . . I feel now . . .
I cannot change . . . But I see . . .
So this is the world . . .
I want . .. But I cannot . . .

Inspired anger lives in art. All of us regret, all of us suffer loss, all of us die. But mad desire is not inspired anger unless and until it is directed creatively. There are many alternatives. Futile desire can fester. Anger can collapse into depression or explode in violence. Or, desire might move us to run marathons, or to look for ways to help. Both of these involve pounding and pushing back; as such they express desire for just anger. These forms of desire insist on *doing* something. They hope for redemption, reconciliation, or peace, and perhaps vengeance. But inspired anger is without hope. And yet, though there is nothing to be *done* about it, perhaps there is something to be *made*.

The American Visionary Art Museum in Baltimore displays folk art. Many of the pieces are contributed by people who are institutionalized, in prisons and asylums. The museum is a treasure trove of inspired anger. Some of the pieces are especially unsettling because they're works of art by people who have directed their anger not only creatively, but also destructively, in some cases exploding with extreme violence. One exhibit featured a piece by an "inmate" who wove a tapestry, about three inches by two inches, entirely from the only materials available to him, the threads from his socks. The detail was stunning. The tapestry depicts the view from his window. We see sky, cloud, tree, and green, green grass. It represents and expresses an aching, mad desire accompanied by pain and sorrow, but without hope. Why without hope? The artist was *in for life.*

"I Hung My Head": Cash, Sorrow, and Regret.

Justified anger is desire, accompanied by pain. Inspired anger is desire accompanied by pain and sorrow. One of the most distinctive features of Cash's voice is its sorrow. Not all sorrow is the same, however. We can distinguish different kinds, and identify the sorrow that accompanies inspired anger.

Sorrow accompanying inspired anger is mournful. We can distinguish mourning from both self-pity and depression. Self-pity does not recognize or accept the painful, sorrowful world for what it is, and for what it can never be. Instead it hopes, or wishes, perhaps in pure fantasy, that what can never be restored will be restored. It waits for somebody to come and make it right. It feels that someone else *should be* responsible for the hurt, and *should* fix it. And self-pity feels sad, not so much about what is wrong, regrettable, or lost, but about the perceived state of the self as a suffering *victim*. Self-pity languishes in anger and sorrow, wanting made right what can never be fixed.

We can also distinguish mourning from depression. Mourning is sorrow about what has been lost, where what has been lost is felt to be lost from the world, as Freud (1856–1939) observed in *Mourning and Melancholia*. Depression is sorrow about perceived loss which provokes a loss of self-regard. In depression, it is the self that feels empty. The sorrow that accompanies inspired anger is mourning, not melancholia. In mourning, we feel a loss in the world. It is the world, or part of it, that feels empty. The empty chair, the empty house . . .

Inspired anger also feels regret, which is inextricably connected with time. In Cash's songs, we find prisoners doing time, working-men putting in time, and folks lookin' for a good time. We also find regret woven in with loss, death, and eternity. But, nobody regrets what they do while they are doing it. Regret takes time. We feel sorrow and regret because we cannot stop time, we can never get a moment back. As we hear in "Hurt": "If I could start again / A million miles away / I would keep myself / I would find a way." Time haunted Johnny Cash. And time haunts us.

But pop culture and pop psychology esteem an attitude of *No regrets!* Why? Because when we don't regret we see ourselves as strong. The idea seems to be that if we feel regret we admit to wrongs, harms, and missed opportunities. But is this strength, or an inability to live with ourselves? Is this strength, or an intolerance of vulnerability and fear of pain and sorrow? Pop culture and pop psychology need to move past the blanket rejection of all regret, and come to understand that some forms of regret are aspects of feeling human in the world. Here we could take another lesson from Aristotle, who says it is the imperfect but nevertheless relatively good person who is capable of regretting, and only the wicked and dissipated who have no regrets, since they stand by all their choices, however bad (NE 1150b30 ff).

"Unchained": The Inspired Anger of a Religious Man

People think of Johnny Cash as a religious man, as a Christian. But what does this mean? In a memorable scene from the film *Walk the Line*, a young and desperate Johnny Cash auditions for record producer Sam Phillips. Cash opens with a gospel tune. Phillips interrupts, "I don't believe you." Cash responds, "You think I don't believe in God? Is that what you're saying? You think I don't believe in God?" Phillips says, "You know exactly what I'm saying. I'm saying if you were just run over by a truck and had just one minute before you were dirt, what would you sing about? What would you say to God about your time here on earth?" Cash stops. Then, he begins, "I hear the train a comin' / It's rollin' round the bend / And I ain't seen the sun shine since / I don't know when." That evening, Johnny Cash records "Folsom Prison Blues" for Sam Phillips's label, Sun Records.

But if Johnny Cash was a Christian, how could he feel inspired anger? Christians believe in redemption. They profess forgiveness of sins. They hope for salvation. How can Christians sing the blues? Can they hurt like Johnny Cash? Do Christians "Cry, Cry, Cry"? We discussed sorrow that feels an absence in the world. We considered regret. We learned that inspired anger is desire for what can never be. Knowing this, we may wonder, is inspired anger at odds with religious belief? But this is the wrong question—a kind of philosophical showdown.

A showdown is a reckoning, a final confrontation. Once the lines have been drawn in the dirt, someone's going down. Someone's getting hurt. But we make a false move when we think about inspired anger and religious belief as two sides of an argument. These are not the terms of a debate. And yet, philosophers and theologians are trained to clarify concepts and evaluate the strengths and weaknesses of arguments. This makes analysis possible. In this discussion, we clarified and evaluated different kinds of anger. We differentiated just anger, unjustified anger, and inspired anger. We distinguished mournful sorrow from the sorrows of self-pity and depression. This is illuminating. But, we must be careful. Riding high on propositions, truth values, and the felt need for logical consistency, we risk forgetting the human person, the person who gets hurt. Instead of asking whether inspired anger is inconsistent with religious belief, we might think of Mr. Cash, a religious man.

When we imagine Mr. Cash as a religious man, who do we see? We see a young boy who sings gospel hymns in the fields with his mother. This same child screams "Do something!" as his brother Jack dies in their family home. We see a young man who falls in and out of love, with music, with women, with himself. This same young man chokes down pills, booze, and tears. We see an old man at his piano, with his memories, with his songs, with June. This same old man, still dressed in black, still blown away by a world of hurt.

How does such a man pray? In "Unchained," he sings:

I have been ungrateful
I've been unwise
Restless, from the cradle
Now I realize
It's so hard to see the rainbow
Through glasses dark as these
Maybe
I'll be able
From now on
On my knees
Oh I am weak
Oh I know I am vain
Take this weight from me
Let my spirit be
Unchained.

The music and his voice express sorrow and regret: *ungrateful, unwise, now I realize*. The lyrics also reflect time: *from now on, on my knees*. Instead of a set of beliefs, a set of propositions that preclude inspired anger, Mr. Cash offers up a prayer. Let us see through dark glasses. Let us feel sorrow. Let us feel weak. Let us feel angry. Let us regret. Let us fall to our knees, unable to change, unable to make right. Let us want. Let us see beauty in this world. With Mr. Cash, let us pray.

14
Johnny Cash and Justice

JOHNNY HUSS

In "Jacob Green," recorded live in a Swedish prison, Cash sings of a young man who is arrested on possession charges. Locked up and awaiting trial, Jacob is subjected to humiliating treatment. The guards confiscate his clothes and for good measure chop off his hair—presumably a hippie's mane. Shorn, shamed, and shaken, he is later found hanging in his cell, an apparent suicide. A team of lawyers hired by Jacob's father calls for an investigation. As a result, the sheriff is persuaded to retire, two guards are fired, and Jacob's cell is spruced up with a fresh coat of paint. Some measure of justice is served, but justice by what measure? Has anything really changed? As in so many of his other songs, Cash directs our gaze beyond the anecdote to its broader implications:

> It happened yesterday
> And if you turn your head away
> Somewhere in some dirty hole
> The scene will be rerun
> Not only Jacob Green
> But many more you've never seen
> It could be someone that you love gets done like Jacob
> Green got done.

What is striking about "Jacob Green" is how Cash manages in such a short song—a hair over three minutes by my iPod—to evoke so many distinct concepts of justice: as desert, as equal treatment, as a property of individuals, acts, and institutions, as social convention, as means to the greater good, and as a political and social cause.

Jacob's very arrest raises the issue of *justice as desert*. This is the idea that justice consists in giving someone what he or she deserves. We might ask whether someone in possession of drugs, presumably for his personal use, deserves to be arrested. Jacob's arrest also evokes the idea of *justice as equal treatment*, or in this case, injustice as biased treatment. We can imagine the police unjustly singling out Jacob for his long hair, funky clothes, or aroma of patchouli oil while some well-dressed, well-heeled ne'er do well walks away scot-free. Justice is also portrayed, both in Jacob's arrest and in his father's lawsuit, as a set of conventions codified in laws. This is the view known as *conventionalism*. To the conventionalist, whether justice has been served is simply a matter of whether the relevant laws were applied.

Yet Cash prods us to ask a further question, one a philosopher would ask, regarding our laws and social institutions—are *they* just? Obviously to answer this question will require going beyond the laws and institutions themselves to some other criterion of justice by which we might evaluate them. Equal treatment is one such criterion, but does it go far enough? After all, to dole out humiliating treatment equally to all—be they Jacob Green, some anonymous individual, or someone near and dear to us—hardly counts as justice. In fact, indiscriminate mistreatment of citizens would be a strong call to bear witness and engage in political action in the name of justice. Moreover, if an identifiable group is systematically treated unjustly, such as Native Americans often have been, we might, as Johnny Cash did, take up their cause in the name of *social justice*.

I Know I Had It Comin': Justice as Desert

The fact that just about any convict mentioned in a Johnny Cash song knows he "had it comin'"—provided he's guilty—is good evidence that "justice as desert" is a widely held principle. In fact, it is one of the oldest ideas of justice—an eye for an eye, a tooth for a tooth. By the time the Greek philosopher Plato (427–347 B.C.E.) wrote his *Republic*, justice as desert was already part of the collective common wisdom, eventually codified in Roman law as "*justitia est cuique suum tribuere*" (justice is ren-

dering to each man what is due to him). But the fact that a principle is widely held does not make it unproblematic. And as it
turns out, to view justice as desert has implications that many
would be unwilling to accept.

Perhaps the most serious problem with justice as desert is
revealed when we begin thinking about the disconnect between
desert and individual responsibility. Today we tend to think that
whether it's right to praise or blame someone for an action
depends on their responsibility for the action. This is perhaps
what Cash means when he refers in "Man in Black" to "a victim
of the times," someone whose actions are due at least partly to
factors outside their control. Such factors tend to reduce culpability for wrongdoing. We excuse someone who acts unknow-
ingly or who could not have acted otherwise than she or he did.
Likewise, someone who by position of birth or dumb luck
achieves something great through little effort of his or her own
is thought not to deserve praise. Yet the link between desert and
personal responsibility has not always been so tight. The ancient
Greeks, for example, thought that the measure of a man was the
quality of his actions, without much regard for individual
responsibility. They had little difficulty accepting that so long as
the wicked suffered and the virtuous were happy, justice was
served.

But what does it mean to say, as we moderns do, that someone deserves praise or blame, reward or punishment, only if he
or she is responsible for the action in question? In part this
depends on how dogged we are in pursuing the question of
responsibility. At a minimum, it means that the person intended
to do what he or she did. By this standard, someone who "shot
a man in Reno just to watch him die" certainly deserves blame,
and justice is served by doling out an appropriate punishment.
Conversely, if a legal system punishes someone for something
they could have done nothing to prevent, we tend to view the
punishment as undeserved and the legal system as unjust. But
how far do we push our inquiry into personal responsibility?

If you think about it, many of the circumstances causally
involved in producing our actions go well beyond our own
efforts and intentions. For instance, nature endowed Johnny
Cash with a distinctive singing voice, and his achievement in
developing a successful musical career depended heavily on this
natural gift. Clearly he can claim no responsibility for possess-

ing this gift, so is his fame deserved? Most people would point out that it was not enough that Cash possessed the gift, but that he took the initiative to develop his talent, and exerted great effort in putting it to use in the creation of music for the public to enjoy. So perhaps we can say that he genuinely deserves praise and fame not for his natural gift itself, but for his efforts to develop it.

Yet this merely pushes the problem back one step further, for even Cash's drive and grit might be considered natural gifts he can claim no credit for. Perhaps his willingness to try, his decision to pursue music, or his very character are themselves consequences of some combination of the hand nature dealt him and how he was raised, neither of them his doing. If we insist that in order for a person to deserve praise or blame, punishment or reward, for a given action, he or she must be personally responsible for *all* of the conditions leading to the action, then the notion of desert collapses. Each time we think we have arrived at a point where we have identified some reason that a person is deserving of something, we can always pinpoint additional factors beyond their control that undercut that judgment.

It seems that the collapse of desert would leave us with two options. Perhaps we could substitute a weaker notion of responsibility, so that we call someone deserving as long as they intended to act as they did and exerted some control over the situation to the point where it cannot be chalked up simply to good fortune or to bad luck. Or perhaps we could admit that no one is ever fully responsible for what they do, and therefore rethink our whole concept of desert. If we wish the greater good to be served, perhaps we could say that for someone to deserve something means that there is some value to society in rewarding or punishing them. The view that the societal good is to be maximized is known as utilitarianism; for more on utilitarianism, see Chapters 7 and 12 in this volume.

Cash's song "Jacob Green" provides us with at least one clear case of justice as desert. The legal inquiry into the treatment of Jacob culminates in the decision that the sheriff deserves to be forced into retirement, and that the guards deserve to be fired. Perhaps justice would have been better served had they been given even stiffer penalties. Obviously the song does not provide us with enough of the backstory to sort out the causes for their actions. For all we know they were scapegoats. Yet Cash here raises a general point that renders the particular fate of this sheriff and these guards moot: it's *the system* that's unjust, and this won't be rectified by a few personnel changes and a fresh coat of paint. As much as we like to peg injustice to particular individuals and their actions, there is an aspect to justice that is closely tied up with our legal and social institutions.

Things Need Changin' Everywhere I Go

But how can we tell whether our social and legal institutions— our laws, jails, courts, prisons, schools, reservations, and instruments of governance—are just? To paraphrase Mahatma Gandhi (1869–1948): a nation can be judged by how it treats its worst off, such as its prisoners. The same goes for the institutions within a society. If an institution systematically mistreats the least empowered members of society—those who have little say in how the system is set up and are least able to defend themselves against it—then that institution is unjust.

Considering justice from this standpoint, as a systemic property of our institutions, we can see that Johnny Cash had a lot to be ticked off about, and why he used his music to draw attention to the system and its victims. "Jacob Green" for example, portrays a world in which we become so engrossed in the details of one particular case that, unless somebody points it out as Cash does in this song, the systemic nature of the mistreatment of criminal suspects goes completely unnoticed. Songs such as "All of God's Children Ain't Free," "Man in Black," "Apache Tears," and even "San Quentin" describe the plight of the system's victims: sharecroppers, the poor, the elderly, soldiers killed in Vietnam, American Indians, and prisoners. Cash's attitude toward these injustices oscillates between fatalism— "there's things that never will be right, I know," he sings in "Man In Black"—and "inspired anger" (see Chapter 13 in this volume), often accompanied by a call to action.

The Long Black Veil of Ignorance: Justice as Fairness

Johnny Cash is to be admired for standing up for those passed over, cast out, or beaten down by an unjust system, but this merely raises the question of what a just system would be. Sure, we might make some concrete and worthwhile proposals for changes in social policy regarding corrections, labor, veterans' affairs, civil rights, and other important issues, but from a philosophical perspective, it would be helpful to have a theory of justice to help us abstract away from specific problems to some general considerations that would pertain to any just institution. In his *A Theory of Justice* (1971), philosopher John Rawls (1921–2002) undertakes precisely this project. Rawls call his view "justice as fairness," and he develops the idea by means of a hypothetical exercise.

Imagine that you and all other members of society are to decide, together, the principles of justice on which society is to be based. These principles will govern the assignment of basic rights and duties, who is entitled to what, and the means for settling disputes. Here is the catch: to keep you from rigging society to your sole benefit, your choice of the principles of justice is made from behind a veil of ignorance. Neither you nor anyone else knows who he or she will be in society—any one of you could be Jacob Green. Together you're deciding the principles of justice without anyone knowing his or her own class, race, gender, job, talents, abilities, likes, dislikes, or values. Behind the veil of ignorance, everyone is in the same position (which Rawls terms the "original position"). Hence, no one can tweak the principles of justice to favor his or her self. Of course, in the resulting society there will still be people who are better or worse off by virtue of the hand that either nature or nurture has dealt them (the very factors that cause problems for "justice as desert"), but at least the principles of justice will have been arrived at by a fair process. Rawls called his conception *justice as fairness.*

Behind the veil of ignorance, there would be a strong incentive to adopt principles of justice that would enjoy the willing consent of even those who are society's worst off. Why? Because *that worst off person could be any one of us.* And if we thought this way, once we stepped out from behind the veil of ignorance into the world we actually inhabit, there is no way we would stomach so-called principles of justice that would allow any one of us to "get done like Jacob Green got done." In fact, this is exactly the call to conscience Johnny Cash dials in "Jacob Green." In theory, the kind of society Rawls describes is the society we live in. Cash reminds us that as long as we turn our heads away from violations of the principles of justice on which our society is founded, our practices are not living up to those principles. We live in a real world of real injustice—there's no hiding behind the veil.

The Ballad of Ira Hayes: Social Justice for Native Americans

The victims of injustice championed in Johnny Cash's music include both individuals and groups. In fact, in some cases the plight of one individual is an ear-grabbing way of drawing attention to the plight of their group. This raises an important question for theories of justice—does just treatment of individuals ensure justice for the cultural groups they belong to? That is to say, is there any additional measure of justice that is needed, given that we inhabit a world of diverse ethnic, cultural and religious groups? Beyond individual justice, is there a need for social justice? It may be instructive to look at the case of Ira Hayes.

"The Ballad of Ira Hayes," penned by Native American songwriter Peter LaFarge and made famous by Johnny Cash on his 1964 concept album *Bitter Tears: Ballads of the American Indian*, tells the real-life tale of Ira Hayes, a member of the Akimel O'odham (the Gila River Pima Indians) and World War II hero. The story has also been retold in James Bradley's book *Flags of Our Fathers* and a movie adaptation of the same title directed by Clint Eastwood. Hayes—an enlisted Marine paratrooper nicknamed "Chief Falling Cloud"—fought in the Battle of Iwo Jima and was one of the five men immortalized in Joe Rosenthal's iconic photo of the raising of the American flag atop Mount Suribachi. Hayes became instantly famous, touring the country, playing himself opposite John Wayne in *Sands of Iwo Jima* (1949) and being feted by Eisenhower at the White House in 1954.

Yet as "The Ballad of Ira Hayes" makes clear, all was not rosy upon Hayes's return from the war. Due to the boost in stateside morale upon the publication of Rosenthal's photo, Ira Hayes and two of his fellow flagraisers, Private First Class Rene Gagnon and Pharmacist's Second Mate John Bradley, were whisked around the country on a tour to drum up War Bond sales. Although he longed to return to the front lines to fight alongside his brothers in arms, Hayes followed orders and stayed on the War Bonds tour, while legions of admirers did what any patriotic American would do—bought the soldier a drink. Upon his return to the reservation—which was among the most destitute in the nation due in part to unjust usurpation of water rights—Hayes tried to lead a normal life, but the obstacles to doing so proved insurmountable.

With every visitor to the reservation who wanted to see "the Indian war hero who raised the flag," Hayes felt increasingly guilty—survivor's guilt. The real heroes, he believed, were his friends and the members of his unit who had died in battle. And to make matters worse, Hayes was a quiet man, who felt uncomfortable with all of the attention. When a reporter, after the ceremony at the Eisenhower White House in 1954, asked him how he liked all of the pomp and circumstance, Hayes hung his head and answered, "I don't." Back on the reservation, Hayes was arrested repeatedly for public drunkenness until one morning, after a night of drinking and playing cards, he was found lying outside in the dirt, pools of blood and vomit nearby, a victim of exposure.

Ira Hayes resisted the hero label—in fact he had threatened to kill his fellow flag raiser, Private First Class Rene Gagnon, if Gagnon identified him in the Iwo Jima photo. Yet there is no question that he embodied, as many people do, a complex mixture of ordinary vices and extraordinary virtues. Perhaps his most extraordinary virtue was an abiding sense of justice as desert, as evidenced not only by his reluctance to accept praise for the circumstances history had thrust upon him at Iwo Jima, but also by the following tale. Throughout the War Bonds tour, a closely guarded secret festered inside of him—one of the figures in that iconic Iwo Jima photograph, Corporal Harlon Block, had been misidentified as Sergeant "Hank" Hansen, and Hayes was perhaps the only one who knew it. In 1945 at the start of the Bond drive, Hayes kept the secret to himself under the order of a Marine public relations officer. Then, in 1946, despite being mired in alcoholism and depression, Hayes's sense of justice impelled him to act. Hitchhiking over 1,300 miles from the Gila River reservation in Arizona to the Texas home of Block's family, he disclosed to them the true story of the bravery of their son, who had been killed in battle a couple hours after the flag was raised. After consoling the Block family, Hayes returned to the reservation.

While this story attests to Ira Hayes's character, it also provides a lesson in the limits of restorative justice. On one hand, Hayes took it upon himself to restore honor to Harlon Block, according him the recognition he justly deserved. Yet curiously, it proved impossible for Hayes himself ever to have restored to him what his gruesome battle experiences and premature withdrawal from combat had depleted (Hayes, like many other veterans, probably suffered from post-traumatic stress disorder in an era before this condition was recognized, a problem aggravated by the destitute conditions and lack of opportunities on the reservation). And this, despite the fact that Hayes was given a hero's welcome, appeared in a movie, and was showered with appreciation. It simply proved impossible for him to recover from the war experience and its aftermath: there was no way to repay him for the effects these experiences had had on him.

But to return to an earlier question, what about social justice? In the case of Native Americans, war veterans, or any other group you might want to name, is there such a thing as justice or injustice toward the group itself, or does it all come down to whether particular individuals are treated justly? It's the latter, according to theories such as Rawls's. Rawls's theory of justice falls within the tradition of political philosophy known as "classical liberalism." The classical liberal holds that our institutions are justified to the extent that they promote the interests of *individuals*. Because individuals value different things, have their own projects they wish to pursue, and nothing guarantees these won't conflict, our system of laws (and other institutions) exist to allow life, liberty, and the pursuit of happiness (or "the good"—that which is worth pursuing, something different individuals may disagree on).

In classical liberalism, what's directly unjust about discriminating against a group like Native Americans is not that it ends a way of life, or that Native American cultures themselves are violated. These are only unjust indirectly. The direct injustice on this view is how a particular individual—the "Old Apache Squaw" Cash sings about on *Bitter Tears,* for example—has his or her liberties taken away by a system to which they never consented nor would have consented. Discrimination against Native

Americans, on this view, is unjust because of its devastating effects on individuals.

But suppose we set aside the classical liberal view and allow that one form of justice—what I have been calling social justice—should be directed at promoting the interests of entire cultural groups, such as the Pima Indians, not merely those of the individual members making up the group. This is a view sometimes known as *communalism*. For example, we might want to allow the group itself to pursue its own projects and its own vision of the good.

The classical liberal finds that while there is no reason to stand in the way of group interests (provided they don't trample any individual liberties), there is no direct duty to promote group interests. The classical liberal has a worry: what happens if the interest of the cultural group itself involves committing injustices to some individuals? We end up here in a bit of a bind, condoning injustice to individuals in the name of acting justly toward a cultural group.

An example of a current controversy that many would find to fit this pattern is the debate over the treaty with the Makah granting them the right to engage in gray whale hunting, despite the fact that gray whales have been on and off the endangered species list in recent decades. Traditional practices many of us would like in principle to leave untouched present a serious ethical challenge. Here liberal principles—animal liberation in this case—may indeed carry the day. Yet at the practical level, sometimes the best way to obtain justice for a group's individual members is to organize and rally around the interests of the group itself. Often, the interests of individuals line up with the interests of the group. Such has been the case with other Native American causes.

"As Long as the Grass Shall Grow": Honoring Treaties

One of the subtexts to "The Ballad of Ira Hayes," if not Cash's entire *Bitter Tears* album, is the White Man's systematic disregard for Native Americans' relationships with the land, not only in the establishment of bounded reservations, but in the breach of treaties by the U.S. government whenever it was expedient to do so. To the end of many treaties was appended a standard time limitation: "as long as the grass shall grow and the rivers flow," a metaphor for perpetuity. How fitting then that many a treaty has been broken by damming up a river and flooding sacred ground, or diverting a river away from Indian lands until grasses wither and die along with the agricultural livelihood that has sustained a people since pre-Columbian times. When the river stops flowing and the grass stops growing, you know the treaty is history.

If ever there was a clear instance of an entire people being treated unjustly, it would have to be the violation of U.S. treaties with native peoples. As legal constructs, treaties are conventions, but at a deeper level, breaking a treaty is not merely flouting a convention—it is breaking a promise, perhaps one of the most egregious ethical breaches since at least the time of Immanuel Kant (1724–1804; see Chapter 11 in this volume). "The Ballad of Ira Hayes" links Hayes's decision to enlist in the Marines to the White Man's diversion of waters that normally would flow down the Gila River onto the land of the Ira's people, the Akimel O'odham:

> Down the ditches for a thousand years
> The water grew Ira's people's crops
> 'Till the white man stole the water rights
> And the sparklin' water stopped.
>
> Now Ira's folks were hungry
> And their land grew crops of weeds
> When war came, Ira volunteered
> And forgot the white man's greed.

Over at least a millennium, the Akimel O'odham, a group of Arizona Pima Indians organized politically today as the Gila River Indian Community, had developed an intimate knowledge of, and relationship with volatile landscape and sporadic flow patterns—flood, drought, shifting channels—that characterize desert river systems. The strategy the Akimel O'odham adopted in the face of an unpredictable environment was to shift their settlements and croplands accordingly, a strategy that resulted in consistently high maize yields even after severe flooding such as the flood of 1905. (A discussion of the Akimel O'odham's remarkable history of cultural adaptation to a dynamic landscape may be found in the June 2004 issue of *American Anthropologist*).

Contrast this attitude toward the land with that of the Anglo-European agricultural industry. The White Man's response to nature's inconstant rhythms? Erect dams and irrigation systems to bring them under technological control. Yet even after these "advanced" agricultural practices got underway in the 1860s, diverting water from native lands, Ira's people were still able to adapt through settlement shift and other strategies. It was not until around 1920 that so much water was diverted for irrigation upstream of the Akimel O'odham that they virtually ceased practicing agriculture altogether, certainly contributing to their extreme poverty, and perhaps also influencing Hayes's decision to leave the reservation and enlist.

"As Long As the Grass Shall Grow," written by La Farge and sung by Cash on *Bitter Tears*, references a treaty signed by the Seneca Chief Cornplanter and President George Washington in 1796, granting the Seneca the Cornplanter Tract—1,500 acres along the Allegheny River in Pennsylvania—in gratitude for Chief Cornplanter's assistance to the federal government in negotiating with various Indian tribes. Chief Cornplanter believed that in the long term, his people's interests would best be served by developing diplomatic relationships with European settlers, working especially closely with the Quakers. Over time, he became increasingly disillusioned with the shabby treatment of his people at the hands of the U.S. government, and moved away from the assimilationist course he had been pursuing. And what of the Cornplanter Tract today? It is under water. In direct violation of the treaty, ground was broken to construct the Kinzua Dam in 1960—with La Farge, Cash, and Buffy Sainte-Marie launching protest in song to no avail—flooding Seneca land and driving the last Native Americans from Pennsylvania.

Cash's commitment to social justice on the part of Native Americans ran deep. He felt one with them, convinced he had at least some Cherokee blood roiling inside his Scots veins. Although this has been disputed, there is no disputing that many Indian nations embraced him as one of their own. In the late 1960s he performed on reservations in Oklahoma and South Dakota. In 1970, New Mexico's Jicarilla Apaches put up two million dollars for the filming of Cash's film "A Gunfight," starring Cash, Kirk Douglas, Jane Alexander, and Karen Black—

despite the fact that the film had nothing to do with the Jicarilla or any other native group. On his death in 2003, Cash's obituary in *Indian Times* lamented that Native Americans had "lost a warrior."

What Is Justice?

While Cash was no philosopher, his music and his own life reflected a complex and nuanced understanding of the richness of moral life. While it is possible to see Cash's populist patriotism (see Chapter 5 in this volume) and social protest as fundamentally at odds, Cash was able to "walk the line" between culture and counterculture by insisting that America, founded on ideals of justice, often failed to live up to those ideals in its unjust treatment of convicts, veterans, Native Americans, and the poor. By drawing our attention to systemic injustices in songs such as "Jacob Green" and protest songs such as "Man In Black," "What Is Truth?" and "Singin' in Vietnam Talkin' Blues" Cash reminds us that principles of justice alone—much as we philosophers fixate on them—are not enough. Justice requires action, and it is up to us to see that justice is served.

PART V

God

15

Resurrection One Piece at a Time

RANDALL M. JENSEN

In the tragically funny song "The Man Who Couldn't Cry," Johnny Cash tells the story of a man who loses his dog, his wife, his job, his arm, and even his freedom and his dignity, but still finds himself without a single tear in his eyes. Cash goes on to describe the redemption and vindication of this poor soul as he goes to heaven and is reunited with his dog and his arm—but thankfully not with his unfaithful wife, who has since died of what must be alarmingly extensive stretch-marks.

Although this song is a comedy, Johnny Cash is dead serious about the possibility of judgment and redemption, as we hear in "Redemption," "When the Man Comes Around," "Kneeling Drunkard's Plea," "Down There by the Train," and so many other classic Cash songs.[1] No matter how bad things may get—and they get pretty bad for the man who couldn't cry, and sometimes for Johnny Cash himself, for that matter—there's always a hope that things will be made right. And, perhaps more importantly, no matter how bad *we* may get, no matter how much evil we do and how many people we hurt, there's always a hope of forgiveness. Even Judas Iscariot is "down there by the train, where the sinner can be washed in the blood of the lamb," and he's carrying John Wilkes Booth.

---

[1] Johnny Cash wrote many of his songs himself, but he sang many songs written by others as well, especially in the celebrated *American Recordings* series. But as a performer he made all these songs his own, and so I'll generally avoid worrying about whether a song is a Cash original or a cover.

We shouldn't be surprised to find this theme of redemption and forgiveness running through so much of Johnny Cash's music (and his other creative endeavors, including the novel *Man in White* and the film *Gospel Road*), given his lifelong love of Gospel music and his wonderfully unconventional and undeniably authentic commitment to the Christian faith during his later years. And no doubt this focus is a big part of why Cash and his music resonate so deeply with folks who find themselves in a prison of one kind or another.

Sometimes the redemption Cash sings about is something we can offer to each other in this life, as when a stranger offers comfort and company to a dying man in "Give My Love to Rose," or when a boy named Sue reconciles with his father after discovering the real reason for his hated name, or when a prisoner exclaims that "I'm Free from the Chain Gang Now." But the powerful core of Cash's view of redemption lies in the hope of the life to come. It's just too abundantly clear that death often comes when we're not ready for it, while we're still fighting personal battles and trying to repair broken relationships. And so Cash sings about heaven and about the hope that when death separates friends and lovers, it's only temporary, as in "If We Never Meet Again This Side of Heaven," "Wayfaring Stranger," and "Daddy Sang Bass." In "Meet Me in Heaven," he sings that "I'll know you and you'll know me out there beyond the stars." And surely the possibility of such a joyous reunion brings great consolation to anyone who's lost a loved one, and it eases the pain of the prospect of having to say such a final goodbye for all of us.

But does it make sense to hope and long for such a reunion? After all, you and I will *die* long before this promised celestial meeting, right? And isn't death the end of us? Dead people are usually buried in the ground—or even cremated in some cases. So, whoever that is out there beyond the stars, how can that be you or me? How can the dead live again? Such an idea seems very difficult to fathom. However, that hasn't stopped most cultures throughout history from believing in some kind of life after death, or *afterlife*, for short.

But it isn't easy to figure out whether belief in an afterlife is so widespread because it's supported by ample evidence or whether the prevalence of this belief should instead be explained by wishful thinking and the fear of mortality. We don't much like the idea that everything we are will come to an end, after all, and we're pretty good at avoiding believing in things that cause us pain. But before we can discern whether it's *rational* to believe in an afterlife or not, we need to figure out whether this belief is coherent—whether it's even *possible* for someone to live after death. Is it even possible for you and me to have a postmortem meeting?

The idea of an afterlife could be like the idea of a round square: you don't have to do any checking to know that there isn't and just can't be any such thing. It's just a logical impossibility. Is it likewise impossible for me to live on after I die? To answer this question about the afterlife, we'll be forced to think more carefully about what it is for me to be me and you to be you. In other words, we'll need to take up the issue of *personal identity*, which is one of the central issues in *metaphysics*, the branch of philosophy that's concerned with the nature of reality.

One Piece at a Time?

Before we discuss the identity of persons, however, we need to say a few things about the idea of *identity* itself, and about what it means for something to be *identical* to something else. You see, we might mean a couple of different things when we say that two things are identical.

Sometimes, what we mean is that two things are exactly like one another, as if we were to say that some freakishly good Johnny Cash impersonator is identical to the real Johnny Cash. This is identity as *qualitative similarity*, and it's what we have in mind when we describe a set of twins as identical twins. This is not the kind of identity we care about at the moment, because our ultimate question is not whether there could be an exact replica of you or me in heaven. Presumably God could manage that without any great difficulty. No, what we want to know is whether two people in heaven could really *be* you and me. With this kind of identity—call it *numerical identity*—what we mean in calling "two" things identical is that they aren't really two things at all, but only one. Sometimes a numerical identity claim reflects our discovery that what we thought were two different things are instead one thing under two different descriptions, as when we learn that the singer we know as Johnny Cash is also the singer we know as "The Man in Black." Other times a numerical identity claim concerns the identity of a thing over time: the Johnny Cash who made the *American Recording* series of records is the same guy we saw play with Elvis in Memphis back in 1955.

Probably it's obvious that what we really want to know is what makes a thing at one time numerically identical to that very same thing at another time. (Hereafter, I'll sometimes drop the "numerical" since it's a bit cumbersome, but you should assume that it's still numerical identity we're talking about.) This is the metaphysical problem known as *the problem of identity over time.* Our particular concern is with the identity of persons over time, and eventually with personal identity across the boundary-line of life and death, but it'll be helpful for us to consider the identity over time of a less complicated thing than a person first. Philosophers often think about this problem with the help of an ancient Greek thought-experiment known as the Ship of Theseus, which involves losing and replacing the parts of a ship.[2] But let's see if we can give this famous thought-experiment a tweak so that it fits better into our Johnny Cash context.

Remember Cash's humorous song "One Piece at a Time"? It's about a guy who works at an automobile factory and sneaks a part out at the end of every day so that he can eventually build himself a new Cadillac for free. What he ends up with, after twenty-some years of this pilfering, is a car that's the automotive equivalent of Frankenstein's monster. As the song closes, Cash is describing it as a "'49, '50, '51, '52 . . . '69, '70 automobile," due to its odd conglomeration of parts. It is indeed "the only one around." Why is it unique and why all the uncertainty about what to call this thing? Probably because we typically identify a car by its parts, at least in part, if you'll forgive the pun. A black 1979 Cadillac Seville and a red 1984 Ford Mustang are different from each other in all kinds of ways: make, model, color, shape, size, and so on, and so there are any number of ways of distin-

---

[2] What, you may ask, is a *thought-experiment?* Well, it's pretty much what it sounds like. We're asked to imagine some scenario that's designed to make us do some interesting thinking about something. Sometimes the point of a philo-sophical thought-experiment is to support a particular conclusion, while other times the point may be to set out a paradox. The Ship of Theseus, which was first reported by Plutarch (around 45–125 C.E.), is more in the latter category.

guishing them. What about two black 1979 Sevilles that are in more or less the same condition? They're the same color, shape, and size. And maybe they rolled out of the same factory. But their parts, although qualitatively indistinguishable, or nearly so, perhaps, are not numerically the same parts. They have eight tires between them, four over here and four over there, for example. Crudely put, the two cars are made of different hunks of metal, plastic, rubber, and whatever else might make up the *matter* of a car. That's what makes them two different cars. But they have the same *form* (or structure), which is how the Greek philosopher Aristotle (384–322 B.C.E.) might put it, if he were to travel through time to take up the issue of the metaphysics of Cadillacs.

If the identity of a car depends on the matter that it's made of, what happens when there's a *change* in a car's matter? We do change various parts on our cars over the years. No one thinks that a car's identity changes—that it actually stops being one car and starts being another car—every time we change the oil or replace a tire.[3] However, and here at last we arrive at our thought-experiment, what about a more complete change of parts?

Consider one of Johnny Cash's cars in the early years, a green '54 Plymouth. Suppose we could travel through time back several decades and monkey with this car in various ways. (While we're out time-traveling, we should be sure to catch Cash in a concert or two!) Let's start by replacing this Plymouth with another one just like it, one night while Cash is asleep. The car he gets into the next morning won't be the same car he got out of the night before, right? One car has been replaced by a numerically distinct car, even if Cash can't tell the difference. Okay. Let's try something different. What if we completely disassemble the car while he's asleep and then put it back together? This time, surely we think the car Cash drives in the morning is the very same car he drove the night before. We can take something apart

---

[3] Well, maybe not no one. The ancient Greek philosopher Heralictus (around 535–475 B.C.E.) is famous for saying that no one can step twice into the same river, because the river is always changing so that it's never the same river. Someone who believed that everything is always changing in that kind of way might very well think that any change in a thing is a change in its identity. But this view isn't exactly popular these days.

and put it back together without destroying it, right? One interesting implication of this seems to be that some things can survive a gap in their existence, because it looks like the car doesn't exist while it's totally in pieces. Or does it? People might begin to disagree here.

Now let's combine these first two maneuvers by again replacing Cash's car with another car of the same make and color, but this time we'll do the replacement piece by piece. If we do all this in a single night, doesn't it seem as though the car Cash drives the next day will once again be a different car? It shouldn't matter if we replace the car all at once or piece by piece. Or should it? Suppose we replace the parts of Cash's car more slowly, over a period of months or even years. As I just mentioned, it's odd to think that we would "create" a different car by replacing just one of its parts. But that seems true no matter where we are in the replacement process, whether the part we're replacing is the first on our list or the last. Imagine that it's the last night of our clandestine operation. At last we replace the final part on the car, which we'll make a hubcap. If the car Cash has been driving each day has remained the same car throughout the change of every other one of its parts, it's very strange to believe that this relatively minor replacement now makes it another car entirely. So it may seem that a fast replacement of a car's parts, all at once, yields a different car, while a car's identity can remain intact with a very slow replacement of its parts, one piece at a time, even if every single one of the parts is replaced. The car Cash is driving, day after day, then, seems to be the same car, even after losing *all* its original parts.

This suggests that the claim that a car's identity depends on its parts is a bit simplistic. Matters get even more complicated when we add another twist to our thought-experiment. Suppose that each night when we replace a part of Cash's Plymouth, we take the original part to a garage where we slowly assemble (or re-assemble?) a green '54 Plymouth that's made of the parts we remove from Cash's car each night. In this way, at the end of the process we have two cars. The car Cash is driving has none of the original parts, while the car in our garage is made of the parts that originally made up Cash's car. So if a thing's parts are all that matter for its identity, this car has a good claim to be identical to Cash's original car, since it's made of the very same collection of parts. But the car Cash has been driving day after day surely also has a claim to be identical to Cash's original car. The bottom line? There's a philosophical puzzle lurking here and so it may not always be obvious whether two things are identical over time.

Here's Johnny!

Now we'll investigate the notion of personal identity, keeping firmly in mind the lessons we've just learned about the problematic nature of identity. To begin with, we need to distinguish the notion of a person's *metaphysical* identity from the notion of a person's *practical* identity, because we're likely to get confused if we don't keep these things apart. Johnny Cash's metaphysical identity is what makes Johnny Cash the particular person he is as opposed to some other person altogether, such as Kris Kristofferson or Billy Graham. Cash's practical identity is what makes him the kind of person he is—which may have to do with his appearance, his personality, his values and preferences, and his character. This distinction is important because claims like the following can be understood in quite different ways:

"I swear, Johnny Cash is two different people."

"Johnny Cash, you aren't the same person you used to be."

The first claim might mean something fairly ordinary: that Johnny Cash is a complicated guy and his mood and manner can change quite a lot, which does seem to have been the case. June Carter Cash tells us that she even called him by different names ("J.R.," "Johnny," or "Cash") depending on how he was acting at any given time. What's going on here has to do with Johnny's practical identity. If we were to interpret this claim in light of his metaphysical identity instead, it would mean that Cash is literally two different people! Perhaps it turns out that the one person we think of as Johnny Cash is actually a set of twins (as in the 2006 film *The Prestige*) or maybe Cash has the sort of multiple personality disorder that seems much more common in B movies than in real life. Things like this are far from ordinary.

Likewise, the second claim might simply mean that the new straight and sober Johnny Cash is a pretty different man than the old Johnny Cash who was nearly always on something. Somebody who utters this second sentence is simply saying that Cash's practical identity has shifted significantly, which is the sort of thing that happens to many of us at some times in our lives. But, again, if this is about his metaphysical identity, the claim is rather startling. Johnny Cash, the man who recorded all those records, no longer exists! Now there's another person here! Maybe the body-snatchers have invaded. Or maybe someone's erased Cash's mind and given him a new set of memories. Either way, something truly bizarre has happened.

Our question, then, concerns a person's metaphysical identity. It wouldn't trouble us overmuch if our practical identities are somewhat altered when we get to heaven. After all, the adult Johnny Cash may be radically different in all kinds of ways from the child he once was. And, in fact, the Christian doctrine of heaven pretty explicitly includes the idea that we'll be new and improved versions of ourselves. What would be alarming is if the people who enter heaven aren't us but someone else instead. Because then we'll have been copied or replaced rather than resurrected. And the thought that after I die there'll be some doppelganger of me wandering around in heaven is creepy rather than comforting. So what would it take for this heavenly wanderer to be identical to me, metaphysically speaking, that is?

I'm Gonna Break My Rusty Cage and Run

With our earlier musings on the identity of cars in mind, let's start by thinking about how our identity as persons might depend on our parts. What kind of parts do we have? *Materialism* states that human beings are wholly made up of material parts. When it comes to what we're made of, human beings are no different in kind from cars and guitars or dogs and hogs. We're just more complicated. *Dualism* is the view that human beings are made up of two very different parts: a body and a soul (or mind, if you like). Now maybe each of these two parts is made of parts of its own, but the key thing for us to see here is this fundamental divide between the body and the soul. We'll spend some time thinking about how each of these two general positions on human nature might handle the notion of personal identity and the possibility of an afterlife.

Plato (427–347 B.C.E.) was one of the first Western philosophers to give a serious account of what might happen after we die. In the *Phaedo*, a dialogue that is set on the day that ends with Socrates throwing back a cup of hemlock in fulfillment of his death sentence, Plato has Socrates suggest that philosophers shouldn't be afraid of death because they've been practicing to be dead all along.[4] Of course, this is something of a dig at philosophers, but we'll allow it since Socrates is one himself. Plato's Socrates is also making a serious point, however, which is that philosophers are all about chasing after wisdom, and for Plato to chase after wisdom is to try to live a life that ignores the body as much as possible.

Now, Plato is a dualist, but as is becoming obvious to us, the body is nowhere nearly as important as the soul. In fact, he tends to think of a person as a soul and of a body as a mere container or vessel, a view that jibes nicely with the theory of reincarnation we encounter in several of his dialogues. Plato even characterizes the body as a prison that drags the soul down from its loftier pursuits—trapped in a rusty cage indeed! The body's desires and demands constantly distract the soul from its quest for the truth. Thus, for Plato, the identity of Johnny Cash the person is tantamount to the identity of Johnny Cash's soul. It's this soul that makes Johnny Cash who he is throughout his life—or lives, if like Plato you go in for the transmigration of souls. And since death does not destroy the soul, but rather liberates it from the body, death is not really the end of Johnny Cash in any meaningful way. Cash's soul, and thus Cash himself, now exists in some Platonic heaven, perhaps awaiting the next trip into the mortal realm.

Not everybody follows Plato all the way down this road, of course, but plenty of folks still believe in the idea of an immaterial and immortal soul. And if we indeed have—or rather *are*—such souls, then death is no problem for us. It looks like we naked souls can meet "out there beyond the stars." Dualists now seem to have a ready-made answer to the problem of identity over time and beyond death. However, various objections

---

[4] Plato *Five Dialogues*, translated by G.M.A. Grube (Indianapolis: Hackett, 1981), especially pp. 97–105. Plato, like Johnny Cash, finds power in telling the story of someone who's been imprisoned.

have been launched against this kind of dualism. Let's have a look at some of them.

First, how can an immaterial soul be *located* out there beyond the stars, or anywhere else, for that matter? We understand what it is for a material thing to be in one place as opposed to another, but it's hard to see how the same can be said of an immaterial thing. How can an immaterial soul be first "in" a body and then "out" of a body? What do "in" and "out" mean for something that isn't physical and takes up no space? It's difficult to understand how an immaterial soul can be connected to and interact with a material body. But it's also hard to figure out how to identify an immaterial soul that's out of a body and how to distinguish one such disembodied soul from another. If we can't make more sense of how this notion of a soul is supposed to work, we might need to abandon it.[5]

Second, we don't need an immaterial soul to help us explain things like how we can be intelligent or self-conscious nearly as much as we used to. A few centuries ago most thinkers believed it was inconceivable that a material thing—mere matter—could be intelligent. But consider what computing technology has made possible for "mere" matter! Sometimes we have a hard time telling what's impossible and what's merely tough to imagine.

Third, and more theologically, some argue that this Greek idea of the immortal and immaterial soul has exerted an undue influence on Christian theology and perhaps on our ordinary ways of thinking about ourselves as well. We need to see the body as part of who we are rather than as a rusty cage to break and run from. And perhaps Christianity is better served by trusting in God for our resurrection after a very real and final death rather than by seeing ourselves as naturally immortal and thus deathless in the way Plato does. The bottom line is that it makes an awful lot of sense to pay more attention to the biblical and creedal idea of the resurrection of the body. One way to do this would be to give the body a more significant role to play within a dualist framework, perhaps by suggesting that we cannot iden-

---

[5] Theists may have a reason to think that it's possible to make sense of the idea of an immaterial soul, since they already believe in an immaterial being: God. However, there may turn out to be important differences between the relationship of soul to body and the relationship of God to the world.

tify Johnny Cash with his soul alone, but rather with the compound of his soul and his body. Maybe a heavenly Johnny Cash needs the earthly Johnny Cash's soul and his body, too, in order to be in business.[6]

Flesh and Blood Need Flesh and Blood

Let's now put on our materialist hats. When I die, there's a corpse here on earth. How can it be that I'll live on in heaven in bodily form? Well, merely having a body in heaven isn't such a big deal. The Christian heaven, unlike the Platonic heaven, isn't a haven for immaterial souls fleeing the prison of earth. Instead, it's the new heavens and the new earth—our own universe made new and transformed. And since Johnny Cash seems to be a kind of down to earth guy, I bet he'd prefer a new heaven and earth to a mysteriously transcendent reality.

The problem arises when we ask how we get *our* bodies to heaven. What happens to a body after death? I apologize for asking, since decomposition isn't a pleasant thing to contemplate. Surely heaven shouldn't look like *Night of the Living Dead*! Actually, by itself this isn't such a problem. An omnipotent God can surely revive, repair, and even revamp a body however he wishes. But matters get worse. Bodies that have been dead for centuries probably aren't even identifiable anymore; in some cases, whatever matter made them up has entirely dispersed. Thus, it isn't simply a matter of fixing them up. What some bodies need is to be completely re-assembled, which is surely an impossible task for anyone but God. Mightn't it even be beyond the reach of omnipotence? After all, it's quite likely that a particular bit of matter served as a part of various human bodies over the centuries. (Cannibalism is only the most direct route by which this can happen.) So God can't simply sort through the matter of the universe and put all the bodies back together as he might assemble thousands of puzzles whose pieces had been

---

[6] Now, part of how this might work is that the "new" body would be connected to the same old soul. If the heavenly Cash has the earthly Cash's soul and quite a bit of the matter that made up the earthly Cash's body, maybe that's enough to support a claim of identity between them. And before Cash gets put back together, Humpty Dumpty style, we might think of Cash's disembodied soul as an incomplete part of Cash the person.

mixed up. Some pieces are needed in more than one puzzle. And maybe even God can't make one thing be in two places at the same time, since to say that God is omnipotent is not to say that he can do what is sheer nonsense.

So, should we give up hope of ever seeing our bodies again after we die? Not just yet. Here's where our reflections about the identity of cars might be of help. Remember that we decided that it wasn't obvious that a car's identity over time is just a matter of being made of the same component parts. The same may be true for human bodies. In fact, it's just got to be true, because we know that our bodies do a more thorough job of replacing their own parts as time goes along than even the most conscientious car-owner does for his car. We also observed that a car could be disassembled and reassembled. What if a few pieces turned up missing during the reassembly process and we replaced them with exact replicas? Would that mean we'd be building a new car instead of reassembling the old one? Arguably not. And a lengthy delay between disassembly and reassembly doesn't seem to be such a problem, either. So maybe a person-as-a-body can die, decompose, and then be resurrected. There's a hope of heaven even for materialists!

Memories Are Made of This

Let's finish on a strong note, with an intriguing closing insight as our final number and a perplexing puzzle as our encore. We've been thinking about the nature and identity of persons as a function of what parts they're made of. Maybe that's not the best way to think about it, in which case worries over replacing parts aren't as serious as we might have thought. After all, what kind of thing is a person?

Being a person seems to be less about what you're made of and more about what you can do. A person is something that can think, and feel, and decide. In more philosophical prose, we sometimes say that a person is self-conscious: a person is the enduring subject of conscious experiences and can see herself as such a subject. If this is where we should begin in thinking about personal identity, it's natural to suggest that I'm the same person over time if the conscious experiences I'm having now are connected to the experiences I had earlier. Perhaps personal identity over time is essentially a matter of *psychological conti-*

nuity. And memory is one of the things that connects our experiences and forms a life out of them. So, persons might be made of memories, although not in the same way bodies are made of cells.

In this case, what makes the earthly Johnny Cash the same person over time is that he remembers his past experiences, which implies that if he were to suffer a total and permanent memory loss, it would be tantamount to the death of the person he was. And what would make a heavenly Johnny Cash identical to the earthly one is if the heavenly Cash had the right kind of psychological connection to the earthly one, including containing the earthly Cash's memories. Never mind what the heavenly Cash is made of. Of course, like any other philosophical idea worth considering, this one has its problems. Chief among them is what's called "the duplication problem."

What if God were to create two bodies in heaven, both of which contained the memories of the earthly Johnny Cash? Which one of them is Cash? There seems to be no good answer to this question. They can't both be Cash. Yet to pick either one would be arbitrary. And surely it'd be odd to think that if God were to create just one of them, Cash would survive, but if God were to create two of them, Cash wouldn't survive at all! A real conundrum! But if it can somehow be resolved, then if the man who couldn't cry finds himself in heaven with two arms and a dog, he's the very same guy no matter what parts he does or doesn't have left in him—as long as he can remember losing his arm and his dog in the first place.[7]

---

[7] Everything we've looked at here could be examined in much more depth, especially this last idea of an account of personal identity based on psychological continuity. For a good place to start, get your hands on John Perry's wonderful little book *A Dialogue on Personal Identity and Immortality* (Indianapolis: Hackett, 1978).

16

Beer for Breakfast: The Role of Suffering in Character Formation

STEPHEN BILYNSKYJ

> Well, I woke up Sunday morning
> With no way to hold my head that didn't hurt.
> And the beer I had for breakfast wasn't bad,
> So I had one more for dessert.

In "Sunday Morning Coming Down," Johnny Cash sang Kris Kristofferson's words mentioning the venerable practice among drinkers known as "hair of the dog," short for "the hair of the dog that bit you." It's the term used for dealing with a hangover by waking up and having another drink. Despite what one might think, there is a remedy, at least briefly, for a hangover's pain by having more of what hurt you in the first place. I adopt "beer for breakfast" as a metaphor for a common supposition regarding *suffering*. Despite what one might think, suffering helps to produce a good life.

Of course, a breakfast beer or two only affords temporary relief from the fatigue, nausea and headache which are common hangover symptoms. No real benefit is derived from treating alcohol abuse with more alcohol. Yet it's often thought that at least some forms of human suffering and even a willing acceptance of or return to such suffering can offer lasting benefit to human development. The experience of disease may foster compassion. Danger may generate courage. And even self-inflicted pain caused by addictive behavior may eventually move one toward self-control and temperance. In short, suffering can have a curative, redemptive, even character-forming role

for human beings—in contrast, of course, to the merely pallia-
tive effect of a literal beer for breakfast.

The supposition that suffering can form character in positive
ways is an attractive interpretation of Johnny Cash's life and
career. His life involved deep personal pain, both innocently suffered and self-inflicted. Biographer Steve Turner says, "Pain was
a necessary part of his growth. Without it he would not have
been the Johnny Cash we know."[1] We suppose that at least some
of his suffering made Cash a better person and a better artist.

Johnny's problem was not beer. He struggled with drug
addiction. The process of his eventual recovery reflects how the
pain he caused himself, his family, and his friends had a
redemptive role in the formation of his person. And, likewise,
his own suffering of loss and personal defeat helped form the
compassion demonstrated in his life and music toward prisoners and other sufferers.

A World with No Hangovers?

John Hick invites us to imagine a world without suffering, a
"hedonistic paradise," where God intervenes and suspends natural laws whenever necessary to prevent all harm and pain
which might arise from any event or action. He then suggests
that human character which developed in such an environment
would be seriously deficient. He writes:

> Courage and fortitude would have no point in a world in which
> there is, by definition, no danger or difficulty. Generosity, kindness,
> the *agape* aspect of love, prudence, unselfishness, and all other
> ethical notions which presuppose life in an objective environment
> could not even be formed. Consequently, such a world, however
> well it might promote pleasure, would be very ill adapted for the
> development of the moral qualities of human personality.[2]

This general suggestion that suffering, or the possibility of
suffering, is necessary for the formation of at least some virtues

---

[1] *The Man Called Cash* (Nashville: Nelson, 2004), p. 228.
[2] *Philosophy of Religion*, second edition (Englewood Cliffs: Prentice-Hall,
1973), pp. 41–42. Hick develops this point and his "soul-making" theodicy at
greater length in *Evil and the God of Love* (New York: Harper and Row, 1966).

is the cornerstone of Hick's case for what he calls a "soul-making" *theodicy* (a justification to human reason of the ways of God): God creates a world in which suffering is possible so that human beings may develop the full range of virtues necessary to a flourishing character. Suffering is necessary for the complete growth of the human soul, so God allows suffering.

Hick implies that courage and its parent cardinal virtue—fortitude—could not develop outside of a context of danger or difficulty.[3] Patience is another virtue in the same complex which, it appears, could not be formed apart from unrelieved pain or some other form of difficulty to be borne over time.

After courage and fortitude, with the exception of prudence, all the other virtues named by Hick cluster around the theological virtue[4] of love. The case that these "love virtues" require a context of suffering for their formation seems less obvious. From a Christian theological perspective—shared by Hick and Johnny Cash—it is common to ascribe love, even perfect love, to God. And, at least traditionally, God does not suffer but has experienced love within His own being (as a Trinity of persons) prior to creation of the world.

However, some subset of love virtues might support Hick's case. Compassion may demand the experience of another's suffering in order to arise. How could Johnny Cash have grown the compassion demonstrated in his prison concerts in a world where no one suffers incarceration? Likewise, a world where there is deprivation and uneven distribution of goods seems necessary for the formation of generosity and unselfishness.

---

[3] Plato (427–347 B.C.E.) developed a categorization of positive character traits, four "cardinal virtues" (see *The Republic* 427c–434d). These are wisdom, fortitude, temperance, and justice. Aristotle (384–322 B.C.E.) and much later Thomas Aquinas (1227–1274 C.E.) took up this same classification of virtue. Fortitude is often equated with courage, but fortitude is a somewhat broader category, including elements such as perseverance and patience.

[4] To the Greek system of four cardinal virtues, Christian theology added three "theological virtues" of faith, hope, and love (charity), which are believed to be gifts from God (see 1 Corinthians 13:13). This theological tradition was carefully systematized by Aquinas (see *Summa Theologica* Parts I–II, Q. 62). The cardinal virtues are moral in nature, and are ordered toward a good life in this world and in relationship toward other human beings. The theological virtues, while possessing moral dimensions (especially in the case of love), are ordered toward a good life in the world to come and in relationship to God.

Generally, then, the argument for a soul-making theodicy turns upon the contention that the experience of suffering (or the experience of a world in which suffering occurs) fosters the development of human character, the formation of desirable virtues. The contention of such a theodicy, as Eleonore Stump puts it, is that suffering and human flourishing are connected in such a way that the former contributes to the latter. Stump argues that even if that connection exists, it is not sufficient to justify God in allowing certain kinds of evil.[5] Moreover, as I will show, if there exists a possibility that human virtues might arise apart from the presence of suffering—if the connection between suffering and virtue formation is not constant—then a soul-making theodicy is further weakened.

Get Tough or Die

One of Johnny Cash's most popular covers is "A Boy Named Sue," by Shel Silverstein. This darkly comic ballad ends with a kind of human fatherly "theodicy" for the suffering inflicted upon a young man by saddling him with the girl's name "Sue."

> And he said: "Son, this world is rough
> And if a man's gonna make it, he's gotta be tough
> And I knew I wouldn't be there to help ya along.
> So I give ya that name and I said goodbye
> I knew you'd have to get tough or die
> And it's the name that helped to make you strong."

The father's role in bringing about teasing and mockery—and perhaps attendant physical abuse—of his son is justified because such suffering produced "toughness," which is clearly understood to be a virtue.

Despite the dimension of theodicy in a "Boy Named Sue," in his autobiography Cash does not seem much inclined to inter-

---

[5] In her unpublished paper, "The Problem of Evil and the Desires of the Heart," Stump argues that, regardless of the connection between suffering and flourishing, a soul-making theodicy is insufficient because human flourishing also requires having the desires of one's heart. Because one form of suffering is the frustration of such desires (if one's desires are not well-ordered to actual or obtainable goods), not *all* suffering can be conducive to flourishing.

pret his own life in terms of character or virtue being formed by the experience of suffering. He tells of his brother Jack's death at the age of fourteen. And he movingly reflects on how the memory of Jack, and contemplation of what Jack might do or say in relation to Johnny's present life, has deeply influenced him. But Cash does not make a direct connection between that experience of grief and his own personal growth.

Indeed, at the conclusion of his reflections on Jack, in describing his mother's grief, he appears specifically to deny the connection between such anguish and the formation of virtue. He tells how the day after the funeral, his whole family was back in the fields, picking cotton. Overcome with sorrow, his mother "fell to her knees and let her head drop onto her chest." He continues:

> Lest you get too romantic an impression of the good, natural, hard-working, character-building country life back then, back there, remember that picture of Carrie Cash down in the mud between the cotton rows on any mother's worst possible day.[6]

So despite "A Boy Named Sue," and the general acceptance of the principle that suffering can help form character, *is* the experience of pain, sorrow or other suffering *necessary* as the occasion for formation of virtue? In particular, could the cardinal virtues of fortitude (which I will assume includes sub-virtues such as courage and patience) or temperance, or the theological virtue of love (which I will assume includes compassion and generosity), form *without* the occasion of suffering?

There has been a great deal of philosophical reflection on the nature of virtue, on the contrast between ethics formulated in terms of virtues and ethics formulated in terms of principles, and on the relations and hierarchies between the various virtues themselves. However, contemporary philosophers have been relatively silent on the specifics of how virtues are formed.

---

[6] *Cash: The Autobiography*, with Patrick Carr (San Francisco: HarperCollins, 1997), pp. 27–28.

Pain, Pleasure, and Habits

The classical locus for philosophical reflection on virtue formation is Aristotle's contention that virtue comes about by a
process of habituation:

> . . . the virtues we get by first exercising them, as also happens in
> the case of the arts as well. For the things we have to learn before
> we can do them, we learn by doing them, for example, men
> become builders by building and lyre players by playing the lyre;
> so too we become just by doing just acts, temperate by doing tem-
> perate acts, brave by doing brave acts.[7]

Aristotle considers the role of pleasure *and* pain in the process
of habituation which forms virtue:

> . . . by abstaining from pleasures we become temperate, and it is
> when we have become so that we are most able to abstain from
> them; and similarly too in the case of courage; for by being habit-
> uated to despise things that are terrible and to stand our ground
> against them we become brave, and it is when we have become so
> that we shall be most able to stand our ground against them.[8]

Thus Aristotle suggests that *both* pleasure and pain can be
circumstances for formation of virtue by a process of habituation. On the one hand, for example, pleasure is the occasion for
temperate acts which will eventually generate a habit of temperance. Johnny Cash's initial experience of the pleasure associated with amphetamines ought to have been the occasion for
him to behave temperately. Instead, he embarked on a course
of further indulgence: "every pill I took was an attempt to regain
the wonderful, natural feeling of euphoria I experienced the first
time."[9]

Cash missed the opportunity to form temperance early in life.
On the other hand, says Aristotle, pain is the occasion for coura-
geous acts which eventually generate a habit of courage. For
Cash, the pain of fatigue and guilt, and later physical pain from

---

[7] *Nicomachean Ethics,* Book II:1, in *The Basic Works of Aristotle* edited by
Richard McKeon (New York: Random House, 1941).
[8] *Nicomachean Ethics,* Book II:2.
[9] *Cash: The Autobiography,* p. 142.

various injuries and ailments, self-inflicted and otherwise, might have helped him to develop fortitude or even courage. Instead, mental and spiritual pain partly prompted his early amphetamine use. Later in life, after being attacked by an ostrich in an animal park near the House of Cash, the physical pain of several broken ribs and a nasty stomach injury became the occasion for adding prescription pain-killers to Cash's repertoire of drug abuse.[10] Again he missed an opportunity for virtue formation.

In Aristotle's account of the formation of virtue, a single act, in itself, is not necessarily a sign of virtue. That Cash was, on occasion, able to abstain from drugs for awhile, does not mean that he had developed the virtue of temperance. For Aristotle, a single act of bravery does not display the virtue of courage unless it meets three conditions. First, it must be known and understood to be a brave act. To commit a brash or foolish act, not recognizing a real danger, is not brave. Second, a virtuous act must be voluntary. An act which is compulsory or based on inappropriate motivation, is not bravery.[11] Third, virtuous actions must proceed from "a firm and unchangeable character."[12] It is this last characteristic of virtuous action which I find most relevant to the question of whether fortitude or compassionate love might arise or exist without being formed by a process of habituation occasioned by suffering.

Virtue, for Aristotle, is a state of character, a stable disposition to behave in a certain way, upon a relevant occasion. Johnny Cash's signature song, "I Walk the Line," is an ode to such stability of character centered around the virtue of faithfulness. There is a certain irony in the fact that the song was written for his first wife Vivian, to whom he was subsequently unfaithful. Johnny had not yet formed a character capable of

---

[10] *Cash: The Autobiography*, pp. 175–76.

[11] Aristotle's insistence on the volitional aspect of virtuous acts raises a paradox, since it appears that, eventually, habitual acts are performed without conscious choice or deliberation of the will. I believe Aristotle's intent is that virtuous behavior must not be contrary to one's will, nor governed by other factors motivating the will. Moreover, Aristotle's formulation of the motivational aspect of this condition is that virtuous action must be performed only for its own sake. However, most would consider brave acts performed for the sake of love for country or family to be acts of the virtue of bravery. But this takes us far afield.

[12] *Nicomachean Ethics* Book II:4.

sustaining such stability in a relationship. Only after suffering the pain of his broken relationship with Vivian did he begin to form a stronger faithfulness to his second wife June.

However, Aristotle's description of the formation of virtue is not meant to cover all possible cases, but, as is often the case in his thought, to describe what occurs generally and for the most part. Even if a process of habituation on the occasion of pain is necessary for the formation of many virtues most of the time, there still remains the possibility that a stable disposition toward certain actions can come to be and exist within a person without any experience of a relevant occasion for the behavior toward which the disposition is directed. Might one learn to "walk the line" without a process of habituation whereby one repeatedly remains faithful in situations that challenge faithfulness or make it difficult? Could one be courageous without ever experiencing any occasion of danger in which to exercise courage? If the answer is yes, then, again, the force of a soul-making theodicy is weakened.

Aristotle's account allows for virtue formation on the occasion of pleasure. Speaking from the Christian tradition in which Johnny Cash's own life unfolded, we may wonder if it would be possible for God to create a world in which formation of virtue was occasioned *only* by the stimulus of pleasure. Such painless virtue formation might be possible for interpersonal virtues like various forms of love which carry a strong positive reinforcement of pleasure. However, some virtues, like temperance, may *require* an element of suffering for their acquisition, particularly for those like Johnny Cash who fail to behave temperately upon first experiences of addictive substances which bring pleasure. Given initial failure to behave temperately, the painful negative consequences of intemperance could be necessary stimuli for the eventual formation of temperance.

Genes or God?

Thomas Aquinas, the most significant Christian expositor of the Aristotelian scheme of virtue, discusses two additional possibilities for the formation of human virtue. In his Question regarding the causes of virtue,[13] Aquinas considers first whether virtue

---

[13] *Summa Theologia* II:I, Question 63.

might be "in us by nature." In contemporary terms, a virtue might be an innate or inherited disposition based in genetics (as in sociobiology's contention that altruism is a survival trait favored by natural selection).

Both virtue and vice appear naturally in varying degrees in different people, apart from any experience of occasions for those habits of character. Johnny Cash succumbed to addiction almost immediately upon his first experience of the pleasures of drugs. Yet others take similar medications and are immediately inclined to moderate their use and become temperate in regard to drugs. Some of the difference in response seems to be innate rather than acquired. There has been success in linking certain genes to addictive behaviors.

Likewise we may imagine a variety of responses by individuals upon a first exposure to a fellow human being in dire need. Some people possess what appears to be an innate compassion which immediately produces acts of kindness. Though Johnny Cash showed little innate aptitude for temperance, there is evidence in much of his music (for example, the 1964 recording of "The Ballad of Ira Hayes," before Native American rights had become a fashionable cause) that he had a natural sensitivity and compassion toward the suffering of others. At his funeral, "artist after artist told how he had bought them food, paid for accommodations, donated guitars, or even clothed them when they fell on hard times."[14] Others, unlike Cash, must make an effort to do compassionate acts, and may find themselves initially revolted by or indifferent toward the needy person, so that the virtue of compassion is only slowly acquired. Different people find themselves, in relation to any particular virtue, beginning with very different aptitudes for or dispositions toward that virtue.

Despite the experience of some natural disposition toward virtue, Aquinas denies that any virtue as such is in us by nature. Noting the differences among individuals in aptitude for virtue, he argues that virtue is nonetheless not a feature of general human nature, though there is a general, natural *potential* for virtue. Insofar as innate capacities for bravery, compassion, temperance and the like differ among individuals, they constitute varying degrees of potential for particular virtues. What

---

[14] *The Man Called Cash*, p. 227.

appears to be innate compassion is an aptitude for compassion, rather than a properly formed virtue of compassion itself. He makes a distinction between virtue appearing in a person *inchoately* by nature, but only *perfectly* by habituation and character formation.

Aquinas maintains that an aptitude for a certain virtue must be perfected by becoming active in a variety of circumstances, thus demonstrating the whole range of the virtue. The person who is initially temperate with regard to addictive substances may subsequently succumb to addiction unless she, through regular practice, forms a habit of temperate behavior on a variety of occasions. Thus the possibility of innate virtue does not count strongly against the connection between suffering and virtue formation.

Aquinas also considers the question whether God might be able to infuse moral virtues in human beings in the same way He infuses the theological virtues of faith, hope and love. In effect, Aquinas asks, would it be possible for God to act supernaturally to form the character of a person so that she possesses a virtue like temperance or compassion, apart from any process of acquisition through experience and habituation? Yes and no, answers Aquinas.

Yes, says Aquinas, God can infuse moral virtues like temperance or fortitude, just as He infuses in humans the theological virtues, faith, hope and charity. However, infused moral virtues will be of a different species from those occurring naturally. Infused temperance, because its source is God rather than nature, will be ordered toward supernatural rather than natural ends. Naturally developed temperance will use food and drink in a properly balanced manner ordered toward the health of the body. Supernaturally infused temperance more rigidly abstains from food and drink in a manner ordered toward the health of the soul. Infused virtue differs from acquired virtue, even when it goes by the same name. Thus Aquinas seems to suggest that if God had infused Johnny Cash with supernatural temperance he would have become an ascetic, rather than merely more moderate in his use of addictive substances.

At the end of his Question on the causes of virtue, Aquinas also states briefly that God could, if He wished, miraculously give a human being "virtues, such as those acquired by acts." That is, God could have, without use of intervening causes like physical pain and mental suffering, directly created a temperate Johnny Cash. Aquinas simply states both here and, by implication in a previous question,[15] that God does not generally choose to do so, except as a special manifestation of His power.

These possibilities of either naturally innate virtue or supernaturally caused virtue are supported by analogy with the causal dispositions of natural agents. In the Aristotelian framework, one may speak of the powers and liabilities of objects in the natural world. These powers and liabilities are dispositions to behave in certain ways under the proper conditions. Potassium of sufficient purity has a disposition to ignite in the presence of oxygen. Sodium chloride has a disposition to dissolve in water. All physical objects have a disposition to move toward each other according to the laws of gravity. And these dispositions exist in the objects regardless of whether there has ever been any occasion for them to be exercised. They are a matter of the physical structure of objects and elements in the material world.

Suppose, then, that there could be a structuring of a human character toward virtuous disposition analogous to the structuring which results in causal dispositions in physical objects. It might very well be the case that virtues like courage or compassion could arise and persist in a person's character, without there ever being any occasion for the behavior towards which that virtue disposes the person. Such structuring of character might have a natural cause such as genes favored by natural selection or a supernatural cause in the miraculous power of God.

Guess Things Happen that Way

We have found there is both a scientific and theological possibility that virtue may form apart from suffering. Despite it being generally and almost always the case that some virtues like temperance, courage and compassion are formed upon experience of suffering, the connection is not absolute. Therefore, we may conclude that the connection between suffering and the formation of character is insufficient to ground a full and robust

---

[15] *Summa Theologia* II:I, Question 52, Article 4.

theodicy. Not all pain, deprivation, mental anguish and the like may be explained by soul-making. We cannot justify God's allowing of suffering solely by appeal to its effect in building character. As seen earlier, Cash seems to have felt that instinctively in response to his mother's suffering.

Moreover, in regard to soul-making theodicy, we might ask *why* God did not simply infuse Cash (or most others) with supernaturally generated virtues of temperance and compassion or constitute the world in such a way that natural selection would form such virtues more reliably. A soul-making theodicy standing alone is too weak. Character formation cannot offer a complete justification for God's allowing of evil and suffering in human life. As one Cash song says—while it nonetheless expresses personal growth in manhood and strength as the outcome of a lost love—some pain and suffering are left unexplained: "Guess things happen that way."

Nonetheless, regardless of its efficacy for theodicy, both general human experience and the life and art of Johnny Cash are solid evidence for a reliable connection between suffering and formation of virtue. Regret for past behavior expressed in songs like "Cocaine Blues" and "Don't Take Your Guns to Town," is occasioned by painful consequences. Such regret can be the seed of developing virtue.

In the addiction intervention by his friends and family described in Cash's autobiography, his experience of mental and physical pain and his apprehension of the suffering he caused his friends and family motivated him toward some further growth in temperance. He tells how his son, John Carter, wrote a letter describing a drunken episode in front of his friends, "embarrassing him and them terribly. I had to hold him and hug him while he read it, to keep his tears back . . ."[16] Thus his natural sensitivity to another's pain, which easily called forth compassion in Cash, ultimately became the occasion for progress in temperance, a virtue he found more difficult. He accepted treatment at the Betty Ford Center then and at other clinics several times later.

Therefore, a "beer for breakfast," understood as a metaphor for confronting pain with a conscious and deliberate acceptance, in conjunction with an attempt to learn from it, often has

---

[16] *Cash: The Autobiography*, p. 180.

a salutary effect upon human life, calling forth the development of good character which would not otherwise exist.

Redemption

One last note regarding theodicy: though "soul-making" and other theodicies are found to be incomplete explanations of human suffering, there may be more to say. Johnny Cash discovered the deepest answers to his own pain in God's participation in suffering through the life and death of Jesus Christ. From his earliest years, he responded to pain by turning to Christian faith. As he sings in "Redemption,"

> And the blood gave life
> To the branches of the tree
> And the blood was the price
> That set the captives free.

Personal suffering is ultimately redeemed in Christ's own suffering:

> And with the numbers that came
> Through the fire and the flood
> I clung to the tree
> And was redeemed by the blood.

These theological convictions may explain why Cash makes so little autobiographical connection between his personal suffering and his own growth in character. He's convinced that his growth and redemption are not primarily the product of successful response to his own suffering, but the gracious benefit of his Savior's suffering. So he sings Kris Kristofferson's song, "Why me, Lord?" addressing God not in regard to suffering in his life, but in regard to his own undeserved experience of "the kindness you've shown." Such humility and gratitude might themselves be further evidence of a character formed by suffering.[17]

---

[17] I am grateful to my wife Beth Bilynskyj, to my friends Terry Glaspey and Jay Wood, and to the editors for helpful comments on earlier drafts of this paper.

17

The Beast in Me: Evil in Cash's Christian Worldview

JAMIE CARLIN WATSON

In a 1982 interview with Johnny Cash for the news show *60 Minutes*, reporter Harry Reasoner pointed out some of the unsavory aspects of some of Cash's songs and contrasted them with his religious lyrics and his professed Christianity. When Reasoner asked Cash whether he had trouble reconciling the two, Cash responded, saying, "No. Roy Orbison had a line in a song . . . that says, 'A diamond is a diamond and a stone is a stone, but a man is part good and part bad.' You know, I recognize the fact that I'm part good and part bad."

In his lyrics Cash looked at controversial social and ethical concerns in light of the Christian convictions he acquired growing up in rural Arkansas. This region was well acquainted with suffering and evil. From drought to disease, labor accidents to death in childbirth. Such hardships might bring to mind the despair of Steinbeck's *The Grapes of Wrath*. But in Cash's case, Christian hope prevailed in the face of evil. Traditionally, however, worldviews that combine the existence of God with the existence of evil raise difficult philosophical questions.

"Ring of Fire": An Augustinian Account of Evil

Traditionally there are three views of the nature of evil: the monistic view, the dualistic view, and the privation view. The privation view was most fully developed in the theology of Aurelius Augustine (354–430), and is what I am calling the "Augustinian view."

According to the monistic view, a single god or deity is the ground of all being, so that everything that exists has its ultimate explanation in the god. On this view "evil" is just one of a myriad of human experiences, and therefore, like "good," "red," "hot," and "loud," has its ultimate origins in the one creator god. Throughout history, few, if any, religions have actually held this as a positive view. More often, belief systems that seem to entail that a god is the author of evil are criticized as inconsistent or untenable.[1]

The seventeenth-century philosopher Gottfried Leibniz (1646–1716) is sometimes seen as a monist about evil. Leibniz divided descriptions of good and evil into three categories: metaphysical, moral, and physical. For Leibniz, God is the author of human freedom, and therefore is the author of all the possibilities for which humans can use their freedom.[2] On this reading, as explained by Protestant theologian John Feinberg, since God is the creator of these possibilities, Leibniz seems forced to say that, in creating Adam, God had to create the possibility of Adam sinning *along with* the possibility of Adam not sinning.[3] To avoid any moral corruption on God's part, Leibniz defends the idea that God, because he is necessarily good, is forced to create "the greatest number and variety of existents" (p. 41), that is, the *metaphysically best* of all possible worlds.

---

[1] In the case of monism, a god's creation of evil need not be contradictory. However, since Christianity holds that God is all good and all powerful, if the existence of evil entails that God must have created evil, or is somehow responsible for evil, then the view entails a contradiction and should be rejected. What is known as the "logical" form of this argument has been refuted by Alvin Plantinga, *God, Freedom, and Evil* (Eerdmans, 1974). The "evidential" form of this argument—the contention that there is enough evil in the world (or enough evil of a certain kind) to make it more likely than not that God does not exist—continues to fuel academic discussion.

[2] Leibniz, *Theodicy*, Part 1, Sections 21, 52. God is constrained to create all possibilities, so it seems that what is possible is not up to him. Leibniz does not think this diminishes God's perfection or freedom, but this deserves much more attention. See also *Theodicy*, Part 1, Section 53, and Part 3, Section 367, and appendices.

[3] John S. Feinberg, *The Many Faces of Evil* (Zondervan, 1994), p. 40, from Leibniz, *Theodicy*, Part 3, Section 275. The idea seems to be that, in order to create the best possible world—one with the greatest amount of good and the least amount of evil—God had to create the possible Adam that sins as opposed to the possible Adam that does not.

The most metaphysical goodness, however, may entail much moral and physical evil, since, given his perfection, he can never create anything as perfect as himself. This has led some critics to argue that Leibniz's theology has the fatal flaw of making God the author of moral evil; that is, it is a monistic view, and should therefore be rejected.[4]

Similarly, the Manichees (Man-ih-keys) criticized Augustine, claiming that Christianity ultimately entails monism.[5] Augustine had been attracted to a sect of Gnosticism led by the prophet Manes (or Mani, or Manichaeus) (215–276), beginning when he was nineteen and continuing, he tells us, for nine years.[6] The Manichees held a dualistic view of evil, which claims that good and evil ("darkness" and "light") are distinct supernatural forces, vying for control of the cosmos. As we will see, Augustine's privation view is an attempt to reject both monism and dualism.

The dualist account of evil goes back to the earliest animistic cultures (such as Native American and pre-Christian Anglo-Saxon religions) and polytheistic religions (such as Mesopotamian and Egyptian religions). According to this view, good and evil are equal and opposing supernatural forces, pitted against one another in a cosmic struggle. Within this struggle, humans find themselves torn between the opponents, acting on behalf of one side or the other, but always subject to the consequences of evil and good actions. Augustine tells us that rather than holding humans responsible for their evils, the Manichees taught, "The cause of thy sin is inevitably determined in heaven," and "This did Venus, or Saturn, or Mars" (*Confessions*, Book IV, Section 4).

Traditional Hebraic, Rabbinic, and early Christian theologies avoided both monistic and dualistic views of evil, placing the blame for depravity squarely in the hands of humans. Though their theological conceptions of good and evil were not fully developed until much later, God was always considered the

---

[4] This extreme concession on Leibniz's part led Voltaire to caricature his position in the absurd character of Dr. Pangloss in *Candide*. When confronted with the evils of war, Dr. Pangloss responds, "All this was indispensably necessary . . . for private misfortunes are public benefits; so the more private misfortunes there are, the greater is the general good."
[5] Augustine tells us this in *Retractions* (A.D. 426–27).
[6] Augustine, *Confessions*, Book IV, Section 1.

ultimate force in the universe. And though there were evil forces, none were powerful enough to compete with the Creator. Though we get glimpses of this view in the Jewish Scriptures, the New Testament, the writings of the early Christian church fathers, and even Greek thinkers such as Plato and Plotinus, the earliest systematic version of the privation view is Augustine's.

"Dark as a Dungeon": The Problem of Evil

Cash's Christianity holds that God is all knowing, all powerful, and all good, which seems to suggest that, he knows about any evil that might exist, that he has the power to prevent it, and that he is willing to do so. Augustine put the point succinctly in *On Free Will*:

> We believe that everything which exists is created by one God, and yet that God is not the cause of sin. The difficulty is: if sin goes back to [or, is caused by] souls created by God, and souls go back to God, how can we avoid before long tracing sin back to God? (Book I, Section 2)

This is the classic Problem of Evil.[7] If God is good, then there should be no evil, but since there is evil, either God does not exist or God is the author of evil, and therefore not good. An attempt to defend God's goodness or justice in the face of evil is called a "theodicy." We can divide Augustine's theodicy into four components: (1) defining evil, (2) justifying God's goodness in light of moral evil, (3) justifying God's goodness in light of the evil suffered by animals and innocents, and (4) justifying God's goodness in light of the immense amount of evil in the world.

In defining evil, Augustine takes cues from Plato, who claimed that "good" is just "what exists," or pure being, and evil is the lack of existence, or non-being. The Platonic view has been criticized because evil seems to admit of degrees, while existence does not. While an act can be better or worse, a thing

---

[7] Augustine attempts to solve this problem in several of his writings, including, *On Order* (A.D. 386), *On Free Will*, (begun in A.D. 388), and *Retractions* (A.D. 426–427).

can only exist or not exist. Augustine revises the Platonic view, explaining that evil is not a species of non-existence, but a tendency toward non-existence, a corruption of that which exists.[8] Augustine writes, "For a thing to be bad is for it to fall away from being and tend to a state in which it is not" (*On the Morals of the Manichaeans*, 2:2). Therefore, evil is a privation, or corruption, of goodness.

As a tendency toward non-being, then, evil has no positive existence. So, just as "darkness" does not "exist," but is just the absence of light, so "evil" does not exist positively as an entity, but is merely the absence of good. And just as the absence of light can come in degrees, so can the absence of good. Since evil has no positive existence, its origin cannot be traced back to God as its creator.

Augustine distinguishes two forms evil can take, "the evil a man has done, and the evil he has suffered" (*On Free Will*, Book I, Section 1). The evil a person does is obviously moral evil, and the evil a person suffers can be the result of moral or natural evil, or punishment by God for sin. Because everyone sins, all suffering is justified as punishment on some level, whether the evil is inflicted through other humans, natural causes (diseases, disasters), or direct divine retribution. Augustine has no trouble saying that God causes evil in the case of punishment for moral crimes. Those experiencing punishment will experience it as "evil," but justice is being served, and therefore God cannot be considered immoral.

It's not clear that Johnny Cash had any knowledge of these views or their development, but we can certainly identify strands of Augustinian thought in his lyrics. To trace an Augustinian view in Cash's lyrics, in contrast to monism and dualism, we need to identify three elements. First, we need to see Cash attributing blame for moral evil to humans alone, and not to God or various other supernatural entities. Second, we need to see a perspective of natural evil that avoids seeing God as unjust in permitting it. And third, we need an explanation for why God permits the amount and heinousness of evil we experience.

---

[8] Christopher Kirwan, *Augustine* (New York: Routledge, 1989), p. 62.

"God Help the Beast in Me": Cash's View
of Moral Evil

In the *60 Minutes* interview Cash asserts that he is "part good and part bad." This claim raises a philosophical question about the origin of our "bad" elements. If Cash means to say that we are *essentially* part good and bad, then it seems he is implicitly adhering to a monistic view of evil, since then we would have been *created* evil. I think the lyrical evidence leads us away from this conclusion. Cash's songs reflect a deep sense of *human* responsibility for moral evil in the world. Therefore, a better interpretation is that we are born with *tendencies* to act certain ways, but we *choose* whether to give in. As Augustine would say, we follow either reason or our passions, and unrestrained passions lead us toward evil.

But how does our ability to choose absolve God from the responsibility for our actions? Isn't he strong enough to prevent us from doing evil, or couldn't he have created humans so that they wouldn't choose evil? Isn't he good enough to care whether we hurt one another?

According to Augustine, God created humans as morally free creatures. Without free will we would not be "human" in any morally significant sense. Philosopher John Hick explains that, "God is able to create beings of any and every conceivable kind; but creatures who lack moral freedom, however superior they might be to human beings in other respects, would not be what we mean by persons."[9] Therefore, it is impossible that God create human "persons" who lack the freedom required for moral responsibility.

In giving humans freedom God gives them the ability to causally determine themselves. This causal separation of human actions from divine actions absolves God of culpability for moral evils.[10] But since God created humans, and if evil is a thing

---

[9] John Hick, *Philosophy of Religion* (Prentice Hall, 1963), quoted in William F. Lawhead, *Philosophical Questions* (McGraw Hill, 2003), p. 113.

[10] This aspect of Augustine's argument is called the "free will defense." Philosopher Alvin Plantinga (*God, Freedom, and Evil*) distinguishes between a theodicy, which he describes as offering a positive reason for God's allowing evil in the world, and a "defense," which he defines as showing that there is no contradiction in God's permitting evil. This is a bit of a technical point, but the idea is that we might not currently have access to all the good brought

humans create, Augustine worries that the creation of evil might still ultimately derive from God. This is partly because God is considered the only force in the universe that can create something from nothing. This is where the privation view does a great deal of work. Since evil is merely a corruption of good, it is not a positive thing in itself. Humans cannot create something without God's help, but they can, through their free will, diminish something good, thereby bringing about evil.

In an Augustinian vein, Cash's "Cocaine Blues" captures its audience's desire for power and reckless abandon, then quickly identifies the corruption inherent in that lifestyle. In the end, Cash urges his audience to avoid his vices. The prisoner in Folsom Prison never displaces blame for his crime, and never complains of any injustice in his incarceration. The blame in "The Ballad of Ira Hayes" is placed squarely on the passivity of citizens indifferent to the injustices of the government. Corruption of conscience leads the protagonist of "The Wall" to commit "suicide" when he finds out that the person for whom he committed so many immoral acts is marrying another. In all these instances, human actions have corrupted good things and the offenders recognize that they are justly paying the price.

There is also an element of *fate* in Cash's conception of moral evil, which might seem ironic or inconsistent on the face of it. In "The Beast in Me" he sets himself in opposition to his inner "beast" that "rants and rages at the stars." And similarly, in "Bird on a Wire," the singer says that, "like a drunk in a midnight choir," he has tried, in his way, "to be free." These words sound as if Cash's characters are lamenting a complete inability to resist sin. But I think this fatalism is better interpreted as an irresistible *tendency toward* sin, rather than an irresistible *compulsion to* sin, the latter of which might then implicate the Creator.

It is true that Cash made public statements implicating, not God or man, but the devil or forces of evil, in certain evils, as

about by evil, or (in our finite mental capacities) we might not be able to comprehend the immense good God brings of evil. Therefore, a defense is a much easier task. But, whereas Augustine's free will defense may not itself be a theodicy, his argument as a whole certainly includes a theodicy. He claims, positively, that God brings good out of every evil that does not arise from immorality or punishment for sin.

he did on his television show. But even here, the forces are enabling rather than compulsory. The "devil" does not *cause* us to sin any more than God *causes* us to do good, since in either case our moral responsibility would be usurped. This is consistent with the Apostle Paul's personal struggle with an inner propensity toward evil. In his letter to the church at Rome, Paul writes, "For I do not do the good I want, but the evil I do not want is what I do. . . . I see in my members another law at war with the law of my mind, making me captive to the law of sin" (Romans 7:18–19; 23; New Revised Standard Version).

For Cash, this tendency is seen as a matter of chance, rather than responsibility. In his cover of Glenn Danzig's "13" the character attributes the fact that he was "born to bring trouble" to a "bad luck wind." This might be true for Paul as well, given that, for Christians, the tendency toward sin is part of fallen human nature. For both the Apostle Paul and Cash, the *temptation* to sin is unavoidable, though, in order to be blameworthy for sin, sin must be avoidable.[11] In the face of temptation, both Paul and Cash turn their attention toward God. Paul asks and answers, "Who will rescue me from this body of death? Thanks be to God through Jesus Christ our Lord!" (Romans 7:24–25). Cash cries out, "God help the beast in me!"

"Bad Luck Wind": Cash's View of Natural Evil

There is much less discussion of natural evil in Cash's lyrics than moral evil. The only unambiguous case seems to be found in "Guess Things Happen that Way." Other cues can be taken from songs about manual labor and rural hardships, particularly "I Never Picked Cotton" and "Five Feet High and Rising," and his public comments on the latter.

Augustine held that natural evil can either have a goal, for instance, to bring about some greater good, or it can be com-

---

[11] In his earlier writings, Augustine argues that humans are free to act, guided by their own wills and desires. Since humans possess the capacity to act but lack divine moral perfection, temptation is inevitable. In Augustine's later writings he is forced to retract full human responsibility for certain theological reasons. But Cash's lyrics resist this later development.

pletely senseless.[12] Augustine doesn't give us any examples of senseless evil, so it is difficult to tell what might count. And, in fact, in one place he says that the "whole range of evil" consists in "sin and its penalty" (*Of True Religion*, Section 12). Most natural evils, such as disease and disaster, appear to possess purpose, so it would be irrational to say that any significant amount of natural evil is just a matter of chance. For Augustine, the foremost purpose natural calamities seem to serve is punishment for moral evil, of which all humans are guilty. And even if we cannot perceive the good natural evils bring about in any specific case, we can be confident that God has something in mind that is better than the good that would have endured without the evil.

While Cash is fully willing to place the blame for moral evils with human free will, the same is not the case with natural evils. At least that is the case in "Guess Things Happen That Way." The story seems to be about the death of the character's beloved. Though he does not mention death specifically, explaining that God "put him on his own," seems to indicate that it was more than just irreconcilable differences that separated the couple.[13] But the nature of the reference to God is particularly interesting. Cash's character blames God for his loss. This wouldn't be such an interesting development if the character was eaten up with rage or grief, but he is quite realistic about the situation, admitting that he will eventually get over his sorrow and move on to be with someone else. We can identify with his emotional protest, "I don't like it," and resignation, "but I guess things happen that way."

The philosophical question here is whether it is legitimate for Cash to attribute blame to God for taking his love away. The answer seems to be yes, since most evils are used to bring about something better or serve as justice for sin. Though Cash's character does not attempt to identify the good that might come of God "putting him on his own," it's clear that he bears no ill will to the person he considers responsible.

---

[12] Hans Schwarz, *Evil: A Historical and Theological Perspective* (Fortress, 1995), p. 102.

[13] This is further supported by songs where a couple does separate over interpersonal problems and the blame is placed with the person who caused the conflict. Examples include, "Cry, Cry, Cry," "Kate," and "There You Go."

Corollary evidence for thinking Cash is Augustinian with regard to natural evil comes from songs about labor and life in the rural South. In "I Never Picked Cotton," Cash's character recounts how, because of celebrity success, he never had to work as hard as his family or endure the hardships that permeate a farming lifestyle. But at the end of the song, reflecting on his fame and wealth in light of facing the gallows for a crime of passion, he regrets that he has nothing to be proud of. The implication is that sufferings and hardships that accompany the difficult farming life engender worth and meaning beyond the meager physical sustenance that lifestyle provides.

And finally, in "Five Feet High and Rising," the child character in the song is transfixed by the power and destructiveness of the flood. The notable element of this song is its intentional lack of reference to a meaning for, or a cause of, the destruction. As onlookers, we are perplexed, wondering why the child does not ask broader questions, such as *why* the event is happening.

Augustine attributes natural evil to either sin or greater good, and Cash offers spotty hints of it in his lyrics. Publicly, however, he was more forthcoming. In a recently released live concert called "The Great Lost Performance" from 1990, Cash told the audience about the flood in "Five Feet High" and recalled his mother's words, "if you look for it and commit it to the Lord . . . there's a blessing that will always come in times of adversity." When Cash's family came back to their home "the blessing was already there . . . the land was covered with rich black river dirt," and that year the cotton "grew taller than ever before." Cash leaves us with the full weight of the Augustinian tension. Despite the hardship of being forced out of his home by flood and all the damage that goes along with it, Cash echoes Augustine (in a Southern drawl, of course) and emphasizes the greater good, the "blessing," that follows adversity.

"A Boy Named Sue": A Cashian Theodicy

A question left looming ever larger behind Cash's accounts of moral and natural evil is why God would allow the immensity of evil we experience. At any given time, the evils we experience seem so heinous that it is almost impossible to imagine what greater good could possibly justify God's tolerance. And even if the good did outweigh the bad in the long run, couldn't we blame God if the distribution of evil seems to be unfair to some?

The simple Augustinian response that humans either deserve what they get or God has something better in store for them seems to fall flat in the face of our experience. But Augustine was so confident in his answer that he never gave it a stronger or more precise formulation. And in responding to critics concerning the natural sufferings of children and animals, he is almost dismissive, relegating the solution to the mysteries of God's will.[14]

Though we typically see the need to hold people responsible for their actions, there is clearly a limit to justice, beyond which a punishment does not fit the crime. Augustine offers nothing to address this concern beyond claiming that the good wrought through suffering is sometimes beyond human ability to conceive. As it stands, Augustine's view of why God tolerates evil is rocky at best. Christopher Kirwan says that the "free will defense," as Augustine formulates it, "is not at all convincing as a justification of God's tolerance of sin."[15] Therefore, Augustine's view leaves us with a very uneasy tension about the amount of evil in the world.

Cash honed in on this Augustinian tension with his masterful rendering of Shel Silverstein's "A Boy Named Sue." The song begins by recounting the plight of a life lived under a gender-challenging name, given by a deserted father. After a bloody father-son reunion, Sue finds out that the painful trials of his life served a greater good. The father says:

> "Son, this world is rough
> And if a man's gonna make it, he's gotta be tough
> And I knew I wouldn't be there to help ya along.
> So I give ya that name and I said goodbye
> I knew you'd have to get tough or die
> And it's that name that helped to make you strong."

Sue doesn't feel that the good wrought in him through his suffering was enough to warrant subjecting his own offspring to

---

[14] Augustine, *On Free Will*, Book III, Section 23.
[15] Kirwan, *Augustine*, p. 80.

a similar trial. Despite coming away with "a different point of view," he announces that if he has a son he'll name him, "Bill or George! Any damn thing but Sue! I still hate that name!"

Perhaps we all feel that the evils of the world are just too great for God to be justified in using them for any conceivable good. Contemporary Augustinian-style defenses against the problem of evil have focused on the nature of the good that is intended for the evil we experience. Philosopher John Hick explains that

> Christianity...has never supposed that God's purpose in the cre-
> ation of the world was to construct a paradise whose inhabitants
> would experience a maximum of pleasure and a minimum of pain.
> The world is seen, instead, as a place of "soul-making" in which
> free beings, grappling with the tasks and challenges of their exis-
> tence in a common environment, may become "children of God"
> and "heirs to eternal life."[16]

Hick defends the idea that humans are created for a better world, so that the evil we experience here is "building" us for a better world to come.

Cash's view seems less sophisticated, expressing only confidence that, regardless of what we have endured, humanity will experience ultimate justice and satisfaction in the afterlife. In "The Circle Won't Be Broken," Cash has faith that the injustice of the tragic childhood death of his older brother will be undone. He implies in "When the Man Comes Around" that there will be *shalom* (peace) after Armageddon (traditionally, the last battle before the end of the world). Even the protagonist in "Let the Train Blow the Whistle," who expects to spend eternity in "the fires," explains that all his debts will have been paid when he has died.

Whether the promise of ultimate justice and satisfaction is viewed simply as a reward for evil suffered, or as the culmination of "soul-making," Johnny Cash expresses the difficult tension between God and evil alongside the Augustinian picture that humans are solely responsible for evil and that God will ultimately make things right.[17]

---

[16] John Hick, *Philosophy of Religion*, in Lawhead, *Philosophical Questions*, p. 114.
[17] Thanks to the editors of this volume for helpful suggestions and corrections on earlier drafts.

18
The Jagged Edge

DAVID WERTHER

The film *Walk the Line* begins with Johnny Cash staring at the blade of a circular saw, waiting to take the stage at Folsom Prison. The blade's jagged edge brings to mind Jack Cash's death. On May 12th, 1944, twelve-year-old Johnny (then known as J.R.) tried to convince his older brother Jack to go fishing with him. Jack refused, determined to spend the day earning some extra money, cutting fence poles on a circular saw. Later that day, their father came looking for Johnny and told him something terrible had happened to Jack. He then took Johnny to the smoke house and showed him Jack's bloody clothes. The saw had torn Jack from his rib cage to his groin. Jack managed to hang on to life for seven days. Shortly before his death, he asked his mother if she could hear the angels, and talked about seeing a river running two ways. Johnny had no doubt that a current would carry Jack to God.

For years the official story was that Jack's death had been an accident. However, in an interview with Nick Tosches, Cash suggested otherwise.

> The story of Jack's death . . . has been retold many times. Now Cash tells me it is not the whole truth. His brother's death, he says, was an accident only 'in the family's mind'. It was murder, he tells me, speaking slowly, deliberately, with the tone of one drawing words from an uncomfortable place.
>
> "There was a neighbor that went down to the shop with him that day and disappeared after the accident. We couldn't prove

anything, but I always thought of it as murder . . . Nothin' was ever done about it."[1]

One wonders how, if at all, Cash could see this murder as something other than a refutation of the Christian convictions he shared with Jack. Couldn't God have prevented this killing and wouldn't God have wanted to do so? Why then the blood-soaked clothing in the smoke house?

Big Foot and the Seventh Cavalry

When philosophers reflect on the existence and significance of evil, they distinguish between two sorts of evil: moral and natural. Moral evil concerns the pain and suffering caused by moral agents: folks like us who have the ability to choose between right and wrong, and-speaking for myself-all too often choose wrongly. Assuming that Cash's theory of Jack's death is correct, Jack's demise would be an instance of moral evil. In contrast, natural evil concerns the pain and suffering caused by—in the language of insurance agents—*Acts of God*: hurricanes, floods, tsunamis and the like. Sometimes natural and moral evils run together, as when poverty forces a family to live on a flood plain with the predictable results: "Five Feet High and Rising."

Thoughtful people allow that some of the evils in our world appear to be—in one way or another—incompatible with the existence of a perfectly good and powerful being. David Hume's (1711–1776) citation of the philosopher, Epicurus (around 300 B.C.), readily resonates with us.

> *Epicurus'* old questions are yet unanswered.
> Is he willing to prevent evil, but not able? then he is impotent. Is he able, but not willing? then he is malevolent. Is he both able and willing? whence then is evil?[2]

Discussion of the apparent incompatibility between the existence of evil and the existence of an all-powerful and all-know-

---

[1] Nick Tosches, "Chordless in Gaza: The Second Coming of J.R. Cash" in *Ring of Fire: The Johnny Cash Reader* (Cambridge, Massachusetts: Da Capo, 2002) p. 233.
[2] David Hume, *Dialogues Concerning Natural Religion*, Part X, (Indianapolis: Hackett, 1982), p. 63.

ing being takes different forms. For ease of exposition and relevance to the life and work of Cash, I will take any mention of this all-powerful and all-knowing being to refer to the one Cash staked his hopes on, prayers on, the Christian God. However, subsequent use of the term "God" does not presuppose that there is such a being, as our concern is whether the existence of one sort of evil or another rules that out.

Philosophers have reflected on the implications of the existence of evil for God's existence in different ways. It is then, more accurate to speak of "the problems of evil" than "the problem of evil." In the case of moral evils, philosophers distinguish between the evidential problem of evil and the logical problem of evil. According to the former, the mere existence of moral evil need not make it unreasonable to suppose that God exists. Rather, it is the quantity and quality of the evils in the world that seem to render belief in God irrational. Concerning quantity, if Jack's murder and Johnny's unfaithfulness to Vivian Liberto, were the only evils that had occurred since the Big Bang, one might reasonably believe that God exists. But, since infidelity runs rampant and recent F.B.I. crime clocks suggest that, in the U.S. alone, there will be a murder every half hour, there's more than enough evil to make one wonder about God's existence.

Concerning the quality of evil, if the worst evil in our world was Ray Cash's shooting of his five-year-old son's beloved dog, because "we didn't need another dog around here"[3] one might still reasonably believe God exists. But, that cruel act is hardly at the top of the scale. To site an example from the Cash corpus, there is the Seventh Cavalry's senseless slaughter of the Sioux at Wounded Knee, a horror Cash sings about in "Bigfoot." When we reflects on both the quantity and the quality of moral evil in our world, we might suppose that the likelihood of God's existence diminishes to the vanishing point.

Walking the Line

In contrast to the evidential problem of moral evil, according to the logical problem of moral evil, any moral evil at all is enough

---

[3] Dave Urbanski, *The Man Comes Around: The Spiritual Journey of Johnny Cash* (Lake Mary Florida: Relevant Books, 2003), pp. 9–10.

to rule out God's existence. To see why consider Cash's infidelity. Suppose it were the only moral evil. That alone may seem enough to exclude God's existence. We can see this by developing a line of argument inspired by Epicurus's questions, focusing on Cash's unfaithfulness.

- If there were a perfectly good being, that being would want Cash to keep his pledge to "walk the line."

- If there were a perfectly powerful being, that being would see to it that Cash freely kept his pledge.

- But Cash was unfaithful.

- So, there is not a being that is both perfectly good and perfectly powerful.

- Cash's Christian God is perfectly good and perfectly powerful.

- But no being is perfectly good and powerful.

- So, Cash's God does not exist.

This line of reasoning seems straightforward enough. A merely good being, much less a perfectly good being, would want Cash to keep his promises. And, it seems incredible to suppose that a being could create the cosmos but couldn't keep Cash in line. So it begins to look like Cash's Christianity is no any better off than his first marriage.

Jack's Life and June's Love

Neither the evidential nor the logical problem of moral evil is as straightforward as it seems. In terms of our sketch of the evidential problem, it is important to distinguish between what is rational to believe relative to some data and what is rational relative to all of the pertinent information. It might be rational for me to believe that Johnny Cash was an inconsequential artist if the only recordings I had to judge from were the ones he made after Columbia let him go and before Rick Rubin took him under his wing. However, relative to all of the pertinent information, including recordings for the Sun, Columbia, and American labels, it would be rational for me to believe that Cash was an uncommonly gifted artist.

In terms of the evidential problem of evil, relative just to Jack's murder, it might have been irrational for Cash to affirm God's existence. But, relative to all of the pertinent data, including the quality of Jack's life, June's love, and the like, it might have been rational for Cash to believe God exists. If we turn to the big picture, relative to all of the rapes, murders, tortures, and more mundane moral evils, it may seem highly unlikely that God exists and so irrational to suppose otherwise. But, if we included in our data not only atrocities and lesser evils, but also the fact that there is universe and that universe is capable of sustaining intelligent life, perhaps there is a different picture.

One might argue (theist William Lane Craig does in a debate with atheist Walter Sinnott-Armstrong) that the improbability of a life-permitting universe points to the existence of God. Craig comments, "British physicist P.C.W. Davies has calculated that in order to be suitable for later star formation (without which planets could not exist) the relevant initial conditions must be fine-tuned to a precision of one followed by a thousand billion billion zeroes, at least."[4] The quantity and quality of moral evil, and the existence of a universe suited for life, are not the only data relevant to the rationality of believing or disbelieving God's existence. The point is: what's rational to believe depends upon what we look at, and we need to look at all of the relevant information.

On the Far Side Banks of the Jordan

The logical problem of evil is a less daunting but nonetheless important topic. If God's existence is incompatible with the mere existence of moral evil, then we don't need to worry about weighing evidence: since there's moral evil there's no God. In order to show that God's existence is compatible with the existence of moral evil, it is enough to show that there is a consistent story, where there is moral evil and God makes at least a cameo appearance. This story needn't be persuasive, plausible,

---

[4] William Lane Craig and Walter Sinnott-Armstrong, *God? A Debate between a Christian and an Atheist* (Oxford: Oxford University Press, 2004), p. 9.

or pleasing as long as it is free of explicit and implicit inconsistencies. To show that something (God's existence, peace in the Middle East or a presidential election with worthy candidates) is possible, it is enough to show that it is part of a consistent story.

Of course, in Cash's case, a story that ran counter to some of his core Christian convictions, say his beliefs about meeting June again in heaven, would be a less than adequate story. It could count as a solution to the logical problem of moral evil in general, but it could not count as a solution for a compatibilty problem concerning Cash's Christian conception of God. To count as a solution in that context, the possibly true story would need to be in harmony with Cash's other key Christian beliefs. If there is such a story it would show that, so far as the mere existence of moral evil goes, Cash's God could exist and Johnny and June could meet on the far side banks of the Jordan.

Crossing the Line

Let's take another look at our expression of the logical moral problem of evil.

- If there were a perfectly good being, that being would want Cash to keep his pledge to "walk the line."

- If there were a perfectly powerful being, that being would see to it that Cash freely kept his pledge.

- But Cash was unfaithful.

- So, there is not a being that is both perfectly good and perfectly powerful.

- Cash's Christian God is perfectly good and perfectly powerful.

- But no being is perfectly good and powerful.

- So, Cash's God does not exist.

This line of reasoning is right in the sense that the two conclusions (the statements following "so") follow from the lines before them. In other words, if we accept the preceding lines, we must accept the conclusions they lead up to. And so, if Cash wanted to avoid denying the existence of God, he would need to call into question the truth of one or more of the lines offered in support of the conclusions. Some philosophers would advise Cash to scrutinize the second conditional in our line of reasoning, in light of a possibly true account of freedom, the libertarian view.

According to the libertarian view, a person acts freely in a situation, and is responsible for her choice, only if she could have done otherwise in that very same circumstance. And so, Cash could freely choose to remain faithful to Vivian only if at the very same time and place Cash could have chosen to commit adultery. If this view of freedom is even possibly true, there is a surprisingly significant result: not even God Almighty could bring it about that Cash *freely* keep his pledge to Vivian.

To see why this is so, imagine Cash tempted to commit adultery. If he has libertarian freedom, he can freely remain faithful in the trying circumstances only if he could also cheat. But the only way God can guarantee that Cash will keep his vows is to eliminate the possibility of his choosing otherwise. And, in order to do that God would have to take away Cash's libertarian freedom.

In describing the full significance of libertarian freedom for the logical problem of moral evil, I can do no better than quote Alvin Plantinga, the architect of this approach.

> A world containing creatures who are sometimes significantly free [have libertarian freedom] (and freely perform more good than evil actions) is more valuable, all else being equal, than a world containing no free creatures at all. Now God can create free creatures, but he cannot cause or determine them to do only what is right. For if he does so, then they are not significantly free after all; they do not do what is right freely. To create creatures capable of moral good, therefore, he must create creatures capable of moral evil; and he cannot leave these creatures free to perform evil and at the same time prevent them from doing so. God did in fact create significantly free creatures; but some of them went wrong in the exercise of their freedom: this is the source of moral evil. The fact that these creatures sometimes go wrong, however, counts neither against God's omnipotence nor against his goodness; for he could have forestalled the occurrence of moral evil only by excising the possibility of moral good.[5]

---

[5] Alvin Plantinga, *The Nature of Necessity* (Oxford: Clarendon, 1982), pp. 166–67.

Chicken in Black

Some philosophers are about as satisfied with the appeal to libertarian freedom as an answer the logical problem of evil as Cash was with Columbia Records when he cut "Chicken in Black." Some critics of theism note that libertarian freedom is not the only game in town. And, when one looks at the logical problem of moral evil from a different angle, the problem becomes even more acute.

The heart of the libertarian view is the claim that genuine moral freedom requires the ability to do otherwise. In contrast to this perspective, compatibilists argue that one acts freely even if one's choices inevitably follow from one's character and beliefs. Julian Baggini and Peter S. Fosl describe compatibilism as

> the view that it is possible to see human actions as being essentially free and at the same time the inevitable consequences of past actions. This works by understanding free will as the ability to act free from external coercion, rather than causes per se. So we act freely if our acts are voluntary-in accord with our natures and desires-even if our acts causally originated in past events.[6]

So, a compatiblist could hold that Johnny Cash freely chose to enlist in the Air Force even if Cash's choice was the inevitable result (= could not have done otherwise) of his desires and character.

If this sort of freedom is, like libertarian freedom, a genuine possibility, then God could create Cash and the rest of us with desires and characters so that we would inevitably act rightly. Given this possibility, it would be morally impermissible for God to create a world where there could be moral evil.[7] Since there's an abundance of moral evil and God is morally perfect, it follows that God doesn't exist.

---

[6] Julian Baggini and Peter S. Fosl, *The Philosopher's Toolkit* (Malden, Massachusetts: Blackwell, 2003), p. 67.

[7] See Keith M. Parsons, *God and the Burden of Proof* (Buffalo: Prometheus, 1989), pp. 107–113, where Parsons summarizes objections raised by J.L. Mackie and Antony Flew, appealing to a compatibilist account of freedom.

What on Earth Will You Do?

In reflecting on this powerful objection it is helpful to consider the question of divine freedom as well as human freedom. There are four possibilities:[8]

1. God has libertarian freedom and humans have compatibilist freedom;

2. God has compatiblist freedom and humans have compatibilist freedom;

3. God has libertarian freedom and humans have libertarian freedom;

4. God has compatiblist freedom and humans have libertarian freedom.

Since the objection under consideration depends upon humans having compatibilist freedom, 3 and 4 are not options. 1 is an option only if it makes sense to attribute not just different degrees of freedom to God and creatures, but entirely different sorts of freedom. In a debate with Antony Flew, Terry Meithe noted that on a Christian view humans are, as moral agents, created in God's image and therefore divine freedom and human freedom cannot be radically different.[9] If so, 1 would not be an option.

To be sure, Meithe's move might seem a tad too convenient. It may come across as concocted for the sole purpose of dodging a difficult objection. If it were, Meithe's move would be illegitimate. But, the doctrine of humans bearing the divine image is part of the Christian tradition, and while there is considerable debate about the content of that image, moral agency is a plausible component of it.

There may be another reason to rule out 1 as a possible way of viewing divine and human freedom. The objection under consideration depends upon the possibility of God equipping humans with a moral nature and a set of desires such that they

---

[8] The line of argument in this section is taken from: David Werther, "Another Look at the Logical Problem of Evil: The Compatibilist Objection," *Philosophia Christi* 5:2 (2003), pp. 555–562.

[9] Terry Meithe and Antony Flew, *Does God Exist? A Believer and an Atheist Debate* (New York: Harper Collins, 1991), p. 172.

inevitably choose rightly. But, one might argue that were God to have given Cash the requisite sort of moral character and desires, it would be inappropriate to call them Cash's. After all, if God did so, the ultimate reason for every one of Cash's choices would lie outside of himself. It would then be no more appropriate to attribute the choices to Cash than it would be to attribute Cash's voice to set of speakers.

With the first, third, and fourth alternatives eliminated, all that's left for the objection is the second: God and humans have compatibilist freedom. If God has compatibilist freedom then divine choices are the inevitable result of God's nature and desires. And, if divine desires are expressions of God's freedom, then all of God's actions and choices are the inevitable result of God's nature.

God's nature is the set of God's essential properties, the collection of characteristics God cannot lack. Typical examples are perfect power, goodness, and knowledge. In keeping with compatibilist freedom, let's suppose that God's choices are the inevitable result of God's essential properties. If so, the choices themselves are essential properties. This is so for, if God's essential properties determine God's choices, then God's choices are just as necessary as God's essential properties. In fact the choices are essential features of God's essential properties. As such they are also included in the divine nature.

God could determine the divine nature, only if, at the very same moment God could exist-so that God could determine the divine nature, and not exist-so that the divine nature could be determined. But Thomas Aquinas (1225–1274) rightly points out that this scenario is absurd, "There is no case known (neither is it, indeed possible) in which a thing is found to be the efficient cause of itself; for it would have to be prior to itself, which is impossible."[10] If God cannot control the divine nature then God has no control at all, for God's choices are aspects of the divine nature. And, if God has no control then it's not up to God whether or not God creates beings with compatibilist freedom. Since that's what the objection assumes, it falls flat.

If ascribing compatibilist freedom to God undermines divine freedom, then the Principle of Charity—interpreting a view in its

---

[10] St. Thomas Aquinas, *Summa Theologiae*, Part 1, Question 2, Article 3.

most favorable light—dictates that we attribute libertarian freedom to God. And, if the Christian doctrine of creation in the divine image requires that human freedom be similar to divine freedom, then as God has libertarian freedom, humans must as well.

Ghost Riders in the Sky

Christians like Cash could not be satisfied with a response to the logical problem of moral evil, unless it was also compatible with their hope in the hereafter. Johnny coped with June's death by going back to work, and recording selections from his mother's hymn book. At least a third of these songs concern Cash's eternal hope, among them: "Where We'll Never Grow Old," "Where the Soul of Man Never Dies," and "If We Never Meet Again This Side of Heaven."

If Johnny and June are to find fulfillment, and not frustration in the hereafter, then it appears that they must forfeit their libertarian freedom. Otherwise they could act wrongly and bring about pain and misery for themselves and others. However, if the inhabitants of heaven lack such freedom, then either nothing of any moral significance happens in heaven or libertarian freedom is not really necessary for morally significant actions. If the former, it's hard to see how a "heavenly" existence could be a fulfillment for moral creatures; it would appear to be a step backwards. If the latter, then libertarian freedom cannot count as a justification for creating a world with moral evil.

There's a sense in which Johnny and June could be free after they've met on the far side banks of the Jordan, even if they could no longer act wrongly. By reflecting on the nature of God and divine freedom, we can see how this could be so. With perfect goodness as a part of God's nature, God cannot act wrongly. But, that does not mean that God's choices are determined ones. God is free to choose between morally permissible actions. God could freely choose Abraham and make a covenant with him, though God would not be morally

---

[11] The Abraham example is from Thomas V. Morris, *Anselmian Explorations* (Notre Dame: University of Notre Dame Press, 1989), p. 29.

blameworthy for failing to do so.[11] Of course, if God makes a promise, as a perfectly good being, God cannot but keep it. However, God's inability to lie to Abraham would neither trivialize a promise to Abe nor rob them of a fulfilling relationship. If we suppose that Johnny freely petitioned God to "lead him not into temptation but deliver him from evil" and God granted that request, a restricted range of heavenly freedom would itself be a function of divine and human freedom, and so compatible with them. Perhaps then, even if Cash couldn't act wrongly in heaven, that need neither demean his heavenly freedom nor eliminate the possibility of his finding fulfillment in the hereafter.

One might wonder though: wouldn't it have been even better for God to create Johnny and June, and especially Jack's murderer, with a restricted range of libertarian freedom to begin with? That way, there could have been a heavenly paradise all along, without any worries that things would take a turn for the worse. If this is a genuine possibility, God couldn't be morally justified in creating individuals who can make moral messes. And it would be a real possibility, if human freedom is indeed a reflection of divine freedom. After all, God has libertarian freedom and cannot act wrongly.

In order to address this concern, we need to note that terms like "freedom" and "goodness" can apply to God and us either univocally, equivocally, or analogically. They apply univocally if they have the same meaning in the divine and human cases; they apply equivocally if their meanings are completely different for God and humanity; and they apply analogically if their meanings are similar but not the same.

"Goodness" applies similarly to God and humanity as it includes the same sorts of actions: faithfulness, generosity and the like. "Goodness" applies differently to God and humanity as God's goodness is essential and ours isn't. Developing a good character is a possibility for us, but not God. "Freedom" applies similarly to God and humanity in that it requires the ability to do otherwise. It applies differently in that for us, but not God, doing otherwise could range over wrong actions.

God couldn't create us with a range of freedom restricted to morally permissible actions, without radically restricting our range of moral development, or eliminating it altogether. However, for beings capable of moral development, a greater range of development seems better than a lesser one. If so, it would have been worse, not better, for God to have created humanity with a radically restricted range of moral development. If these musings are on the right track, God needn't be morally culpable for creating us with the ability to choose wrongly.

Christmas in Jamaica

At six o'clock on December 25th, 1982, the Cash family was celebrating Christmas in their home in Jamaica, Cinnamon Hill, when three visitors arrived, wearing nylon stockings over their faces and armed with a pistol, hatchet, and knife.[12] They gave "Somebody is going to die here tonight" as their holiday greeting, and demanded a million dollars. The gunman put his pistol to the head of eleven-year-old John Carter Cash. Eventually the Cash family and friends escaped with their lives, minus some money and jewelry.

The thieves were not so lucky. All of them died, victims of what Cash referred to as "unofficially sanctioned summary justice in the Third World."[13] Cash had a great deal of sympathy for these young men, pegging them as junkies.

> My only certainties are that I grieve for desperate young men and the societies that produce and suffer so many of them, and I felt that I knew those boys. We had a kinship, they and I: I knew how they thought, I knew how they needed. They were like me.[14]

The robbery and its aftermath remind us again of Epicurus' questions:

> Is God willing to prevent evil, but not able? then God is impotent. Is God able, but not willing? then God is malevolent. Is God both able and willing? whence then is evil?[15]

---

[12] The account of the robbery is from Johnny Cash with Patrick Carr, *Johnny Cash: The Autobiography* (New York: Harper Paperbacks, 1997), pp. 49–58.

[13] *The Autobiography*, p. 55.

[14] *The Autobiography*, p. 56.

[15] Hume, p. 63.

Construed as queries regarding the logical problem of moral
evil, Cash could answer them, by appealing to libertarian freedom and character development. And, in doing so, he wouldn't
have to abandon his hope of a meeting on the far side banks of
the Jordan.[16]

---

[16] I am grateful to Mark Linville and Susan Werther for comments and corrections, and to David Ramsay Steele and George Reisch for email discussion on
the problem of evil. Thanks too to Jessica for playing my Johnny Cash
requests.

About the Authors

GORDON BARNES grew up in Tennessee, but he never rode a Tennessee Stud. His mama didn't sing tenor, but his Daddy did sing bass. His brothers and sisters all Picked Cotton, in their own way. Ten years ago he fell into a Ring of Fire with Marnie Liebert. Now he teaches philosophy at the State University of New York College at Brockport, and he has published articles in journals like *Philosophical Studies* and *The Monist*.

STEPHEN S. BILYNSKYJ holds a Ph.D. in philosophy from the University of Notre Dame. He is the pastor of Valley Covenant Church in Eugene, Oregon, where, besides listening to Johnny Cash, he engages in pastoral care, philosophy, and fishing, three distinct but related activities. His first experience of the connection between Johnny Cash and philosophical thought occurred in college when a philosophy professor discussing aesthetics offered, "Johnny Cash singing 'Folsom Prison Blues' is better than Bach," as an example of a true value judgment. His web site is www.bilynskyj.com.

JESSE BUTLER is a philosophy professor at the University of Central Arkansas, a mere one hundred miles from the birthplace of Johnny Cash. He enjoys carving out spaces for first-person perspectives in the world of science and singing rounds of "Ring of Fire" while on road trips with his family.

SAMUEL A. BUTLER has lived in New York for the past four years, where he is a Ph.D. student in philosophy at the State University of New York at Stony Brook. He is exceedingly worried about getting his nourishment in New York, but makes frequent forays down South to get cornbread, fried okra, and some sand in his shoes. He works in social and political philosophy, and his dissertation examines the role of care work in the formation of solidarity in the public sphere.

YOLANDA ESTES was born in Winchester, Kentucky, in 1962. She has spent twenty-three years studying or teaching philosophy. As an associate professor at Mississippi State University, she teaches in all areas of philosophy but specializes in German idealism and ethical philosophy. Her scholarly work includes *Fichte and the Atheism Dispute* (1798), edited with Curtis Bowman (forthcoming) and *Marginal Groups and Mainstream American Culture*, edited with Arnold Lorenzo Farr, Patricia Smith, and Clelia Smyth (2000).

STEVEN GEISZ preached the Dao of Johnny Cash and country music over the airwaves from a bunch of college radio stations, beginning in the late '90s at WXDU in Durham, North Carolina. In those heady, bygone days of turn-of-the-millennium alt.country, Geisz spent a good amount of time listening to music, watching college basketball, and writing a dissertation on an adverbial view of language and mental representation. Sometimes he did all three at the same time. In the mid '00s, Geisz lived in Beijing for an academic year or so. He can't remember hearing any Johnny Cash while in China, but he did see The Tribesmen—a band from Xinjiang that knew how to get the jiuba rockin'—do their cover of John Denver's "Country Road" a few times, and that was something to write home about. (He did write home about it.) Geisz now lives in Florida, where he is Assistant Professor of Philosophy at the University of Tampa.

DAN HAGGERTY holds a Ph.D. in Philosophy from Syracuse University. He is Assistant Professor of Philosophy at the University of Scranton. His research interests include philosophy of mind and emotions. They say he shot a man in Reno, but that was just a lie.

JACOB M. HELD is Assistant Professor of Philosophy at the University of Central Arkansas. He specializes in Political Philosophy, Philosophy of Law, and Nineteenth-century German Philosophy. He is co-editor, with James South, of *James Bond and Philosophy: Questions are Forever* (2006), and has contributed to various other volumes in the Popular Culture and Philosophy series. He has recently taken a part-time job with GM and hopes to have his very own psycho-billy Cadillac by 2037.

JOHN HUSS is Assistant Professor of Philosophy at the University of Akron. For years his band, The John Huss Moderate Combo, provided a suburbilly alternative to alternative country music in Chicago. John also co-wrote the cult classic film *Use Your Head* (Off Ramp Films) and contributed to *Monty Python and Philosophy: Nudge Nudge Think Think!* (2006).

RANDALL M. JENSEN is Associate Professor of Philosophy at Northwestern College in Orange City, Iowa. His philosophical interests include ethics, ancient Greek philosophy, and philosophy of religion. He has recently contributed chapters to *South Park and Philosophy: You Know, I Learned Something Today* (2007), *24 and Philosophy: The World According to Jack* (2008), *Battlestar Galactica and Philosophy: Knowledge Here Begins Out There* (2008), and *The Office and Philosophy: Scenes from the Unexamined Life* (2008). He used to be a Man in Black, until he got married and his wife told him that black just isn't his color.

DAVID KYLE JOHNSON is an assistant professor of philosophy at King's College in Wilkes-Barre, Pennsylvania. His philosophical specializations include philosophy of religion, logic, and metaphysics. He also wrote a chapter in *Quentin Tarantino and Philosophy: How to Philosophize with a Pair of Pliers and a Blowtorch* (2007), and has numerous articles in other volumes on popular culture. He has taught many classes that focus on the relevance of philosophy to pop culture, including a course devoted to South Park. (One that incorporates Johnny Cash is on the schedule.) Kyle is currently looking for the son-of-a-bitch that named him Sue.

GREG JOHNSON is Associate Professor and Chair of the Philosophy Department at Pacific Lutheran University, Tacoma, Washington. He grew up in East Tennessee listening to Johnny Cash. While he teaches and writes in the areas of ethics and existentialism, every now and again he tries to mimic Luther Perkins's guitar playing to keep the rhythm of life steady.

In the late 1970s, a rockabilly craze swept through Finland, and MIKA LAVAQUE-MANTY got rhythm and installed a mic on a washboard so he could imitate the sounds of early homegrown rockabilly and country. (The washboard was pretty much the extent of Mika's musical prowess.) Since then, his taste has developed, rockabilly has gone the way of other youthful foibles (heavy metal, mullets, and motorcycles), but an abiding appreciation for Johnny Cash remains. A philosopher by training, he has walked off the line into social science and is Associate Professor of Political Science at the University of Michigan.

CRAIG LINDAHL-URBEN earned a B.A. in philosophy from Reed College. He has spent many years in the computer industry both owning a computer software company and as an executive for large computer companies. He was Publisher and Editor-in-Chief of a weekly newspaper where he really had to walk the line, spending most of his time like a bird on the wire.

ROB MICKEY grew up in Austin, Texas, and lets everybody know it. He first saw Johnny Cash play with the Highwaymen at one of Willie Nelson's Fourth of July picnics. He doesn't remember the year, but it was the time he went with this really cute girl named Sharon from east Texas who was tripping on mushrooms and they drank beer and fell asleep under the broiling sun. He's loved Cash ever since. Now he's a happily engaged assistant professor of political science at the University of Michigan; Sharon got married and must've changed her name because he can't find her.

M.J. MULNIX is Assistant Professor of Philosophy at Dean College in Franklin, Massachusetts. He first heard Johnny Cash's music on a road trip from Colorado to California with his parents when he was only six. Listening to "Don't Take Your Guns to Town" repeatedly on the trip had a lasting effect. Unlike Cash's foolish characters, Mulnix always followed the advice of his parents and has yet to find himself behind bars. His current research interests include utilitarian defenses of individual liberty; the metaphysics of justice; and ethical issues surrounding patient autonomy and medical paternalism in healthcare.

Rev. **LANCE A. SCHMITZ** is the minister of Social Justice at Oklahoma City First Church of the Nazarene. Besides being a huge fan of the Man in Black, Lance finds much resonance with the ethos of Cash's concern for the poor and beaten down. Lance has often said that, "Two of the biggest influences in my life have been Jesus and Johnny Cash." Lance works with several organizations that work to create a more peaceful and just society for the poor and marginalized and hopes to carry off a little darkness on his back.

JAMES SENNETT is associate professor of philosophy at Brenau University in Gainesville, Georgia. He has published extensively in epistemology, metaphysics, and philosophy of religion—including a chapter in *The Chronicles of Narnia and Philosophy: The Lion, the Witch, and the Worldview* (2005). He's an avocational guitarist and singer and plays regularly at a local coffee shop. His repertoire includes "Cry, Cry, Cry" and "Cocaine Blues." When he performs, he always wears black.

CHARLES TALIAFERRO, Professor of Philosophy at St. Olaf College, is the author or editor of eight books, most recently *Evidence and Faith:*

Philosophy and Religion Since the Seventeenth Century (2005). Taliaferro once fell into a burning ring of fire, but repeated listening to Cash's music helped him survive. He is now married to the American artist Jil Evans.

JAMIE CARLIN WATSON was born and raised in the South on fried chicken and country music. He is currently a doctoral candidate in philosophy at Florida State University, where he represses (most of the time) the urge to offer impromptu renditions of "Big River" and "Long Black Veil," and tries (with no little difficulty) to avoid adding syllables to words already containing an adequate number of syllables. His research focuses primarily on *a priori* justification and the epistemology of science.

DAVID WERTHER is a faculty associate in Philosophy in the Department of Liberal Studies and the Arts, University of Wisconsin-Madison. He also teaches theology in the extension program of Trinity Evangelical Divinity School. Though there has never been a warrant for him in Old Cheyenne, sometimes he feels like a wanted man. He plans to turn himself in when the man comes around.

Index

The editors gratefully acknowledge the help of Bob Sullivan, Lou Robin, and Lana Toliver in arranging for permission to quote from the following Cash songs:

"Folsom Prison Blues" written by John R. Cash. © 1956, 1984 (renewed) HOUSE OF CASH, INC. (BMI) ADMINISTERED BY BUG. ALL RIGHTS RESERVED. USED BY PERMISSION.

"Get Rhythm" written by John R. Cash. © 1956, 1984 (renewed) HOUSE OF CASH, INC. (BMI) ADMINISTERED BY BUG. ALL RIGHTS RESERVED. USED BY PERMISSION.

"What Is Truth?" written by John R. Cash. © 1970, 1998 (renewed) SONG OF CASH, INC. (ASCAP) ADMINISTERED BY BUG. ALL RIGHTS RESERVED. USED BY PERMISSION.

"The Man In Black" written by John R. Cash. © 1971, 1998 (renewed) SONG OF CASH, INC. (ASCAP) ADMINISTERED BY BUG. ALL RIGHTS RESERVED. USED BY PERMISSION.

"I Walk The Line" written by John R. Cash. © 1956, 1984 (renewed) HOUSE OF CASH, INC. (BMI) ADMINISTERED BY BUG. ALL RIGHTS RESERVED. USED BY PERMISSION.

"Wayfaring Stranger" written by John R. Cash and John Carter Cash. © 2000 SONG OF CASH, INC. (ASCAP) ADMINISTERED BY BUG / AURIGA RA MUSIC (ASCAP). ALL RIGHTS RESERVED. USED BY PERMISSION.

"The Man Comes Around" written by John R. Cash. © 2002 SONG OF CASH, INC. (ASCAP). ADMINISTERED BY BUG. ALL RIGHTS RESERVED. USED BY PERMISSION.

"God's Gonna Cut You Down" written by John R. Cash. © 2006 SONG OF CASH, INC. (ASCAP) ADMINISTERED BY BUG. ALL RIGHTS RESERVED. USED BY PERMISSION.

"Jacob Green" written by John R. Cash. © 1974, 2003 (renewed) SONG OF CASH, INC. (ASCAP) ADMINISTERED BY BUG. ALL RIGHTS RESERVED. USED BY PERMISSION.

"San Quentin" written by John R. Cash. © 1969, 1997 (renewed) SONG OF CASH, INC. (ASCAP) ADMINISTERED BY BUG. ALL RIGHTS RESERVED. USED BY PERMISSION.

"Redemption" written by John R. Cash. © 1994 SONG OF CASH, INC. (ASCAP) ADMINISTERED BY BUG. ALL RIGHTS RESERVED. USED BY PERMISSION.

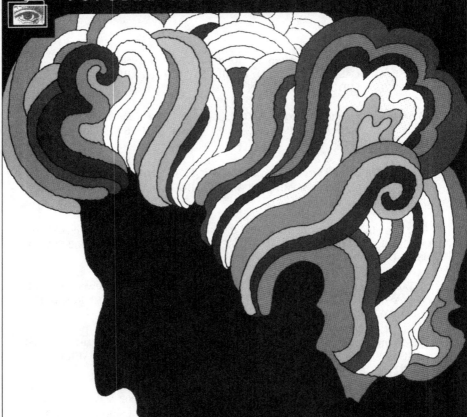

POPULAR CULTURE AND PHILOSOPHY

BOB DYLAN
AND PHILOSOPHY

IT'S ALRIGHT, MA (I'M ONLY THINKING)

EDITED BY PETER VERNEZZE AND CARL J. PORTER

A L S O   F R O M   O P E N   C O U R T

Bob Dylan and Philosophy

It's Alright, Ma (I'm Only Thinking)

VOLUME 17 IN THE OPEN COURT SERIES,
POPULAR CULTURE AND PHILOSOPHY

The troubador who has given English more phrases than any poet since Shakespeare has also warned us that "counterfeit philosophies have polluted all of your thoughts." So here's the genuine article: pure philosophy applied to the provocative, mercurial thoughts of Bob Dylan.

Who is Dylan when he doesn't have his Bob Dylan mask on for Halloween? If a killer is only a pawn in their game, is the killer relieved of moral responsibility? Was Dylan's born-again experience a break or a continuation in his vision of the world? Is it morally defensible to bootleg Dylan recordings? If to live outside the law you must be honest, is freedom more of a burden than conformity? Has Dylan's thinking moved from Enlightenment social protest to postmodern paralysis?

"Sometimes a song is just a song. Sometimes it's a vision of life. Read this book. Do think twice, it's alright."

— ALAN CHEUSE, author of *Listening to the Page*

"Dylan's work persistently re-examines some of the oldest and newest philosophical questions. The authors of this book do not treat him as a mysterious fount of wisdom but as a participant in a philosophical colloquy ranging across space and time. They respect him as an artist and address his work with the knowledge and rigor it deserves."

— MIKE MARQUSEE, author of *Wicked Messenger: Bob Dylan and the 1960s*

AVAILABLE FROM BOOKSTORES OR BY CALLING 1-800-815-2280

For more information on Open Court books, go to
www.opencourtbooks.com